NATURAL WATERCOLOR
PAINT MAKING

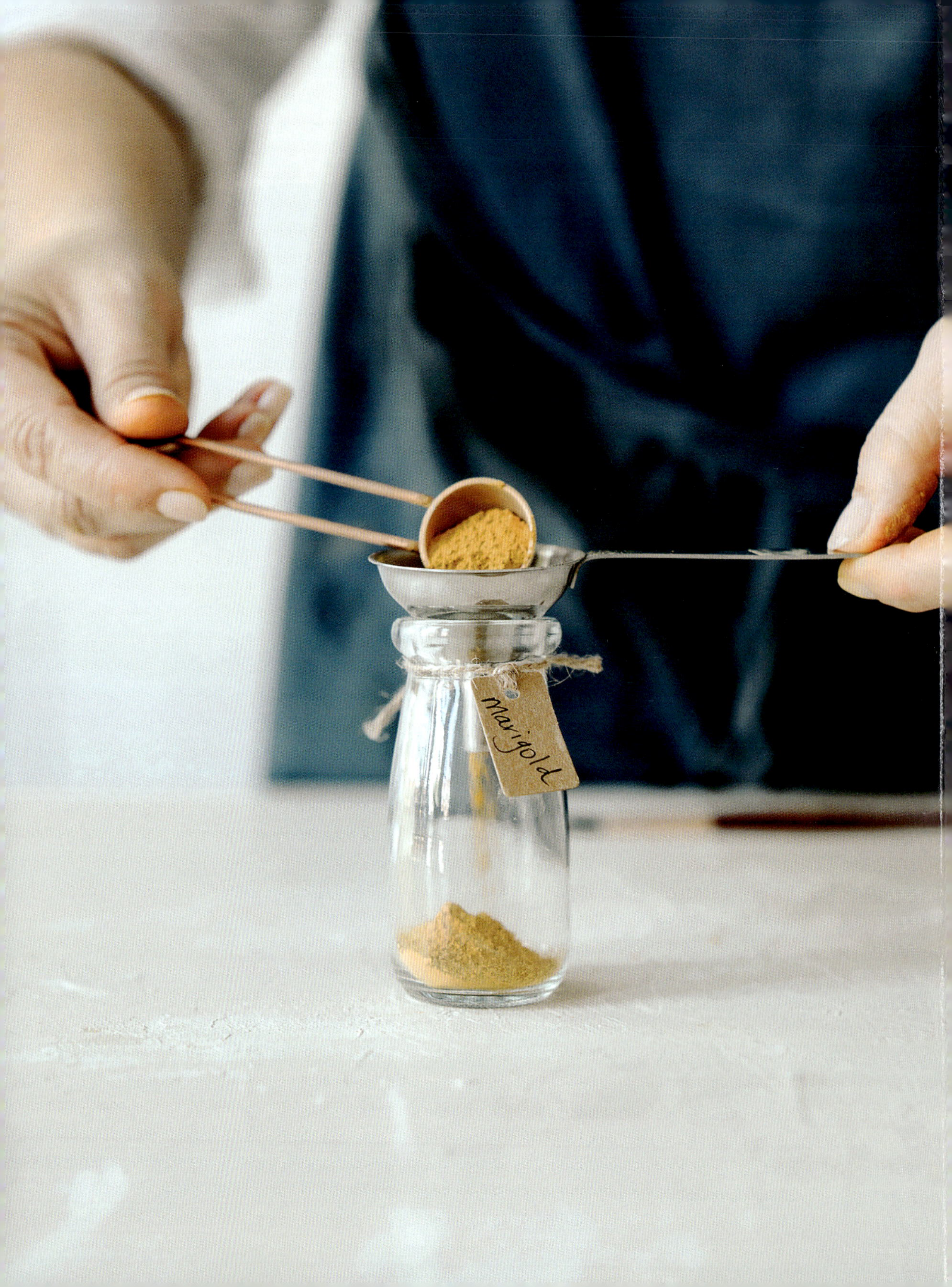

Marigold

NATURAL WATERCOLOR
PAINT MAKING

Create Beautiful Pigments at Home Using
Botanicals, Vegetables and Other Foraged Materials

JOANNE GREEN, Creator of Joanne Green Art

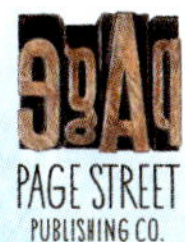

PAGE STREET
PUBLISHING CO.

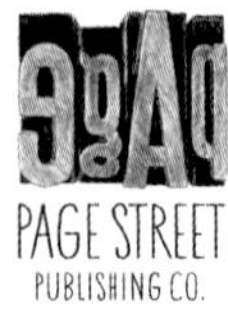

PAGE STREET
PUBLISHING CO.

Copyright © 2025 Joanne Green

First published in 2025 by
Page Street Publishing Co.
27 Congress Street, Suite 1511
Salem, MA 01970
www.pagestreetpublishing.com

Distributed by Macmillan, sales in Canada by The Canadian Manda Group.

29 28 27 26 25   1 2 3 4 5

ISBN-13: 979-8-89003-245-4

Library of Congress Control Number: 2024945322

Edited by Franny Donington-Ayad
Cover and book design by Elena van Horn for Page Street Publishing Co.
Photography by Tegan McMartin
Stock photography on page 16 by Stanislav71; on page 144 (top right to bottom left) by KANNOI, kuruneko, LFRabenedo, Naywan, High Mountain, and Manfred Ruckszio; and on page 145 (top right to top left) by milart, Rojan1, and Meunierd.

Printed and bound in the United States of America

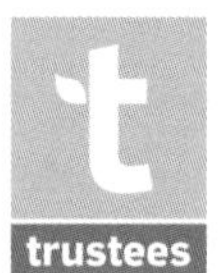

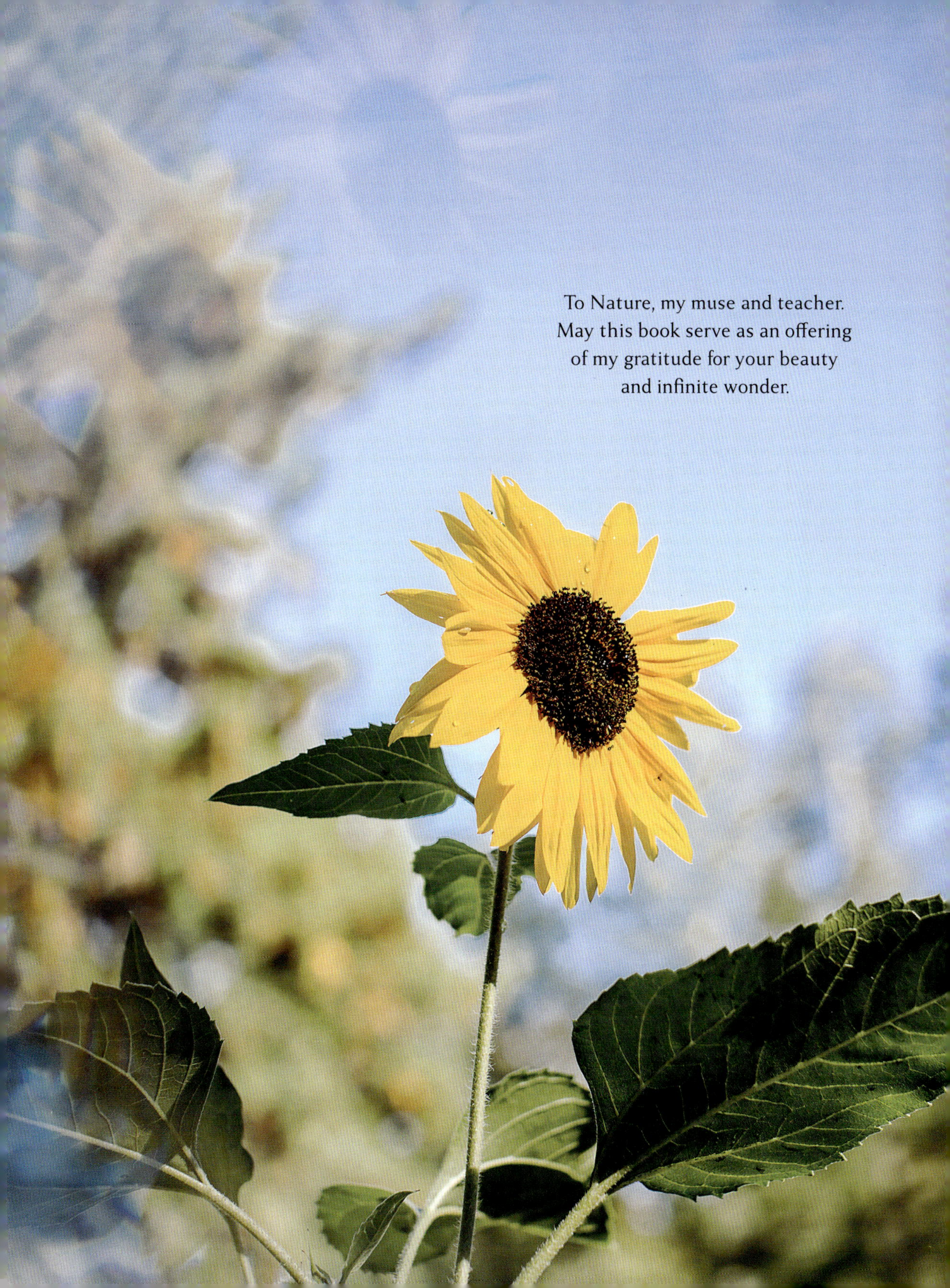

To Nature, my muse and teacher.
May this book serve as an offering
of my gratitude for your beauty
and infinite wonder.

CONTENTS

PART 1: GATHERING THE ESSENTIALS | 15

PART 2: THE PAINT RECIPES | 63

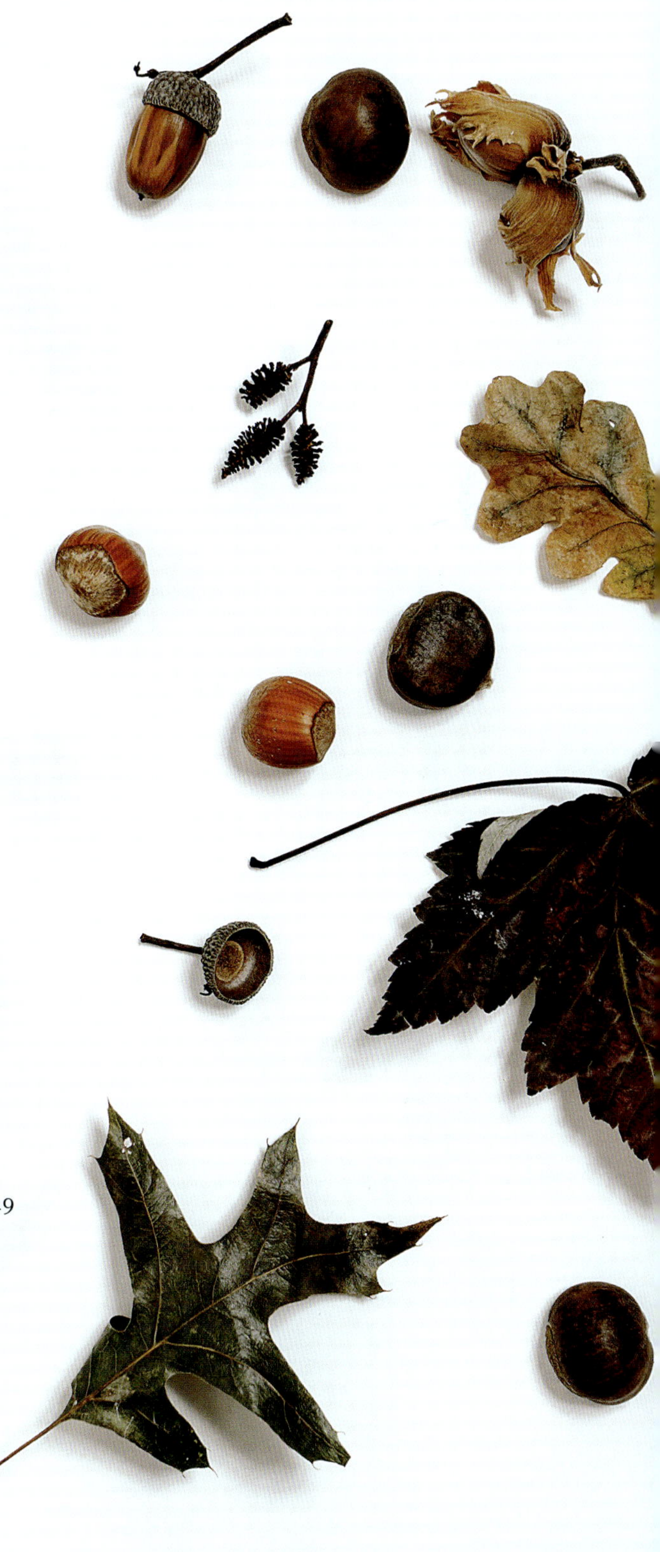

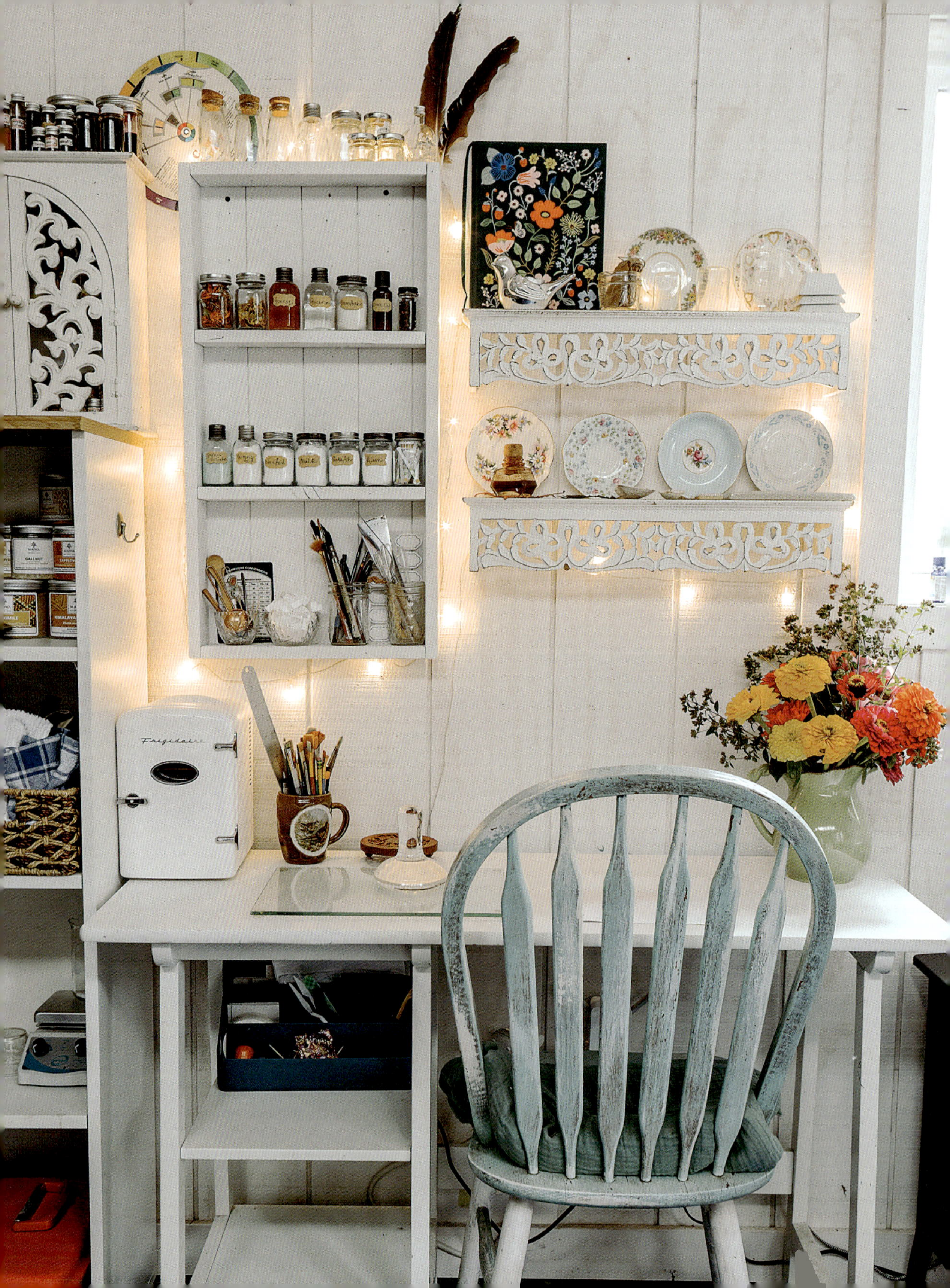

INTRODUCTION

Are you a creative spirit who loves art, color and nature? Or perhaps you are an artist who is seeking more ecological or mindful approaches for your art practice. Whatever the case may be, I have no doubt that this book has landed in the right hands, and I'm absolutely thrilled to share the world of making natural watercolors with you! It is my hope that this book helps you on your journey into painting with the colorful realms of nature's pigments.

The origins of this book started in my childhood. I was that little kid who raided the kitchen for spoons and bowls and then escaped into nature. I mixed up potions using flowers, sticks and leaves and, in doing so, I discovered a deep love for nature's smallest details, especially its colors.

I fondly remember devouring summer cherries and delighting in the deep purple cherry juice that would stain my fingers and lips. I had discovered natural lipstick! I also remember the simple delight of picking yellow buttercups and reflecting the glowing light of their petals under my friends' chins. Especially thrilling was finding an empty shell of a robin's egg and marvelling at that distinctive shade of blue!

As we grow up, we often drift further from the playfulness and wonder we experienced as children and redirect our curiosity into more grown-up pursuits. As for me, I began my professional career as an archaeologist working in British Columbia, Canada. I pressed the pause button on my archaeological career to raise a family and make art full-time. When I discovered that some of my art supplies, particularly the microplastic-laden water from my acrylic paints, were environmentally harmful, I embarked on a journey to find more eco-friendly alternatives. I soon found myself taking a deep dive into the realm of natural color sources and emerged in the world of botanical dyes.

I began experimenting with the flowers in my garden, evoking the spirit of the little girl I used to be. My first homemade paint was made with dandelions. I naively crushed up the petals and made an insipid yellow "paint." Clearly, I needed to know more, so I began learning and developing my skills. I have humbly drawn inspiration from the knowledge of plant experts, natural textile dyers and ink makers. I am also grateful for the discoveries and contributions made by indigenous cultures from around the world and throughout history. Clearly, the love of color and the quest to capture it is innately human. From this foundation of knowledge, I've been able to learn and develop my own unique methods for creating natural watercolor paints.

Turning plants into watercolor paint is a transformative process. But it's also been personally transformative as well. I've not only deepened my connection to the natural world, but I've also found a deeply satisfying and mindful art practice that has rekindled my childhood sense of wonder and play. I've recaptured that magical feeling of creating alchemy and making potions, and truth be told, I didn't realize how much I had missed it. The added bonus is that the paints I create inspire me to paint regularly, allowing me to hone my skills. There's nothing more satisfying than using the paints I've made from ingredients foraged from nature, grown in my garden or even found in my own kitchen!

The personalized paint palettes I create reflect the story of my home and the changing seasons. Each pigment holds the secrets and wisdom of the natural world. I hope this book inspires you to tap into this magic and share your own color stories.

With gratitude,

Joanne

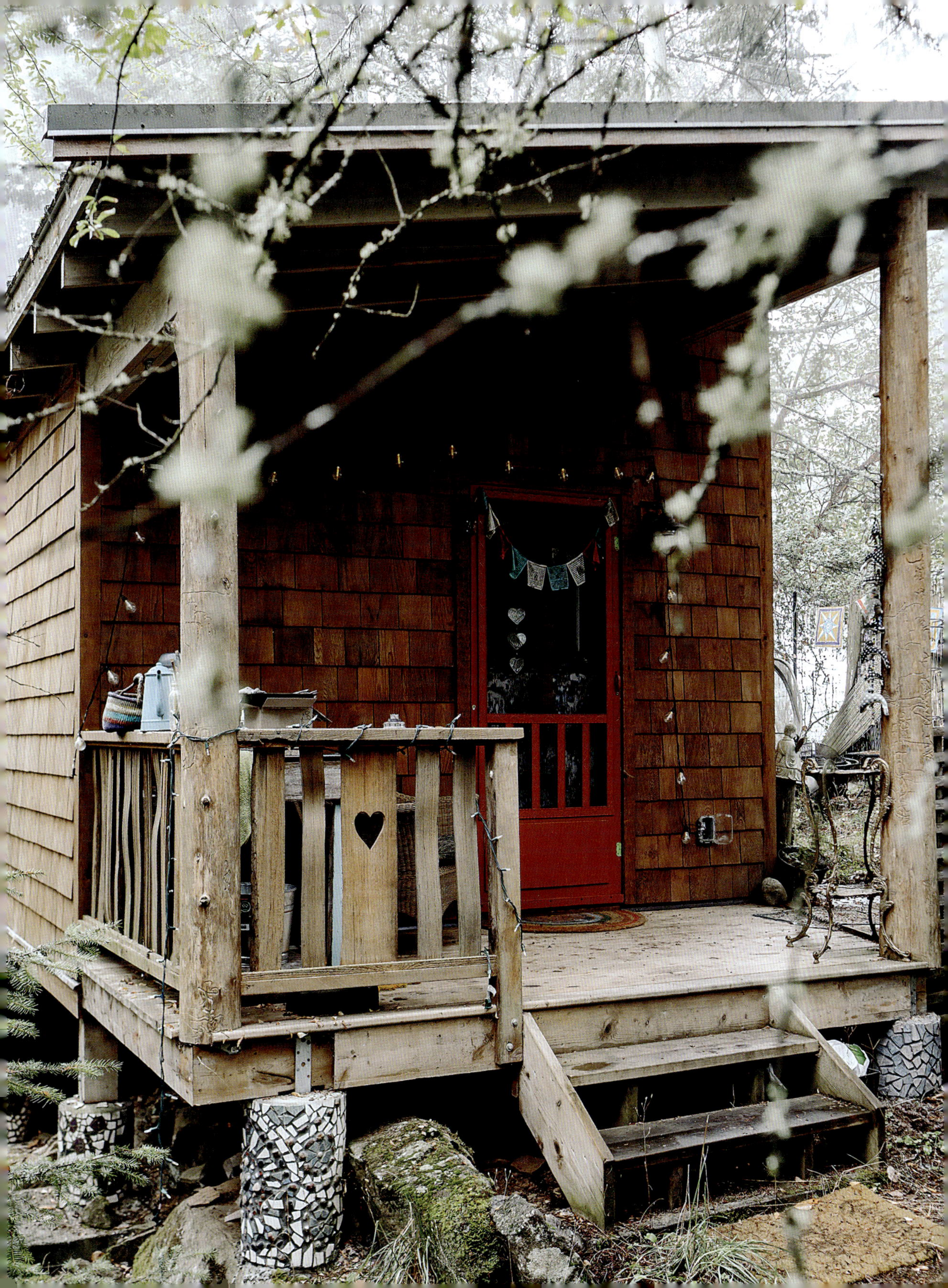

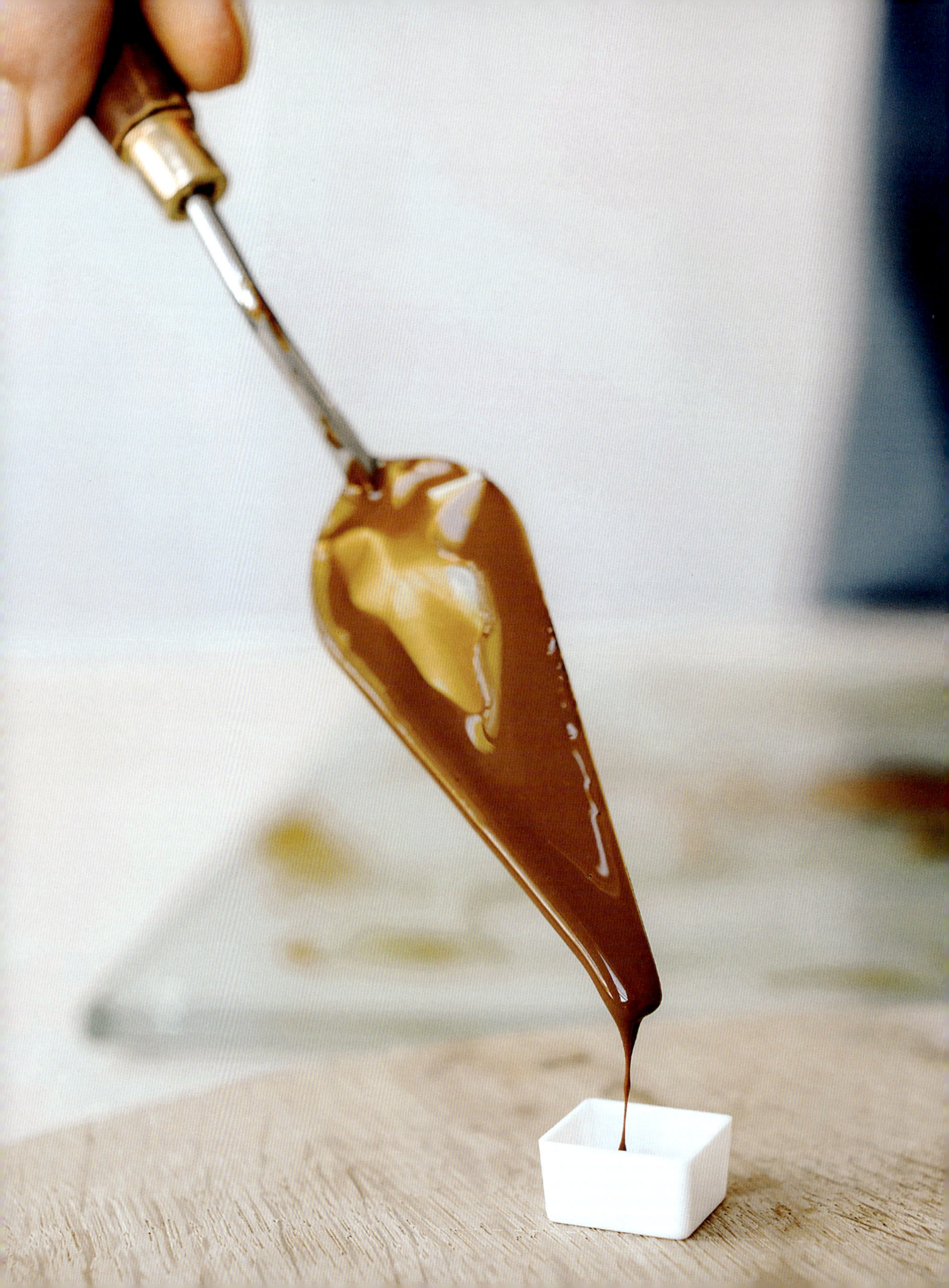

THE PURPOSE OF THE BOOK

This book is an introductory guide to making botanical watercolor paints from start to finish. It will share the tools, ingredients and the step-by-step methods needed to create beautiful natural pigments. By the end of the book, you will have learned how to make a watercolor palette with a variety of mixable watercolor paints, each sourced from either flowers, vegetables, nuts or trees.

Many natural paint makers use inorganic materials like earth minerals (i.e., rock, ochre, soil, clay, etc.), and these are wonderful sources of natural color. This book, however, focuses only on **botanical** sources of pigment.

This book strives to be environmentally considerate. You will soon see that it often requires a lot of plant matter to create a relatively small amount of paint pigment. To avoid being wasteful with precious plant matter, the recipes in this book create small batches of paint that provide the perfect amount for your personal painting needs.

Paint making is not an exact science, so it is my goal to keep things as simple and down to earth as possible. You likely already have many of the tools listed in this book in your kitchen, and some of the more traditional paint-making tools (like a glass muller or grinding slab) can be improvised with things found in your home. Anything else you will need can easily be found in art or natural dye supply stores.

Making botanical pigments is, by its nature, an unhurried process that offers a mindful and sensory-rich experience. Over time, you'll develop your own unique style of paint making, personalizing and possibly modifying the methods I share in this book. Until then, you can use this book to kick-start your paint-making journey. Before you know it, you'll be creating paints from plants that are unique to your local landscape, beyond the recipes provided here.

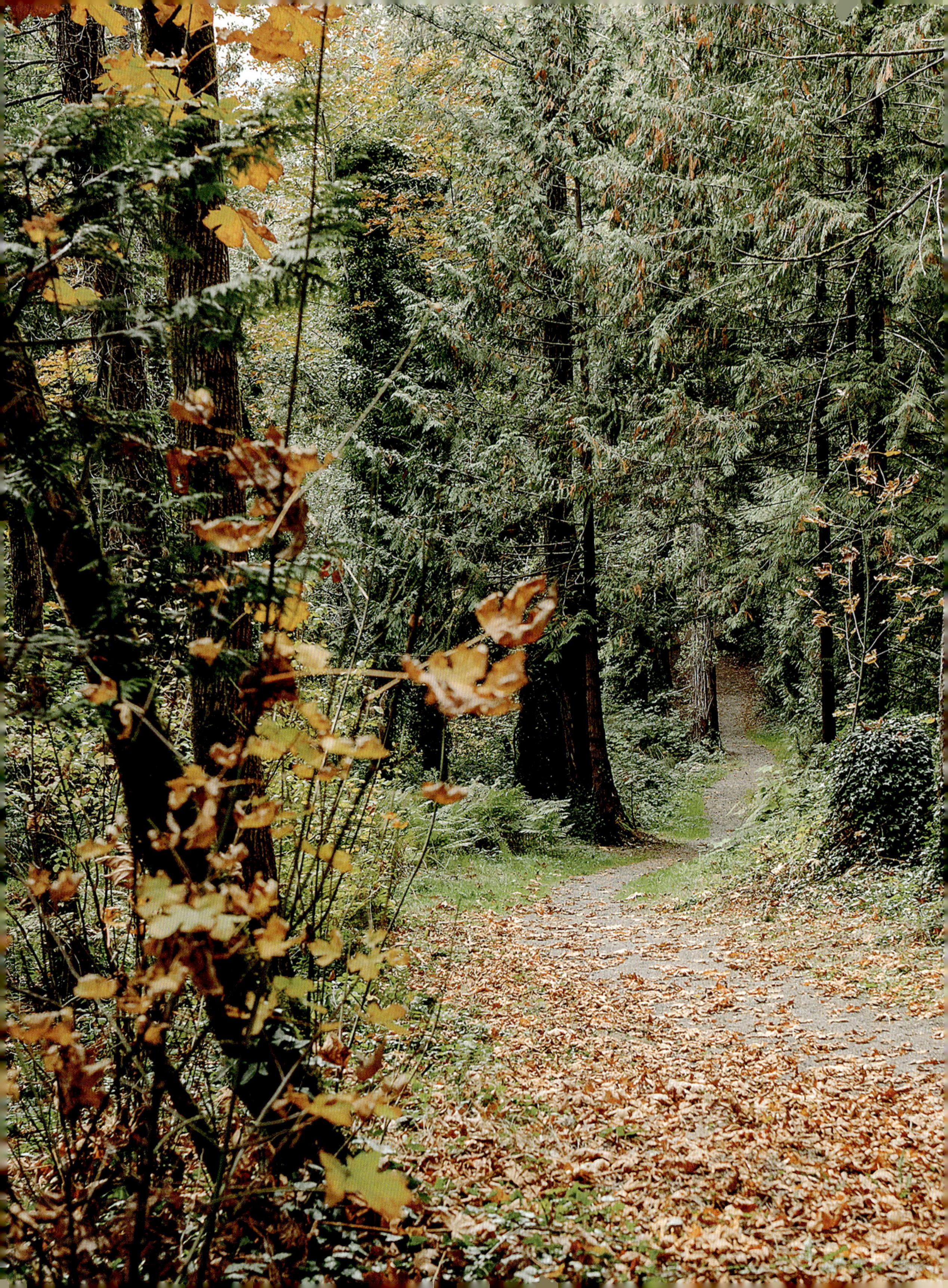

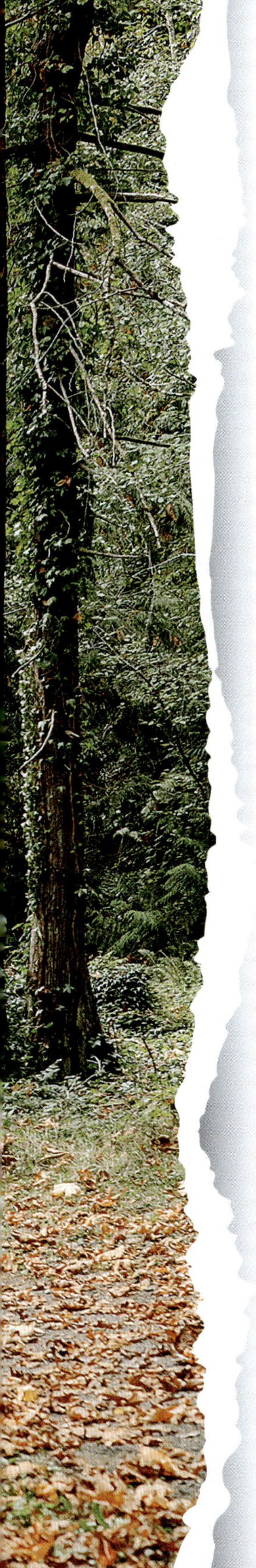

PART 1

GATHERING THE ESSENTIALS

Getting Started

Creating botanical pigments is a captivating blend of art and science. It provides artists with a unique opportunity to connect deeply with the scientific world of plants and it also hearkens back to a time when art supplies were limited only to what nature had to offer. For many artists, this return to simplicity and ecological balance is appealing. The following sections touch on the philosophical considerations that help us place this art form within a wider historical, cultural and ecological context. We'll also go over the core supplies and materials you need to have at the ready to make your own paints. At the end of this chapter, you'll be ready to do some experimenting!

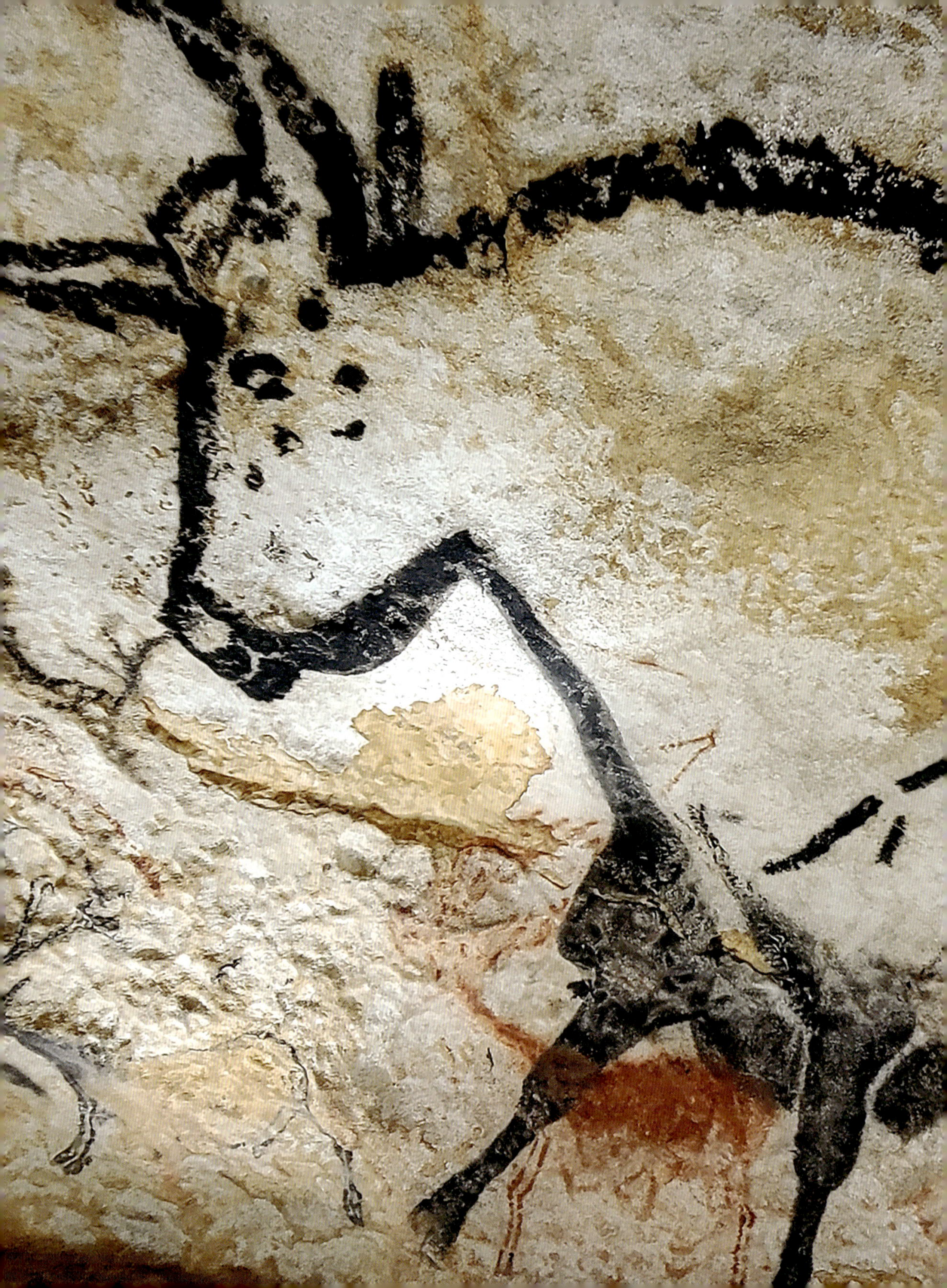

A BRIEF HISTORY OF COLOR

The archaeologist in me is fascinated by the history of color, dyes and pigments. Humans have been harvesting sources of color going as far back as the Paleolithic and Neolithic periods. This can be seen in prehistoric cave paintings dating back to around 40,000 years ago.

Over the course of time, humans learned to harness many sources of color from plants, earth minerals and animals such as cochineal bugs and even a highly coveted purple pigment which came from Tyrian snails. Historically, color became so sought after that pigment resources became valuable global trade items. Unfortunately, this global appetite for color led to some problematic ecological and societal consequences, and in the zeal to expand the artist's paint palette, pigments were often made from highly toxic chemicals.

Fortunately, we have opportunities to source colors in a way that can eliminate harmful chemicals in our art supplies and reduce their negative environmental impacts.

THE CHEMISTRY OF COLOR (IN BRIEF)

Botanical watercolors are simply paints made from pigments derived from the chemical compounds within plants. Each of these colorful compounds has its own unique characteristics, or "personality." The good news is that a background in chemistry is not necessary to become a successful paint maker. However, having a basic understanding of the chemical compounds can help us appreciate their essential "aliveness," then we can anticipate how they will "behave" throughout the paint-making process. We can work with, rather than against, their unique qualities. Don't worry: This book guides you on how to work with these colors and explores the fascinating personalities of each one through a collection of paint recipes. The following information may be used as a reference if you're interested in delving deeper into the chemistry behind the botanical colors discussed in this book.

PLANT	CHEMICAL COMPOUND	COLOR	
Marigold	LUTEIN		Carotenoids
Carrot	B-CAROTENE		Carotenoids
Dandelion Flowers	ANTHERAXANTHIN		Carotenoids
Red Cabbage	ANTHOCYANINS		Flavonoids
Red Onion Skins			Flavonoids
Butterfly Pea Flower			Flavonoids
Hibiscus Flower			Flavonoids
Sunflower Seeds			Flavonoids
Yellow Onion Skins	QUERCETIN		
Weld	LUTEOLIN		
Turmeric	CURCUMIN		
Black Walnut	JUGLONE		

PLANT	CHEMICAL COMPOUND	COLOR
Orange Pekoe Tea	TANNINS	
Autumn Maple Leaves		
Pomegranate Peel		
Algae & Green Plants	CHLOROPHYLL	
Beet Root	BETALAIN	
Madder Root	ALIZARIN	
Logwood	HEMATOXYLIN	
Sappanwood	BRAZILIN	
Green Spirulina	PHYCOCYANIN	
Blue Spirulina		
Indigo	INDIGOTIN	
Burnt Wood	CARBON	

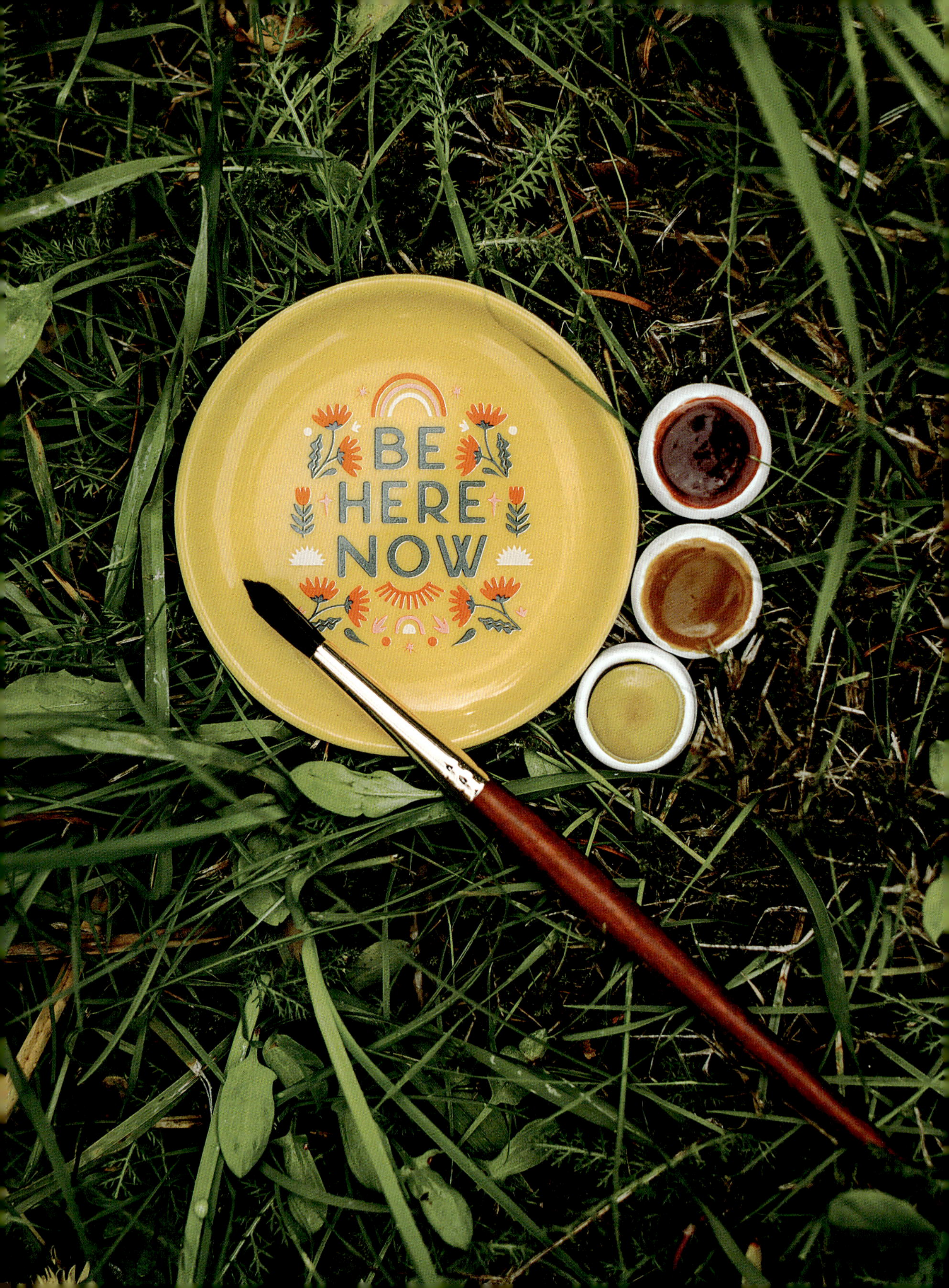

BE
HERE
NOW

HOW THESE COLORS AGE OVER TIME

Because these botanical pigments are chemical in nature, they have an "aliveness" that reacts to changes in their environment. Certain pigments are more sensitive than others to light, heat or changes in pH (the measure of acidity or alkalinity). Consequently, the process of capturing certain plants' colors can sometimes feel like a wild goose chase! With practice, you will learn to harness many of these wild colors, and yet with others . . . you may never be able to fully tame them. For artists and plant lovers alike, this wildness is part of their allure.

Because each pigment has its own chemical "personality," they each come with their own degree of lightfastness—a term used to describe how durable a dye or pigment is when exposed to sunlight. The more enduring a color is over time, the more lightfast it is. Some natural colors are more lightfast than others. Early in my paint-making journey, I experimented with pigments from blackberries, only to watch the vibrant purple shift to gray and then brown within a few hours. Through these experiences, I learned which plant pigments create resilient paints, and which ones are more delicate and ephemeral. The most lightfast sources of natural color are made with *inorganic* pigments made from earth sources, like naturally colored soils and rocks, ochre and minerals.

In modern times, artists have become accustomed to buying "archival" art supplies, specifically designed to endure the test of time. However, many natural textile dyers and paint makers, like me, choose to work with botanical pigments for their inherent beauty and vibrancy. Naturally sourced colors possess a unique luminosity that synthetic ones can't replicate. This choice comes with the understanding and acceptance that, because they are derived from nature, these pigments come with their own life cycle—with a beginning and an end. This notion of impermanence teaches us that change is constant and nothing lasts forever. Botanical colors have shown me how to appreciate and savor life, to be present in the moment and ultimately, how to let go of things beyond my control, like change. At its core, botanical paint making carries a soulful poetry, allowing us to learn valuable life lessons from nature itself.

THE IMPORTANCE OF RESPONSIBLE AND SAFE HARVESTING

I reside on the traditional lands of the Coast Salish people who have been stewarding this area for thousands of years, long before my relatives arrived to Canada. Indigenous cultures have taught me that our survival is deeply connected to living in harmony with the land. Drawing on this wisdom, I believe it's important to be mindful of the land's prehistory when foraging for natural colors. I encourage you to adopt sustainable and thoughtful harvesting practices. Here are my "golden rules" for harvesting:

1. Collect only the minimum number of plants that you need. Excessive harvesting can create stress for the plant or for the overall ecological health of an area. It is better to harvest lightly from a larger area than intensely from one spot or plant.

2. Collect leaves, nuts or bark which are already separate from the plant. Storms provide great opportunities for harvesting windswept plants from the ground. Avoid pulling plant material directly from a living tree or plant. Plants need their parts more than we do.

3. Familiarize yourself with local harvesting rules and guidelines. Many areas and specific plants have special protection status or harvesting laws. These rules vary widely from region to region.

4. Know your plants! Many plants (or parts of the plant) can irritate the skin or be toxic if accidentally ingested. Do your research and consult plant experts when in doubt. Just because something is natural doesn't mean it is harmless.

5. When purchasing dye plants, I encourage you to buy from reputable companies that harvest ethically and do not sell endangered or threatened plants or tree products.

6. Offering your gratitude to the land and the plants you harvest is a beautiful way to acknowledge this exchange.

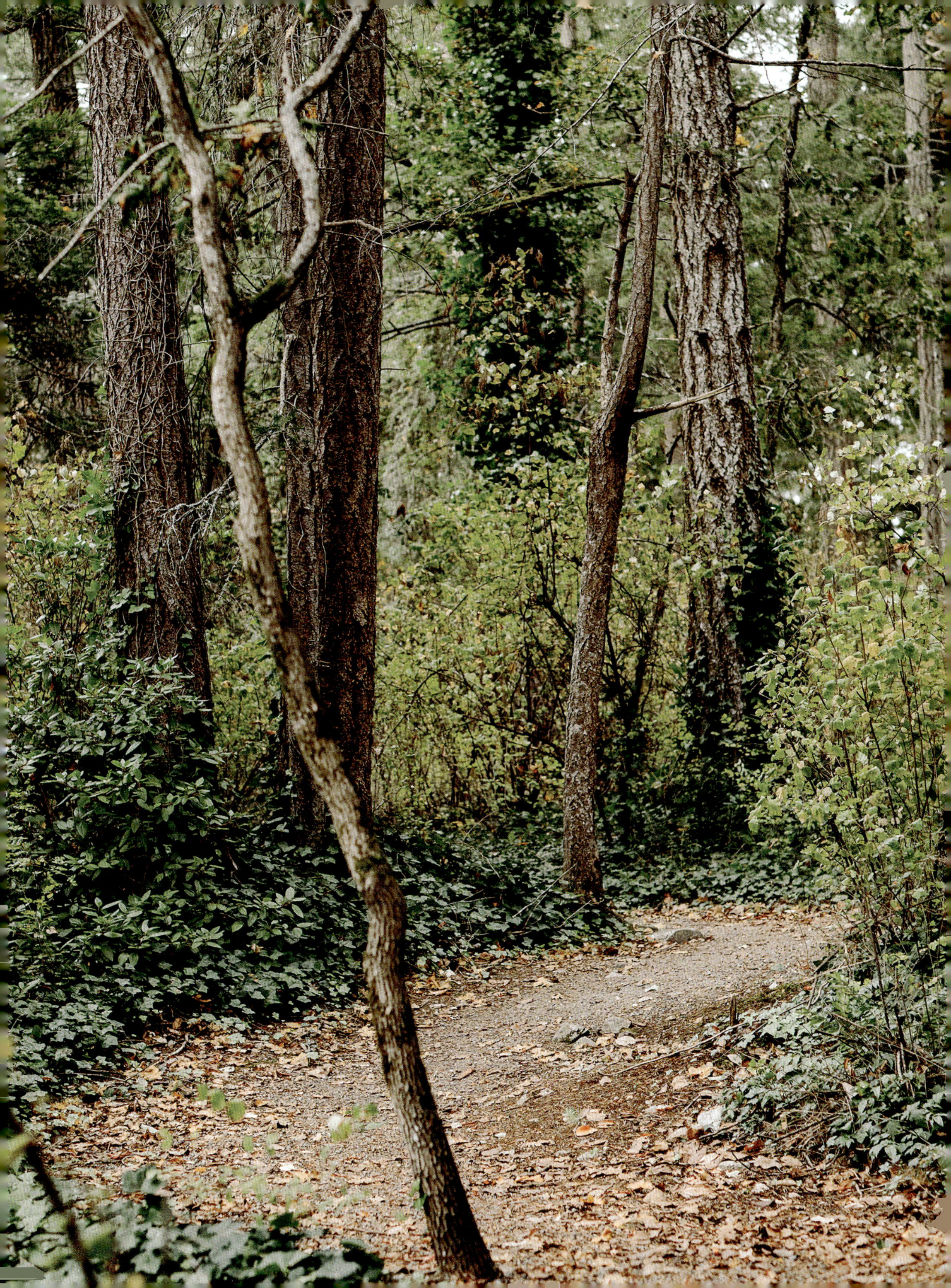

SUPPLIES

At first glance, the supply lists may seem a bit overwhelming—but rest assured, you don't need fancy or expensive tools to get started. There's plenty of room for creativity and improvisation while gathering your supplies. If you find yourself truly falling in love with paint making, you may choose to invest in more special-ized tools down the line. The ingredients for the recipes in this book are also used by textile dyers, so you can easily find these at textile dye supply stores. Other supplies can be sourced from art stores or online. Enjoy gathering your materials and clearing a bit of counter space for your very own paint lab!

FOR THE PAINT LAB

- *Glass canning jars (4-cup [1-L] big jars and 4-oz [125-ml] to 8-oz/half-pint [250-ml] small jars)*
- *Measuring cups and spoons*
- *Stirring spoons*
- *Extra-fine meshed metal or nylon kitchen strainers and/or sieves*

  I prefer nylon kitchen strainers and recommend having a few mesh sizes/ gauges on hand, including 100-, 200- and 400-mesh strainers.

- *Kitchen funnel*
- *Turkey baster or kitchen-grade syringe*
- *Large basket-style paper coffee filters*

  Alternative: squares of very fine-woven fabric

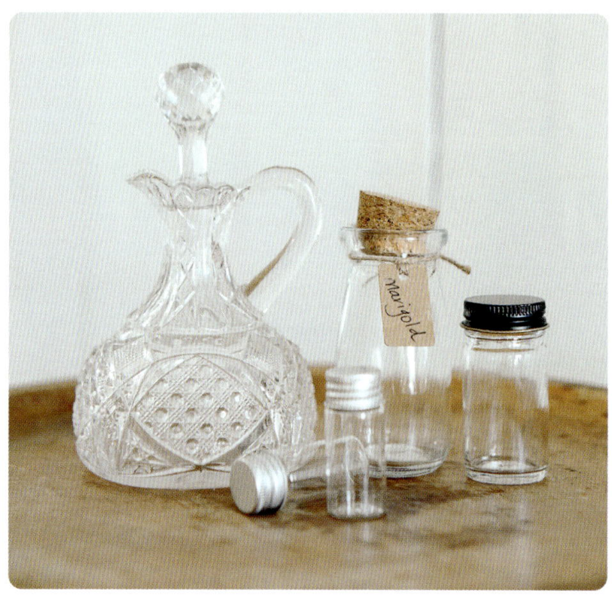

Natural Watercolor Paint Making

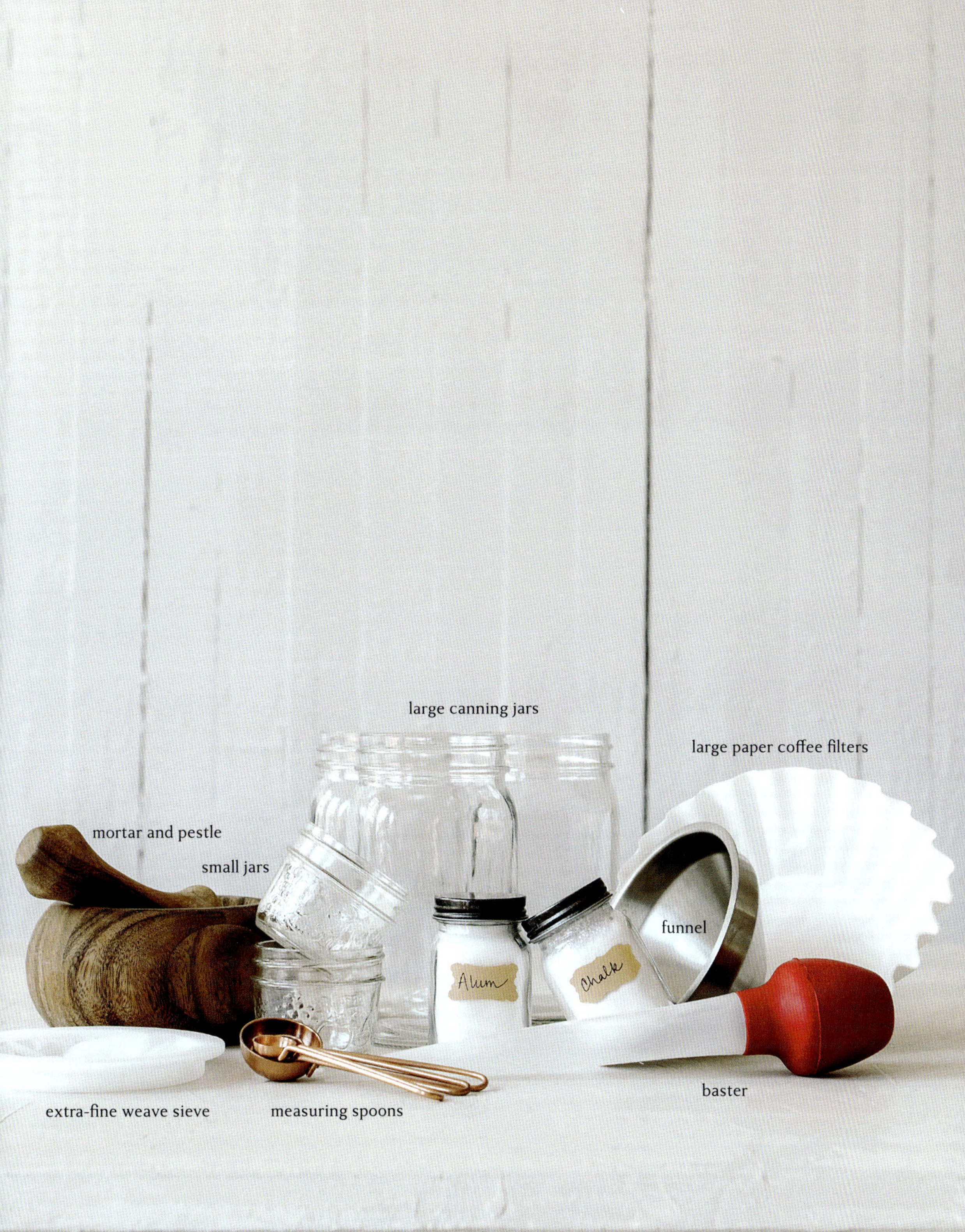

large canning jars
large paper coffee filters
mortar and pestle
small jars
Alum
Chalk
funnel
extra-fine weave sieve
measuring spoons
baster

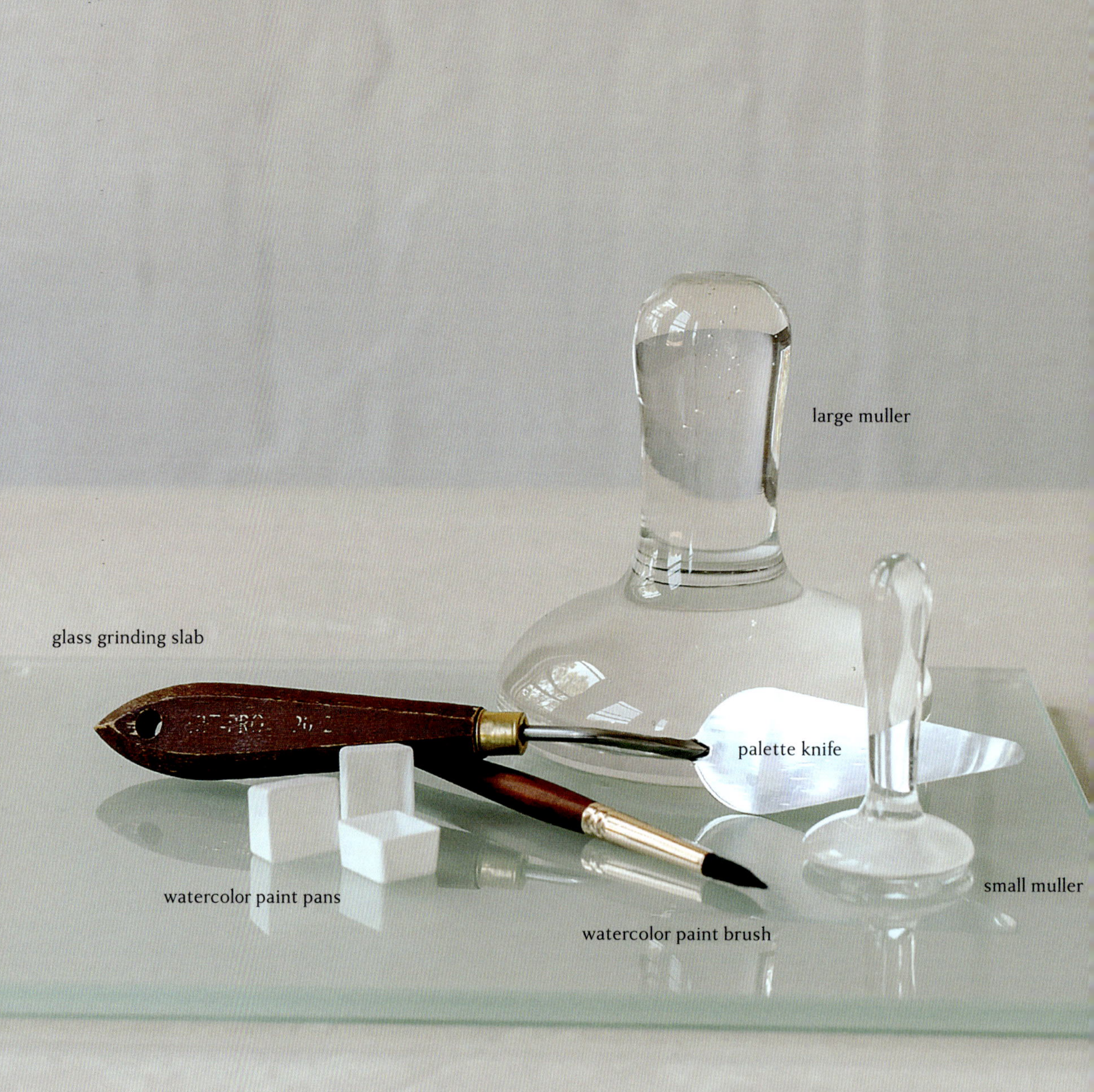

large muller
glass grinding slab
palette knife
small muller
watercolor paint pans
watercolor paint brush

- *pH test strips (optional but helpful to test the pH of your tap water)*
- *Candy thermometer*
- *Palette knife*
- *Heat resistant silicone spatula*
- *Glass mulling slab*

    Alternatives: a flat porcelain plate or a smooth tile
- *Glass paint muller*

    Alternatives: any flat-bottomed glass jar, tumbler or shot glass
- *Watercolor pans (half or full pans)*

    Alternatives: bottle caps or any repurposed small container
- *Large stainless-steel pot*

    Do not use an aluminum pot as this can negatively affect botanical colors.

    To prevent cross contamination with food, designate this pot exclusively for working with plants.
- *Colander/strainer for washing plant matter*
- *Kettle*
- *Small airtight containers or jars (for storing dried pigment)*
- *Mortar and pestle*
- *Old rags for cleanup*
- *Paint brushes*
- *Watercolor paper*
- *Empty watercolor palette(s)*
- *Writing journal*

SAFETY GEAR

- *A high-quality dust/particulate mask or respirator*
- *Safety glasses*
- *Long handled tongs*
- *Rubber gloves*
- *Oven mitts*
- *Ventilation during the dye extraction process*

    This can be achieved by working under a stove's exhaust fan, near an open window or outside.

- *Alum, also known as alum sulfate (I use Jacquard® Products brand)*
- *Calcium carbonate powder, also known as chalk*
- *Sodium carbonate powder, also known as soda ash*
- *Gum arabic powder (I prefer Jacquard Products brand)*
- *Gum arabic liquid (Winsor & Newton® brand is a good option)*
- *Clove oil (typically sold in health food stores and pharmacies)*
- *Whole cloves*
- *Vegetable glycerin*
- *Raw liquid honey*
- *Distilled water*

  I can use the tap water where I live, but distilled water might be a better choice if your tap or well water isn't close to neutral (7 pH) or contains additional minerals. These factors can impact the color outcomes of more chemically sensitive pigments.

- *A variety of pH modifiers, such as vinegar, lemon, baking soda, soda ash or citric or tartaric acid crystals*
- *Ferrous sulfate crystals (iron crystals)*
- *Plants and organic matter*

Natural Watercolor Paint Making

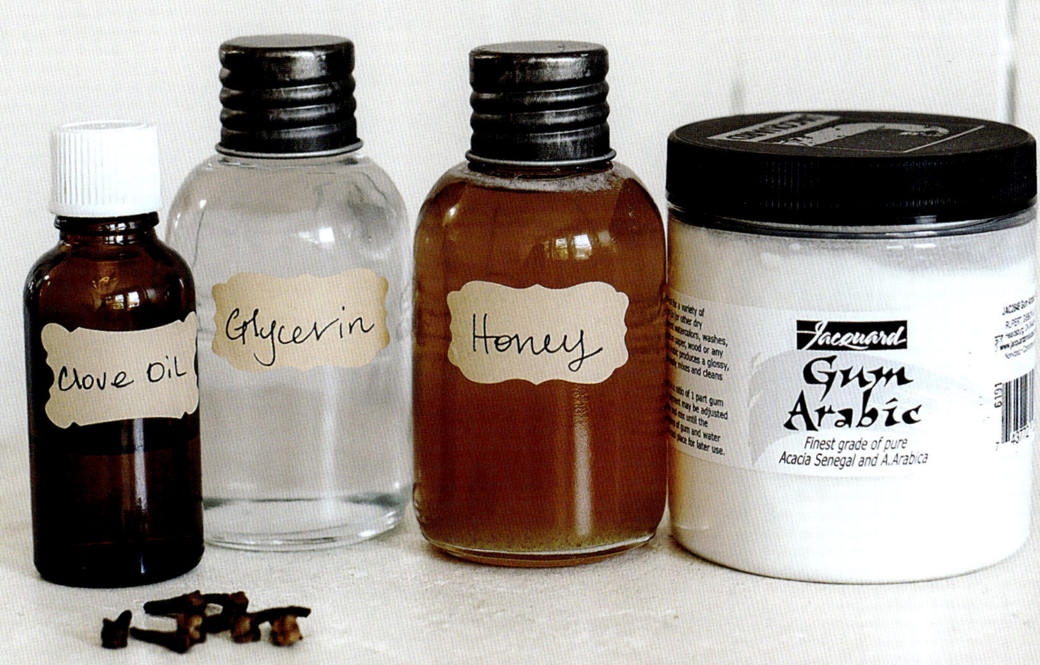
Clove Oil
Glycerin
Honey
Jacquard
Gum
Arabic
Finest grade of pure
Acacia Senegal and A.Arabica

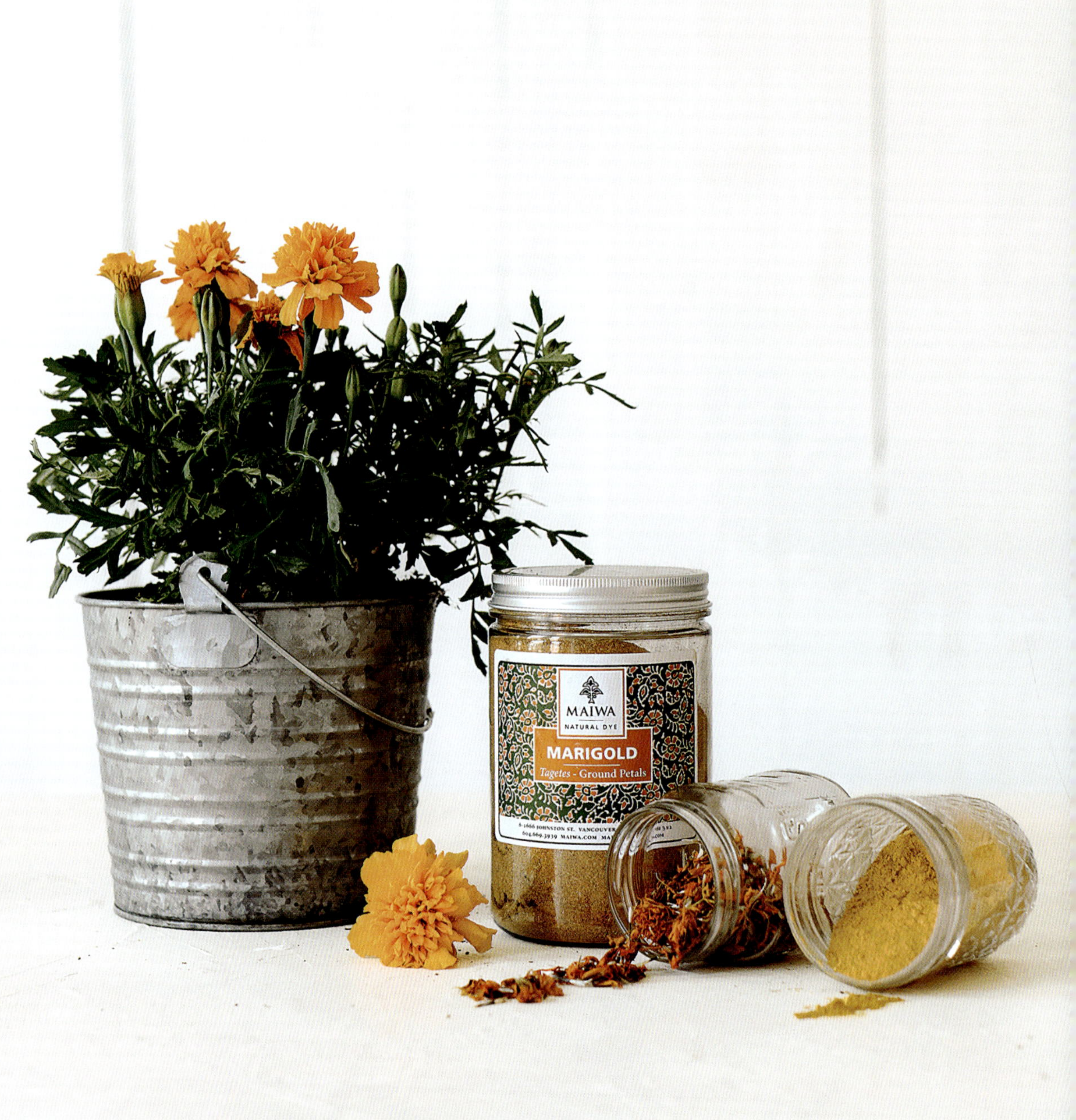

MAIWA
NATURAL DYE
MARIGOLD
Tagetes - Ground Petals
6-1666 JOHNSTON ST. VANCOUVER
604.669.3939 MAIWA.COM

Capturing Color

Once your paint lab is set up and ready, it's time to dive into the fun part—making paint! The following pages will guide you through the process of transforming a plant into a watercolor pigment. While there are several steps involved and it may feel overwhelming at first, don't worry—it's actually quite simple and just requires patience and practice. You'll quickly discover that the process of creating watercolor paint from most plants follows a similar sequence: First, you'll draw out the plant's color in a hot water dye "bath," then filter out the sediment. Next, you'll extract the vibrant pigment, add a watercolor binder and mix everything together to create your own watercolor paints. The following pages are the result of hundreds of hours of experimentation and testing in my own paint lab. Take it one step at a time and at your own pace. Now, let's dive in!

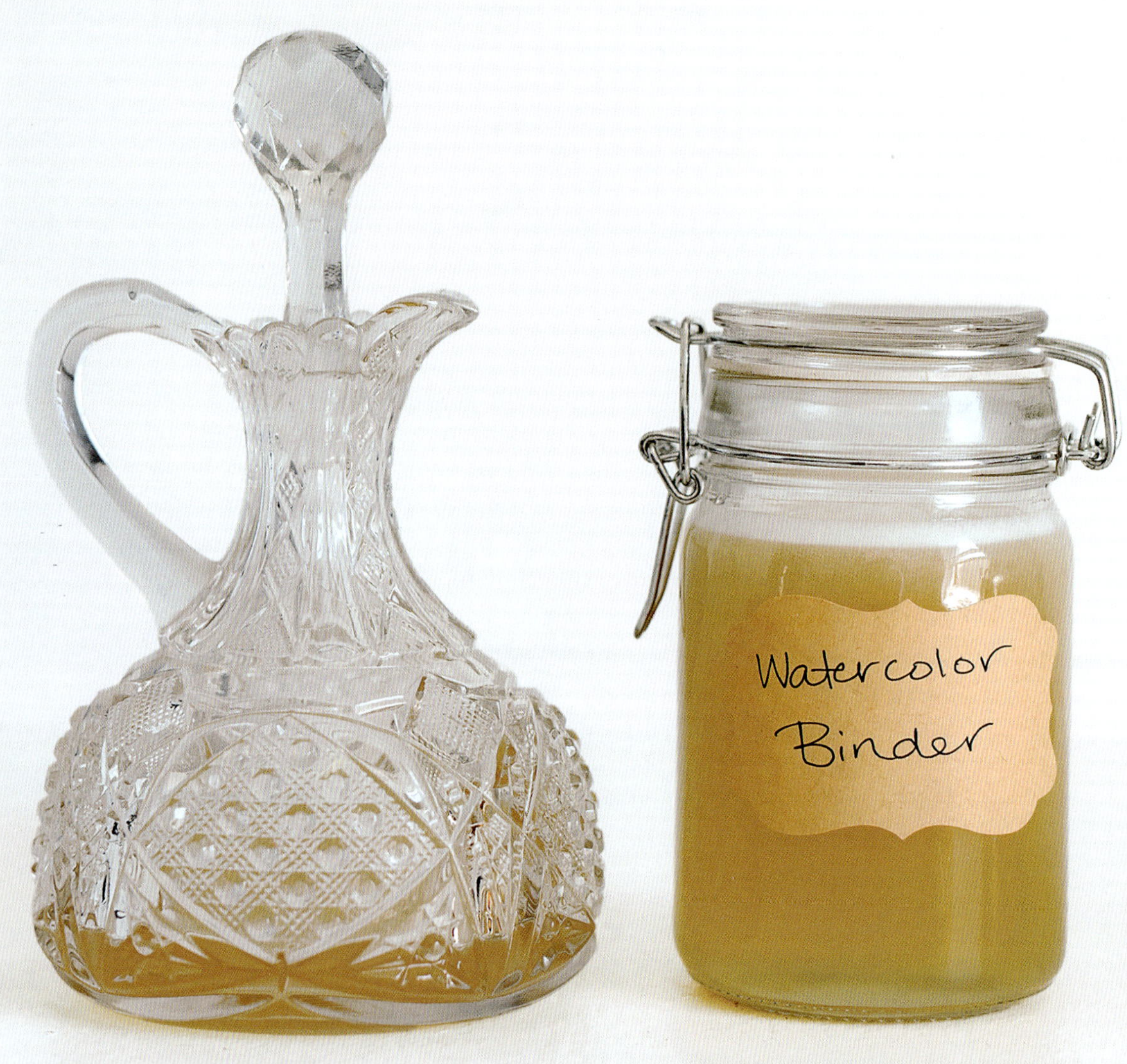
Watercolor
Binder

HOW TO MAKE YOUR OWN WATERCOLOR PAINT BINDER

In this section, I'll guide you through creating the two essential components of watercolor paint: the watercolor binder and the vibrant powdered plant pigment. Pigment powder, whether from organic (botanical) or inorganic (earth mineral) sources, needs to be combined with a liquid binder to become usable paint. Essentially, the watercolor binder acts as the "glue" that binds and coats the pigment particles, allowing them to flow smoothly as a paint medium.

Watercolors are traditionally made with gum arabic as the binder base, and this is derived from the sap of the acacia tree. It can be purchased in liquid and powder form. Having store-bought liquid gum arabic in your tool kit is handy, but the powdered form is essential for the recipes in this book and it's helpful for fine-tuning your paint's texture and thickness. The following watercolor binder recipe will be used for most of the recipes shared later in the book.

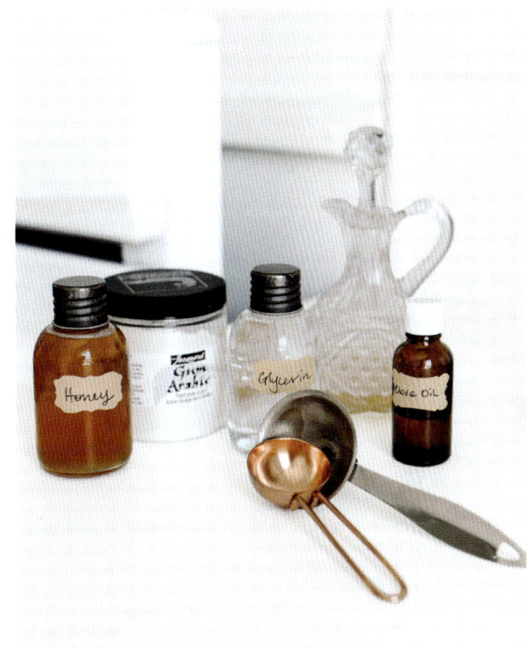

INGREDIENTS

- *½ cup (42 g) gum arabic powder (well-packed into measuring cup)*
- *1 cup (240 ml) of boiling water*
- *1 tbsp (15 ml) of glycerin*
- *1 tbsp (15 ml) of unpasteurized liquid honey*
- *5 drops of clove oil*

In a mixing bowl or saucepan, add the gum arabic powder, then very slowly pour in the boiling water and whisk gently to blend. Clumps will form but they will slowly dissolve. You may also notice foam developing at the top. You can skim this off or wait for it to dissipate.

Once the hot water and gum arabic are mixed, add the glycerin and honey and stir to combine. If you prefer to make a vegan binder, you may omit the honey.

- *The glycerin helps to retain moisture within the watercolor paint and helps give it a glossy and smooth finish.*
- *The honey helps the dried watercolor cake to "wake up" when the wet brush meets it. It is also known to be a natural preservative and helps to prevent cracking during drying. I have omitted honey before and didn't miss it too much.*

Next, add the drops of clove oil and stir. Don't skip this step because clove oil acts as a natural preservative (anti-fungal and anti-bacterial) and is needed to prevent the binder and your future paints from spoiling.

Once the ingredients are fully combined, pour the watercolor binder into a sealable container. Be sure to wipe the lid clean after each use as it can become quite sticky. Store it in the fridge to extend its shelf life; typically, it will last up to a couple of months when refrigerated. You'll likely find that a little binder goes a long way, and this recipe should provide enough to mix a significant amount of watercolor paint.

NOTE: This watercolor binder recipe can be made thicker by adding more gum arabic powder at any point. For more flowing pigments, similar to an ink consistency, you simply add more liquid watercolor binder or thin with alcohol (to make alcohol inks). You'll soon develop your own perfect paint binder blend depending on the application you need it for.

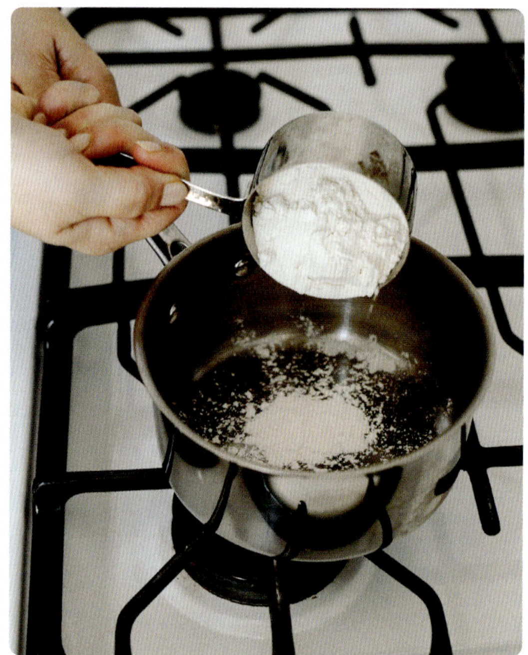

Adding gum arabic powder

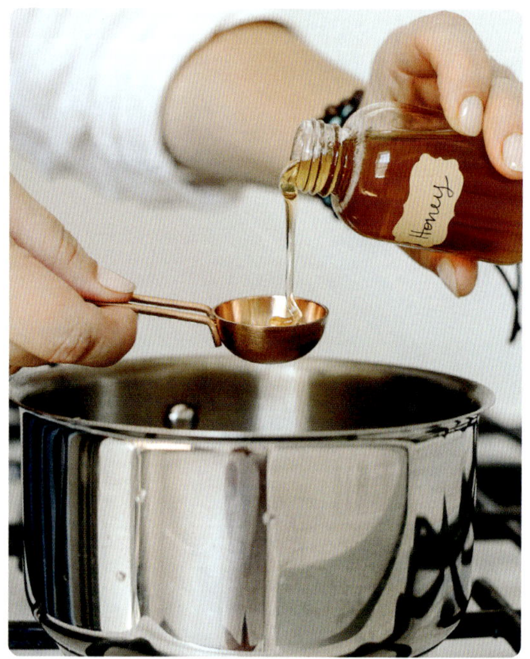

Measuring honey

Natural Watercolor Paint Making

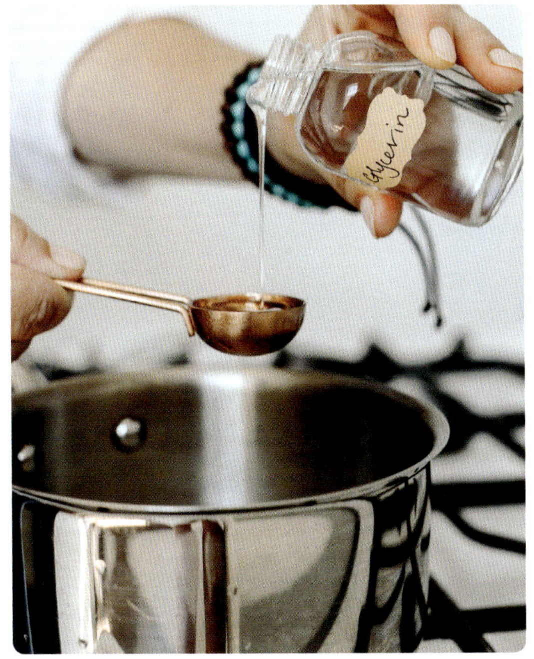

Measuring glycerin

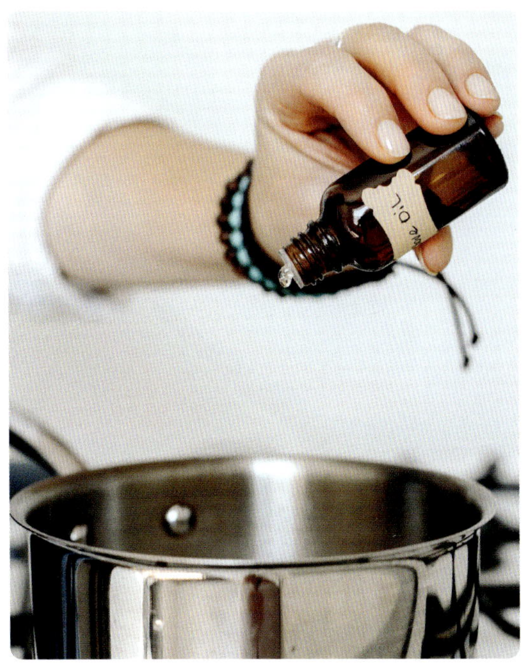

Adding drops of clove oil

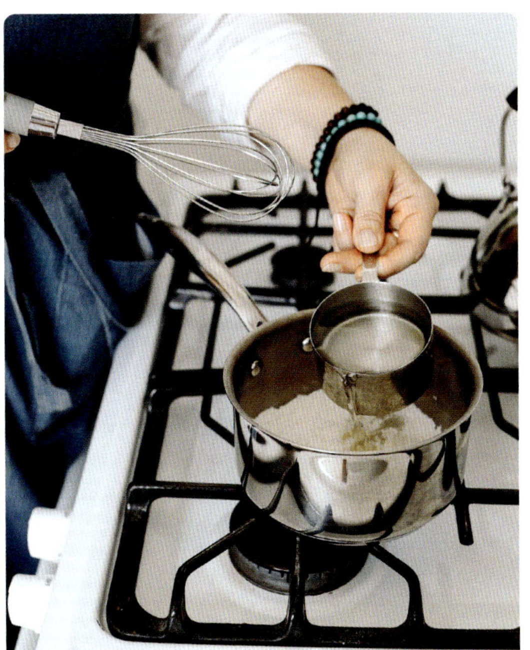

Stirring in hot water

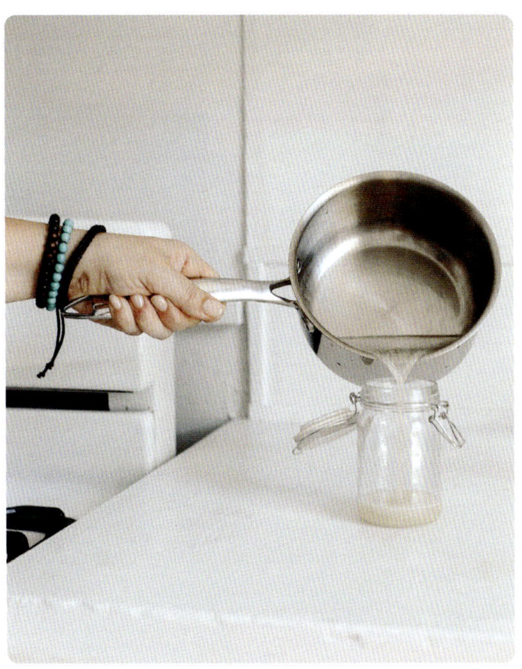

Transferring watercolor binder to a jar

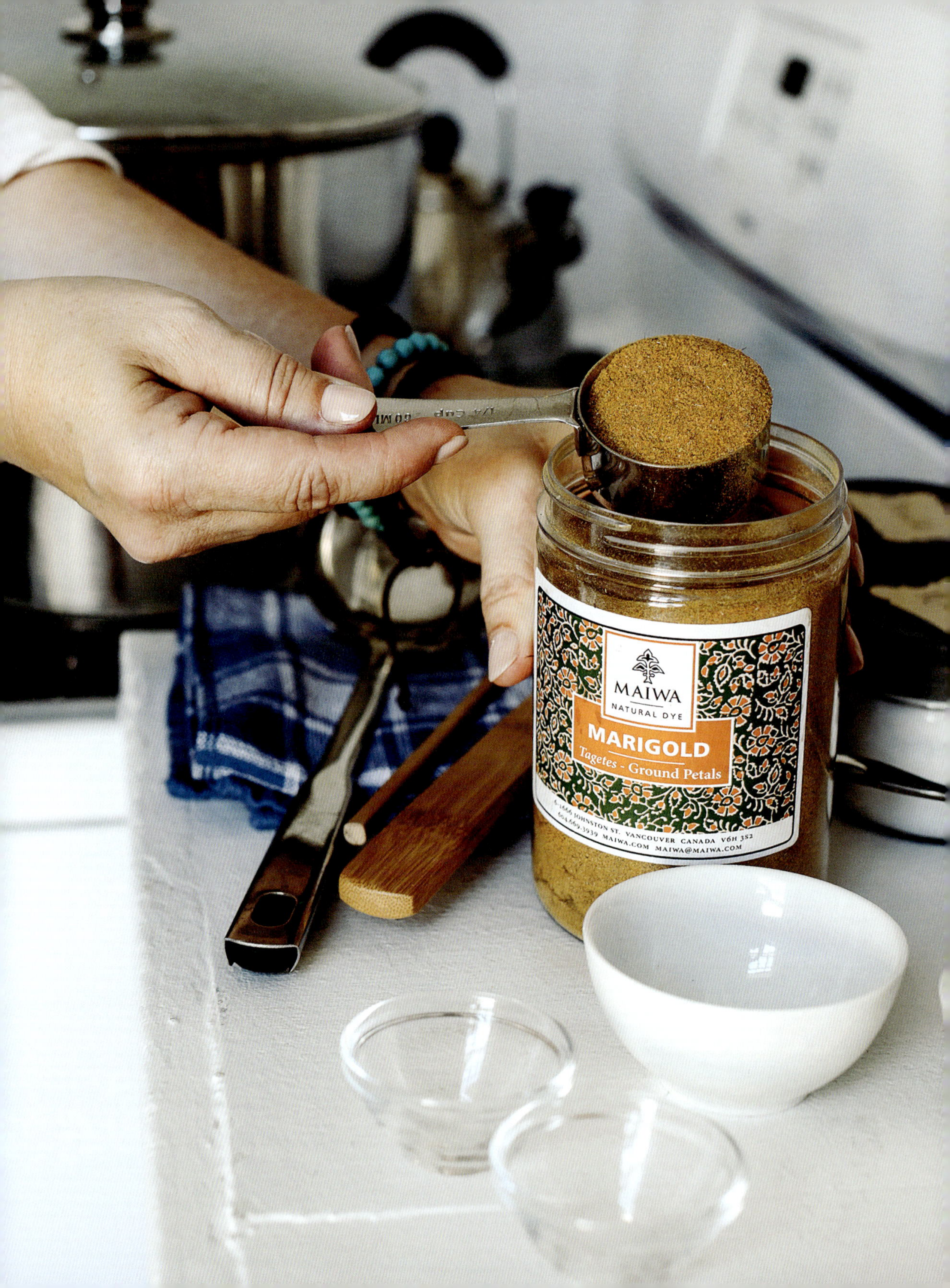

MAIWA
NATURAL DYE
MARIGOLD
Tagetes - Ground Petals
6-1666 JOHNSTON ST. VANCOUVER CANADA V6H 3S2
604.669.3939 MAIWA.COM MAIWA@MAIWA.COM

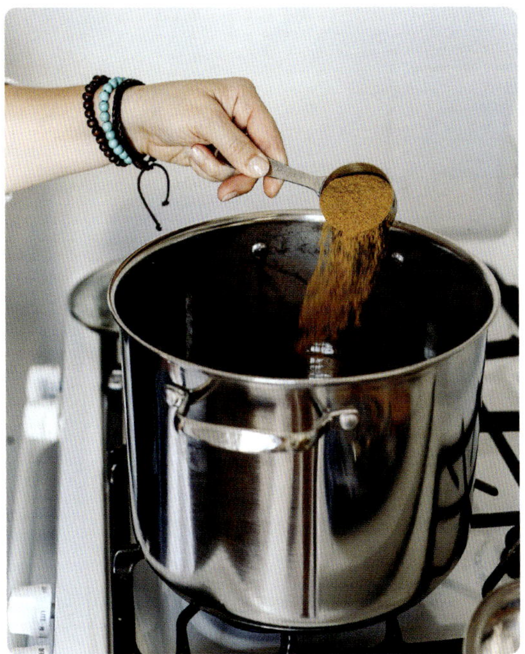

Adding plant material to a large pot of water

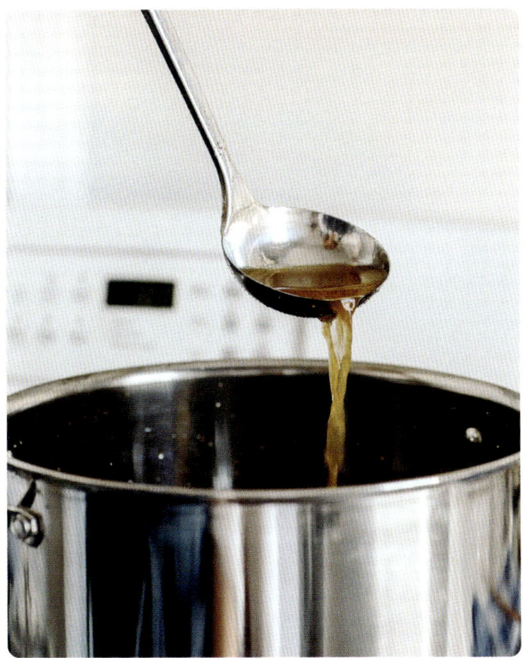

Dye extraction or the "tea"

EXTRACTING DYE FROM PLANTS: MAKING THE PLANT "TEA"

After you have gathered your plants, whether they are flowers, roots or perhaps tree bark, you will need to extract the plant's colorful dye in a hot water bath. You may use dried or fresh plants, some of which may be harvested yourself or purchased. In the second part of the book that covers paint recipes (page 63), I will go into more detail and provide specific instructions on what organic materials to use. But for now, I will explain the general way dye is extracted from plants.

The typical dye extraction process involves simmering plant material in a large pot of water, much like brewing a big pot of tea! The hot water bath helps release the color or dye from the plant matter. The goal is to "exhaust" the plant of its dye, meaning you want to extract as much color as possible. This way, you'll achieve the strongest extraction with minimal waste. Generally, the minimum simmering time is 1 hour, though some plants may require more time and can benefit from an overnight soak, all of which I explain in each paint recipe.

I find that some plants need a more vigorous extraction process—either more time in the dye pot or more heat. This often applies to tougher plant matter, like tree bark, nut husks, wood chips and roots. Conversely, when using more delicate plants, leaves or fresh flower petals, for instance, I start by simply soaking them in hot water and letting them soak for a few hours. Extracting the dye from plants is like every other aspect of natural paint making. You simply need to experiment a little and observe how your plant is behaving in its dye bath.

FILTERING THE "TEA"

Your colorful dye bath now needs to be filtered to remove all of the plant sediment. Having a lineup of large canning jars ready can help you manage the liquid effectively.

To streamline the process, it's useful to have various mesh sizes of sieves on hand. Start with a coarser mesh to capture the larger plant particles, then filter the liquid a second—and possibly a third—time through a finer mesh size. I use a 400-mesh nylon kitchen strainer, which produces a perfectly clear, sediment-free tea. You'll need to rinse your strainers frequently during this process to keep the liquid flowing. While this can be a slow process, it's an essential step toward creating high-quality paint pigments.

For the recipes in this book, the final amount of filtered "tea" will vary, but it's helpful to have at least four large (4-cup [1-L]) canning jars ready to hold the liquid. From here, you can proceed directly to the next steps of pigment extraction. If needed, you can cover the jars with lids and store them in the fridge for up to a few days. However, for the best results, it's ideal to work with these extractions when they are at their freshest to capture the color at its peak.

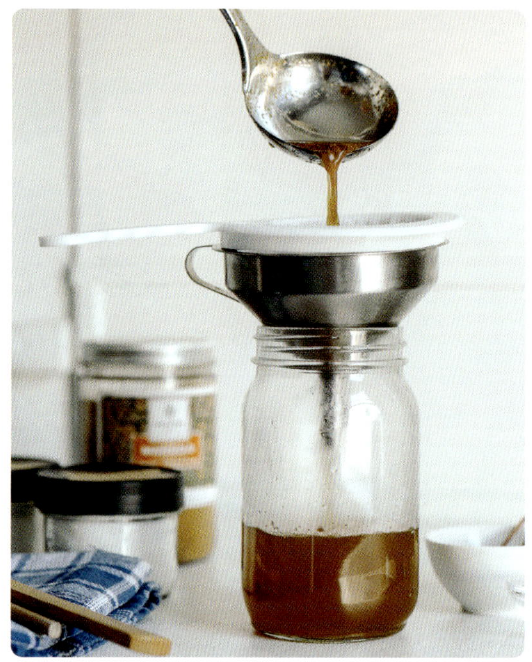

Filtering out plant sediment

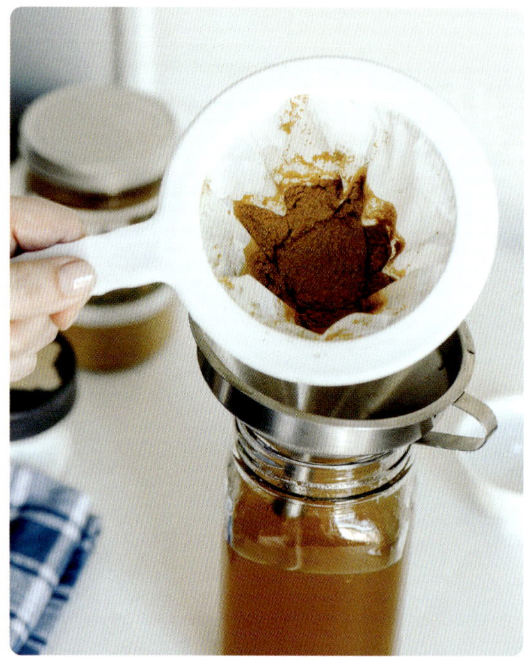

The filtered plant sediment

Natural Watercolor Paint Making

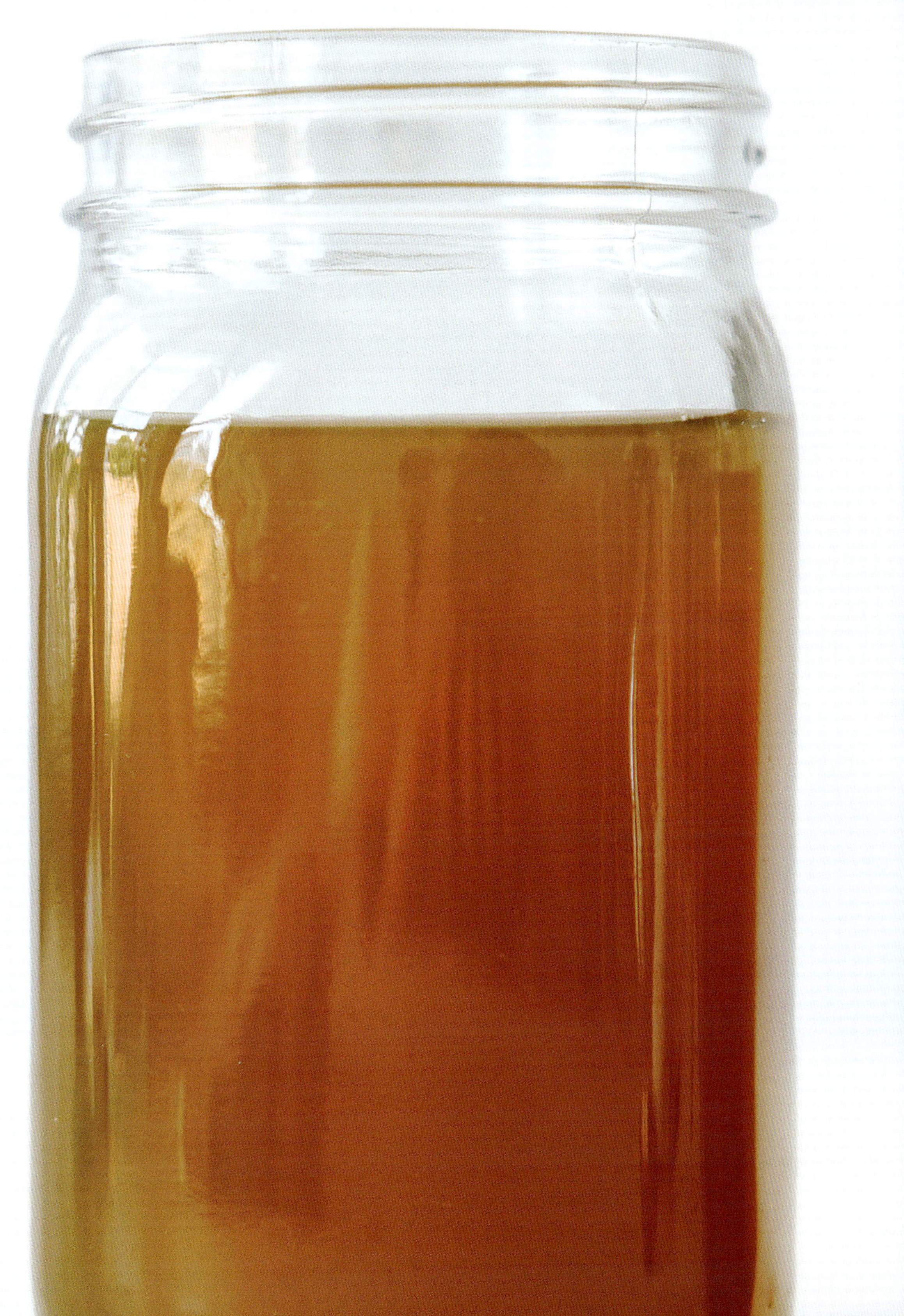

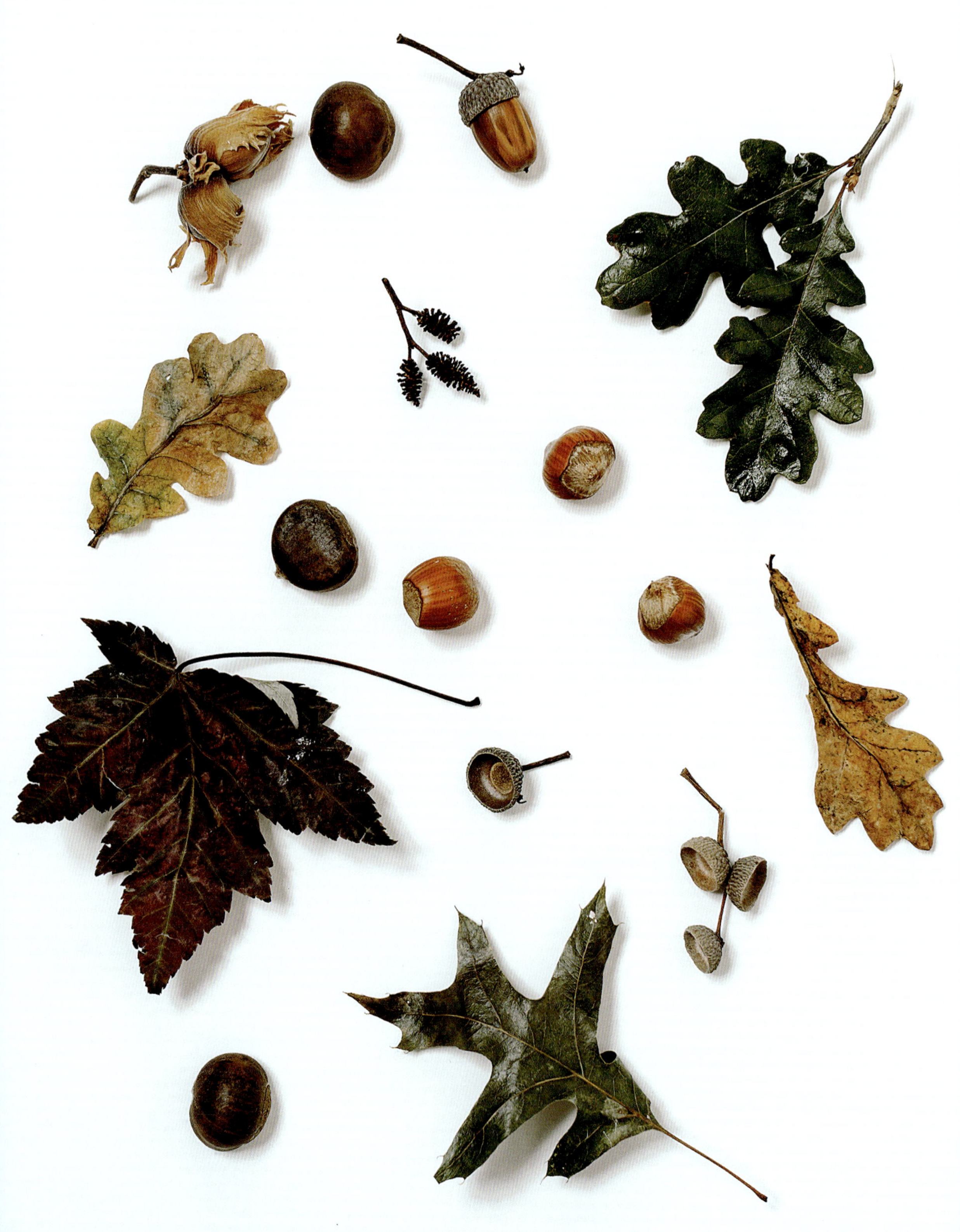

THE TWO CORE METHODS FOR PIGMENT EXTRACTION: AN INTRODUCTION

Once you have extracted and filtered the plant "tea," you will be left with beautifully colored liquid! The next step is to transform this watery brew into a concentrated and useable paint pigment. Below I will introduce the two methods I use that will be explored in more detail in the following chapters.

HEAT REDUCTION

With the heat reduction method, you are essentially taking the plant "tea" and reducing it to create a thicker and more vibrant liquid, which we then thicken further with gum arabic powder. The result is a smooth flowing ink that we can use directly as a watercolor paint, and we store in liquid form. This method is especially useful for the chemically sensitive anthocyanin pigments, such as the purples, blues and reds found in many plants. The Red Onion Skins (Green) recipe (page 71) and the Sunflower Seeds (Deep Rose, Grey, Umber Brown) recipe (page 93) provide further details on the heat reduction method.

LAKE PIGMENT

Most of the other watercolor paints in this book are created using the lake pigment technique where the liquid dye extraction, or the "tea," is transformed into a pigment powder. This powder is then mixed with the watercolor binder to create beautiful botanical watercolors. At first glance, this process may seem intimidating, but with a bit of practice, it becomes quite easy! While it is somewhat time-consuming, it's also a deeply satisfying experience that allows you to connect with nature and color in an immersive, sensory-rich way. With a little practice, you can create highly pigmented, quality watercolors with lake pigments made from the plants, trees and flowers around you. It's my grown-up version of potion making!

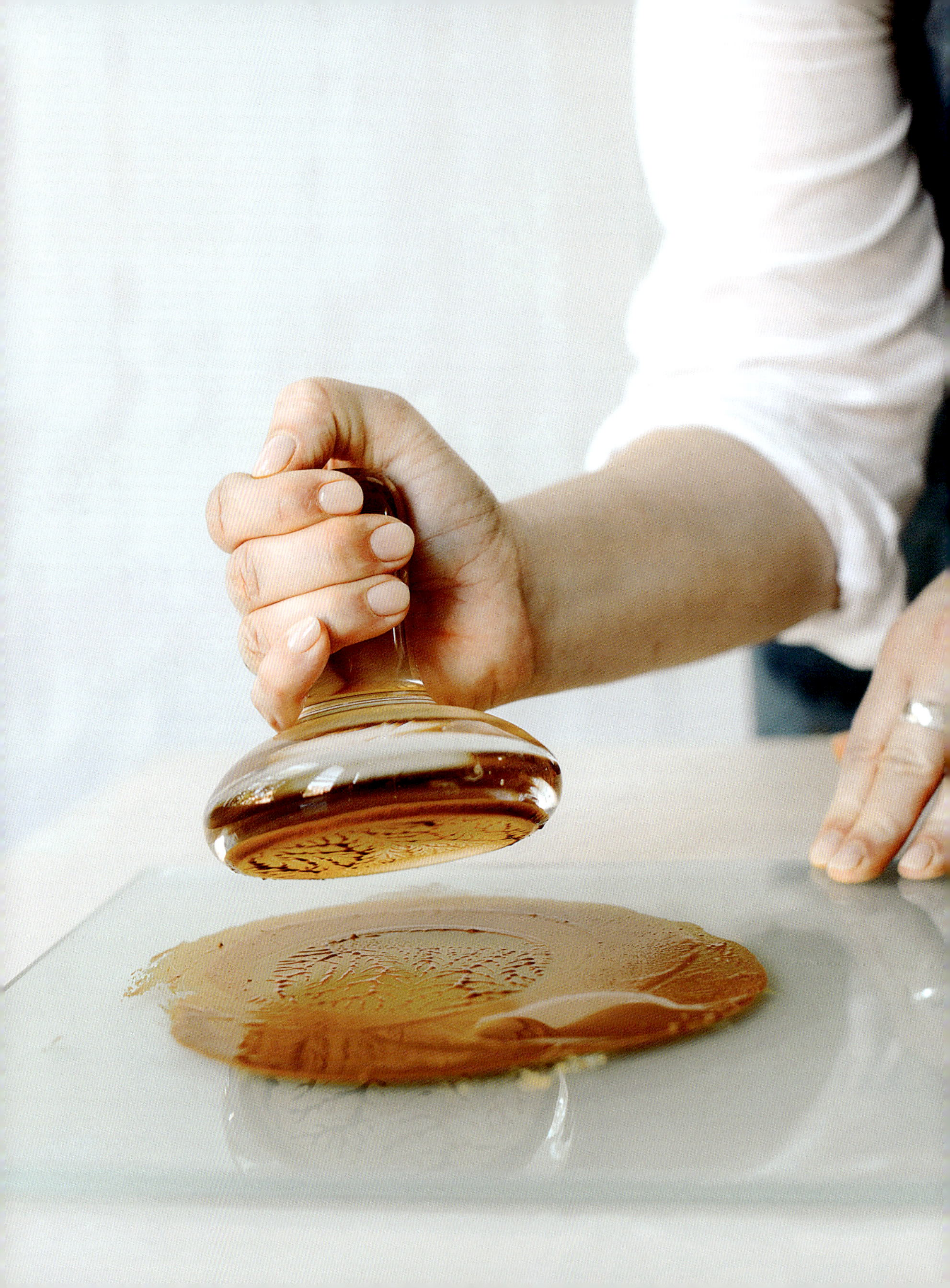

Master Lake Pigment Recipe

This chapter is the heart of the book because it outlines the essential steps for creating a "lake pigment," which lies at the core of natural paint making. Most of the recipes in this book rely on the lake pigment method because it is an effective way to extract high-quality pigment from plants, which in turn can be mixed into watercolor paint or a more fluid form like a watercolor-based ink. While you are learning and making the recipes in this book, I encourage you to use this chapter as a reference guide and return to it as often as needed. Learning how to make a lake pigment is an important step in unlocking the full potential of natural pigments, and it opens up a whole new world of paint-making possibilities.

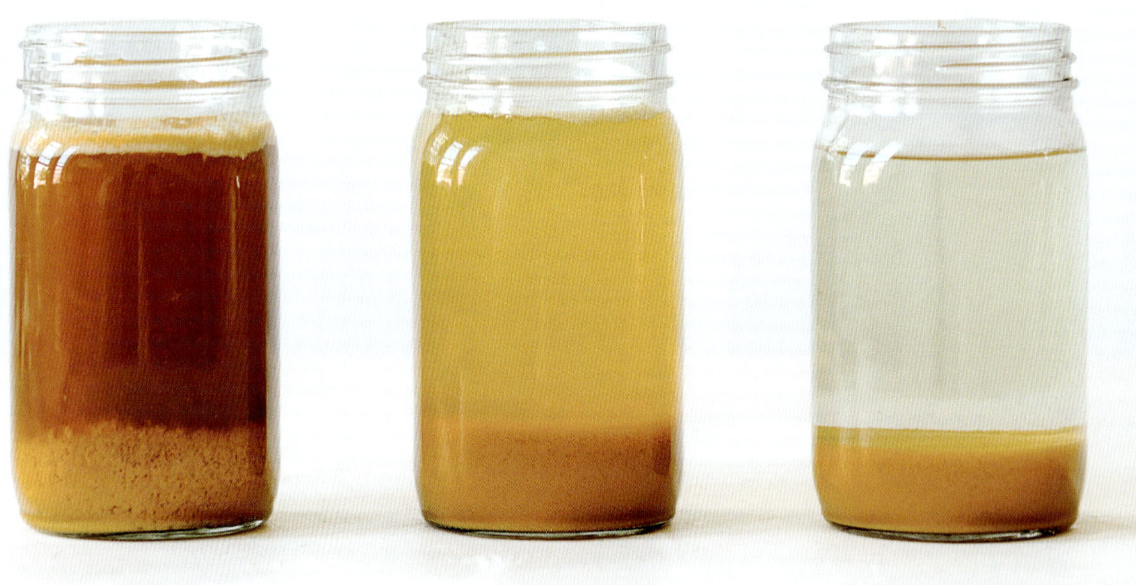

What is a lake pigment? It is a pigment created from a chemical process whereby two ingredients are added to the dye extraction liquid: a metallic salt (alum) and an alkaline (most commonly chalk or soda ash). This chemical reaction causes the liquid to "precipitate" (fizz and bubble) and the colorful pigment solids begin to separate from the liquid. Essentially, it makes the soluble dye particles insoluble. And in turn, this allows us to capture the plant's pigment. I know it's science and chemistry, but to me it feels like alchemy and magic! Lake pigments made from plants are an effective way to produce stunning and vibrant colors that may be mixed into beautiful watercolors. This pigment can also be dried, ground and stored for later use.

The following instructions explain the general methods and materials used for ALL future lake pigments you will make because the process and chemical formula are generally the same. However, once you start exploring the world of plant colors, you may need to adjust the recipe slightly. But this ability to modify comes with practice and a willingness to experiment. I have learned more from my paint-making "failures" than from my successes! But fear not! The following instructions will arm you with all the knowledge you need to begin this exciting journey of making lake pigments with plants.

INGREDIENTS

- *Dye extraction (the "tea")*
- *Alum*
- *Calcium carbonate (chalk) powder*
- *Distilled water*
- *Watercolor Binder (page 33)*

MATERIALS

- *A minimum of 6 large (4-cup [1-L]) canning jars*
- *2 smaller jars (for mixing chemicals)*
- *Stirring spoons*
- *Measuring spoons*
- *Kettle for boiling water*
- *Kitchen syringe or a turkey baster*
- *Kitchen funnels, small sieves or reusable coffee filter baskets*
- *Large basket-style paper coffee filters*
- *Absorbent old towels*
- *Palette knife*
- *Dust mask*
- *Eye protection*
- *Mortar and pestle*
- *Glass mixing slab/plate*
- *Glass muller*
- *pH indicator test strips (optional)*
- *Watercolor pans*
- *Watercolor paper*
- *Paint brush*
- *Small storage containers with airtight lids (for dried pigment)*
- *Permanent marker (for labeling)*

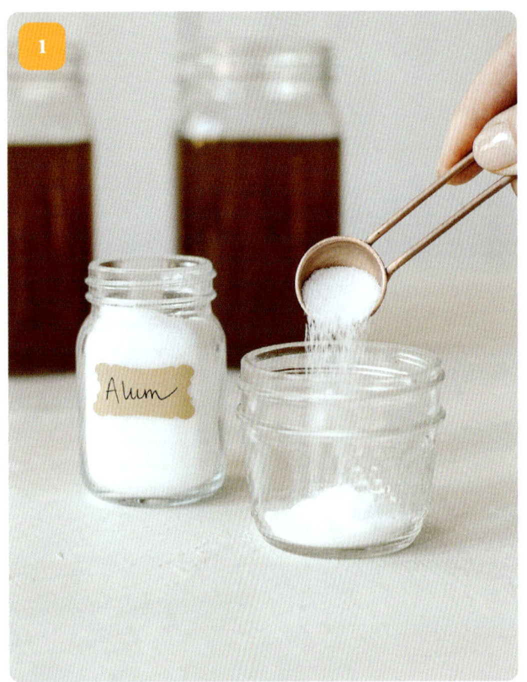
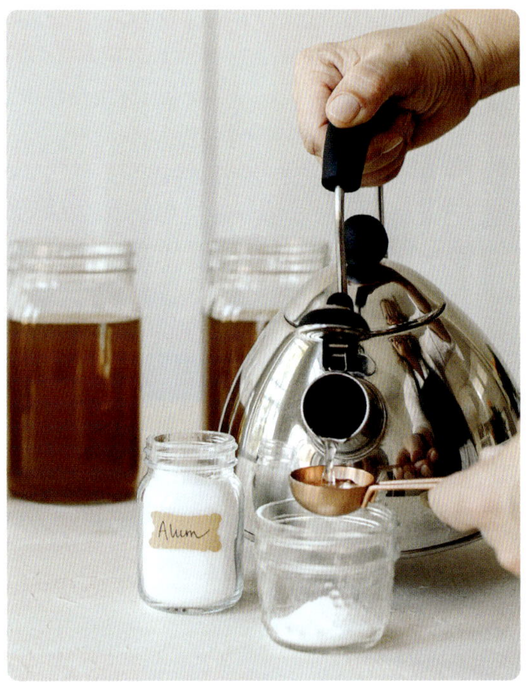

MEASURING OUT THE "TEA"

Begin by measuring 3½ cups (840 ml) of the well-filtered dye "tea" (see page 38) and pour it into a 4-cup (1-L) glass canning jar. You will need several jars to measure out and divide all the liquid. I usually have a minimum of six large jars on hand.

PREPARING AND ADDING THE CHEMICALS

Next, we need to prepare the two lake pigment chemicals: alum and chalk.

NOTE: Many paint makers use soda ash or washing soda instead of chalk. Because I prefer the lake pigment results from using chalk, all the recipes in this book are fine-tuned using chalk as the alkaline ingredient.

The following steps will be repeated for each jar.

Step 1: In a small glass jar, add 2 teaspoons (10 g) of alum. Next, add around 5 tablespoons (75 ml) of boiling hot water and stir well to dissolve the alum crystals. Add the dissolved alum to the first jar of dye extraction and gently stir. In your dye journal, make note of any color changes you observe. Chemically sensitive pigments can dramatically change color when alum is added.

Natural Watercolor Paint Making

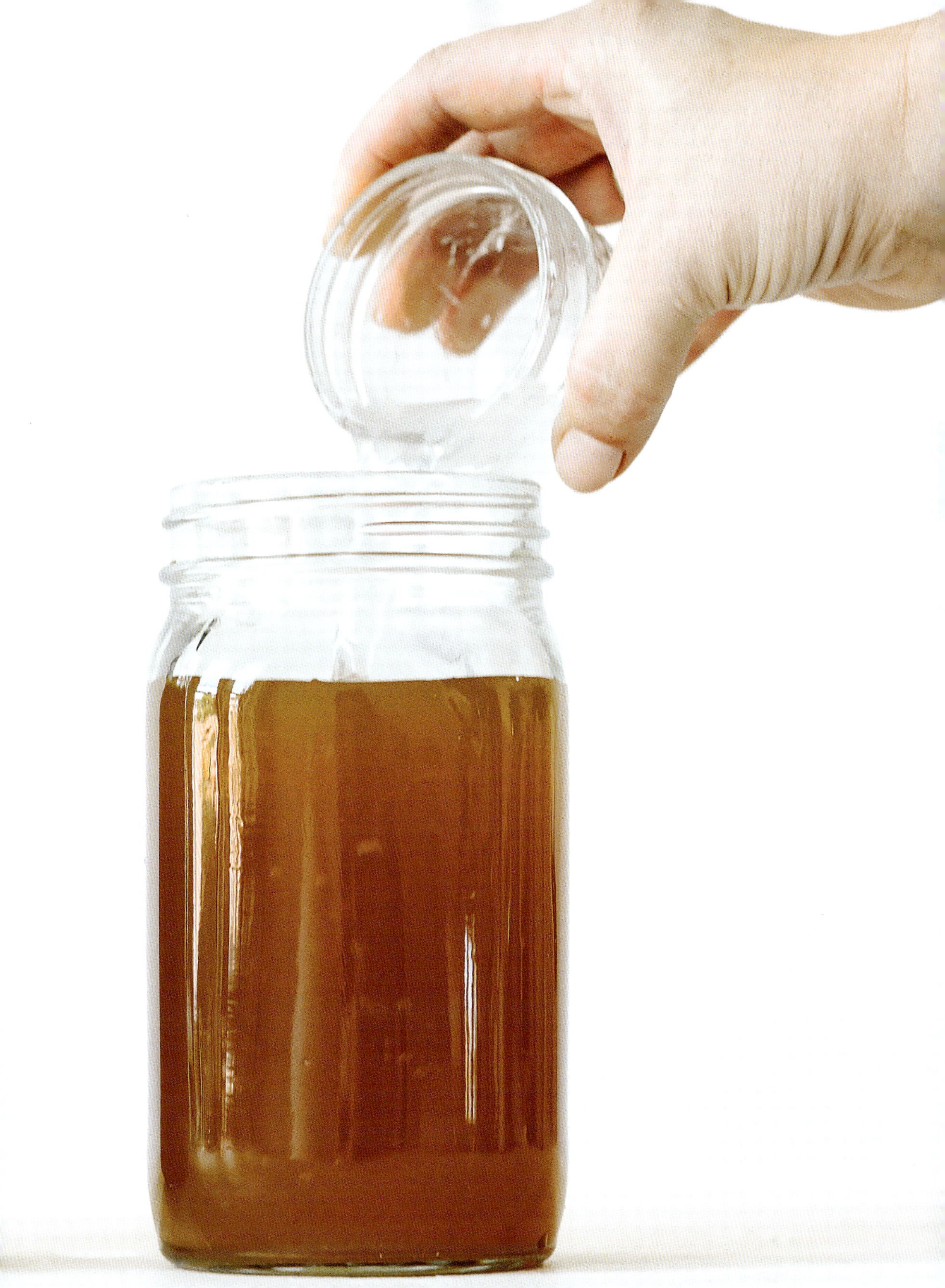

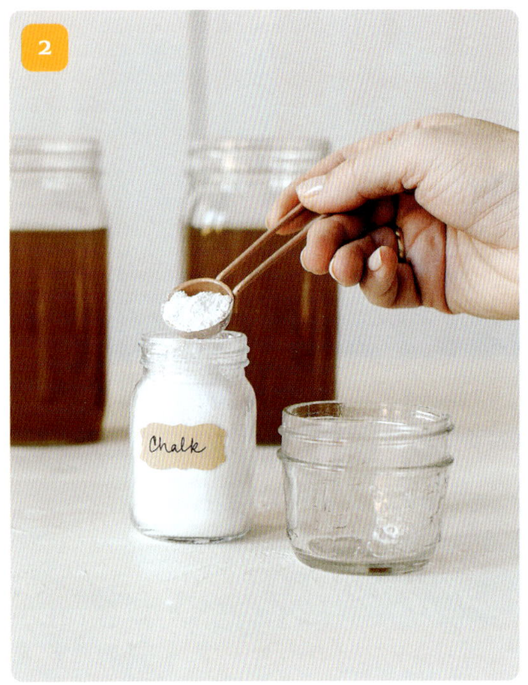

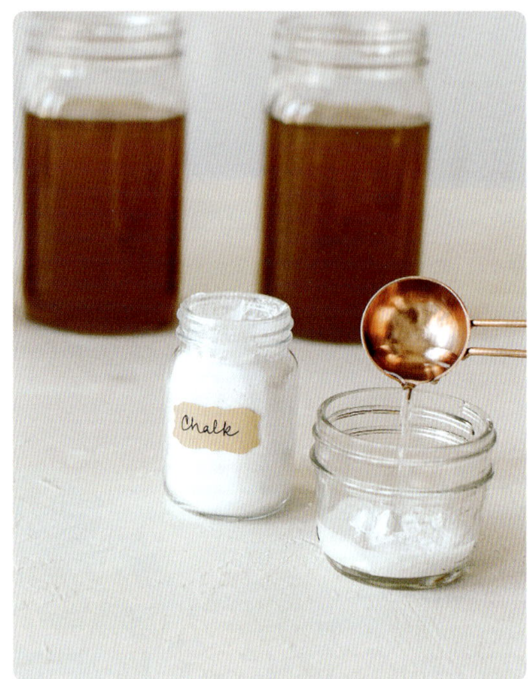

Step 2: Measure out 1 teaspoon (3 g) of chalk and add about 1 tablespoon (15 ml) of very hot water, then stir together well to create a smooth, clump-free slurry. Then add a few more tablespoons (15–30 ml) of hot water and stir *very* well. Pour this slurry into the first jar (where you just added the alum) and gently stir.

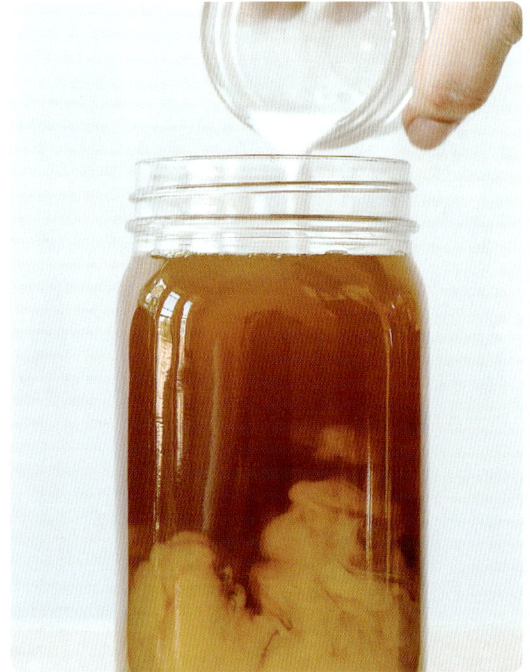

Natural Watercolor Paint Making

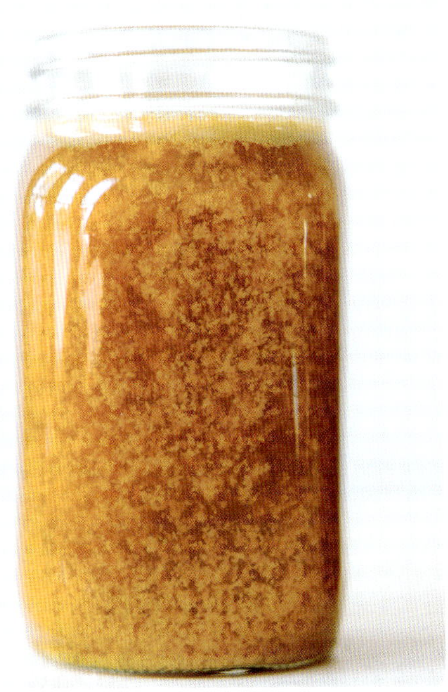

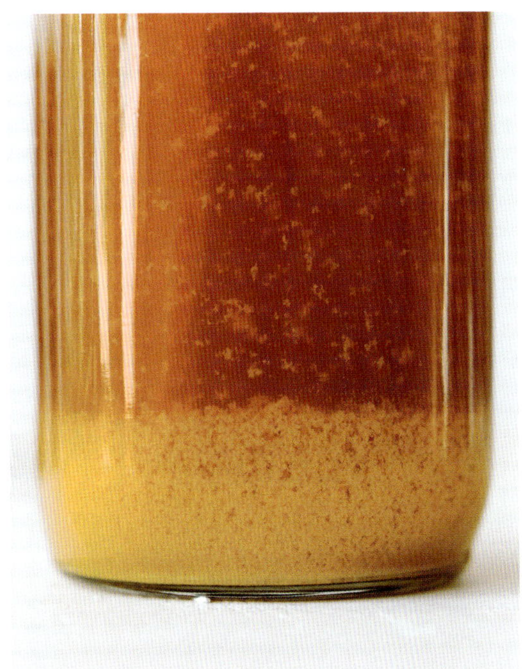

Step 3: Repeat this process of adding dissolved alum and chalk for each 3½ cups (840 ml) of dye extraction. If you have a jar with less than 3½ cups (840 ml) of liquid, simply adjust by lowering the amounts of alum and chalk proportionally. Only proceed to add alum and chalk to the remaining jars of dye "tea" once you see a chemical reaction happening in the first jar.

NOTE: The general rule for lake pigments is to add twice the amount of alum to chalk.

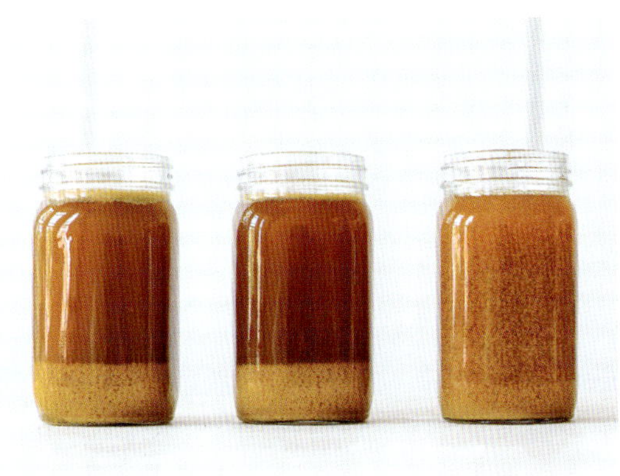

This is where science and art unite! The liquid should begin to fizz soon after the chalk slurry is added to the alum-infused dye extraction. You may notice foam developing on top and sometimes the fizzing can be so dramatic that it causes the jars to overflow. Be ready with rags to wipe up! This fizzing will begin to separate the colorful solids (pigments) from the liquid.

The solids should begin to settle at the bottom of the jar. This can take as little as an hour but the longer you leave it to settle, the better. Some lake pigments can benefit from resting overnight. The sediment at the bottom is the plant pigment that will become your watercolor paint, but first, it needs to be washed.

TROUBLESHOOTING

1. If your first jar of pigment shows no chemical reaction after adding both alum and chalk, start by increasing the amount of dissolved alum in ¼-teaspoon increments. Monitor closely and document any recipe alterations and observations in your dye journal. If you think you need more chalk, you can also add it in ¼-teaspoon increments. In my experience, my jars often benefit from an extra boost of dissolved alum, which is why I prioritize that first. Once you observe a chemical reaction in the jar, you'll know you've found the right chemical combination. By recording these adjustments, you can easily replicate the altered recipe for the remaining jars of dye extract.

2. A lack of chemical reaction may also occur if the dye "tea" is too concentrated, making the pigment load too "heavy." This can happen if the dye bath has lost too much water during boiling or if too much plant matter was added to the dye pot. Fortunately, this is an easy fix! Try diluting the dye "tea" in the jars by adding more distilled water. Hint: When the dye "tea" is in the jars, it should be well-colored but transparent enough to see through. If your extraction is nearly opaque, it may indicate that your "tea" is too strong.

WASHING THE PIGMENT

The purpose of washing the pigment is to remove the chemical residue of the alum and chalk. I find that a well-washed pigment creates a finer-quality watercolor paint. Some pigment makers skip the washing step entirely, but I encourage you to give your pigments this extra TLC.

Step 4: Once the pigment has fully settled at the bottom of the jar, you can start siphoning off the clearer liquid at the top. Remove as much of this liquid as possible without disturbing the pigment below. It's normal for this liquid to be quite colorful.

I often save this vibrant water by transferring it to new canning jars and adding another round of alum and chalk following the previous instructions. However, the resulting pigment from this second extraction won't be as vibrant. While you're learning the art of botanical paint making, it's perfectly fine to discard this colorful water. Over time, though, you may choose to process all the siphoned liquid to capture every last drop of precious pigment.

Step 5: You can now "wash" the pigment solids that are remaining in the jar by refilling the entire jar of pigment with fresh water. Stir well and allow the pigment to once again settle to the bottom of the jar. Repeat this process of siphoning and refilling with fresh water as many times as it takes for the liquid to become clearer and less colored. I typically repeat the washing cycle one to three times.

Natural Watercolor Paint Making

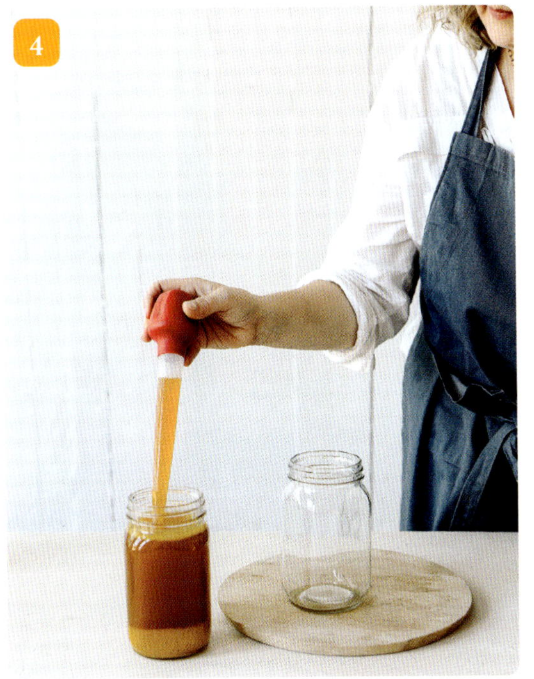

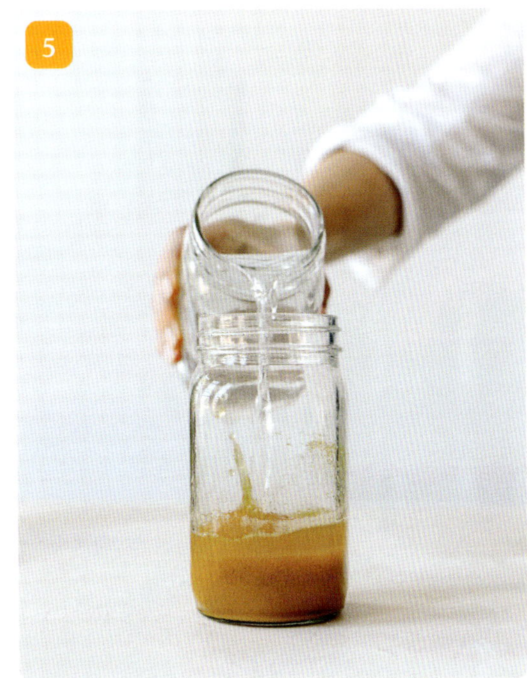

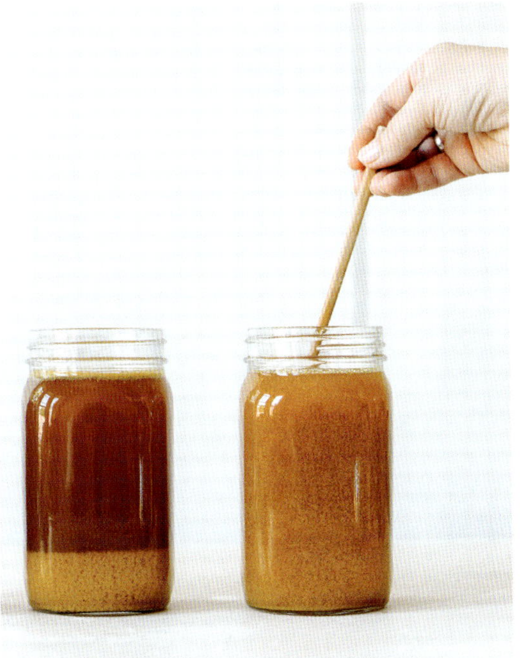

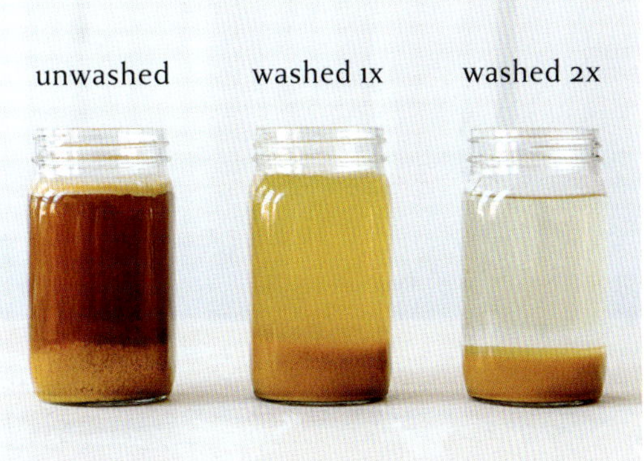
unwashed
washed 1x
washed 2x

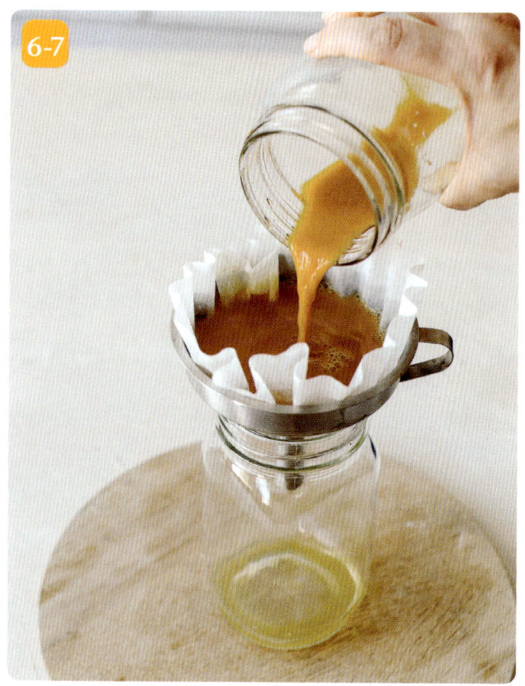 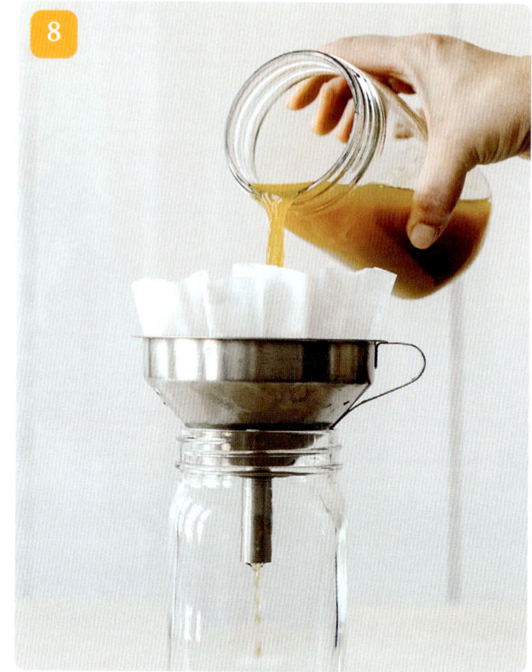

FILTERING THE PIGMENT

This is my favorite part of the entire paint-making process. You now get to collect the beautiful, smooth and silky plant pigment.

Step 6: Place a small funnel or sieve over the mouth of an empty canning jar. Next, add a paper coffee filter. A very fine woven piece of cloth may also be used.

Step 7: Slowly pour the washed pigment into the filter. If you notice any undissolved chalk at the bottom of the jar, try to avoid pouring this into the filter.

Step 8: Allow the water to drain through the filter. Watch the filter carefully, and only add more washed pigment once the water is drained out. The more pigment that is captured in the filter, the slower the filtering becomes. It may be helpful to continue this process with a new coffee filter. Several filters may be needed for one jar of washed pigment.

Natural Watercolor Paint Making

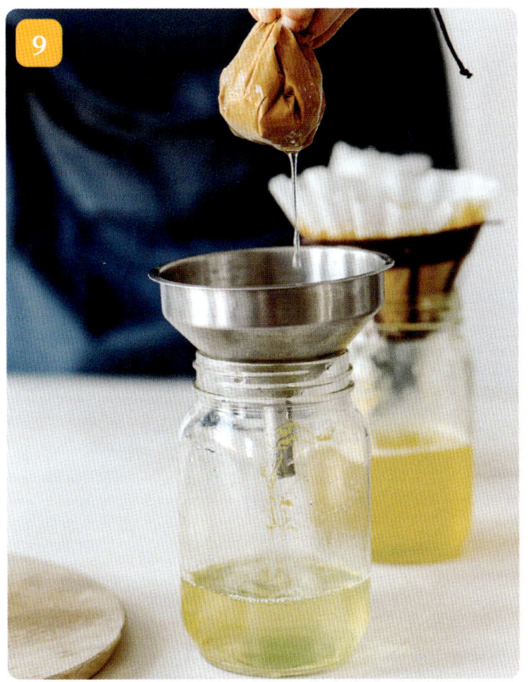

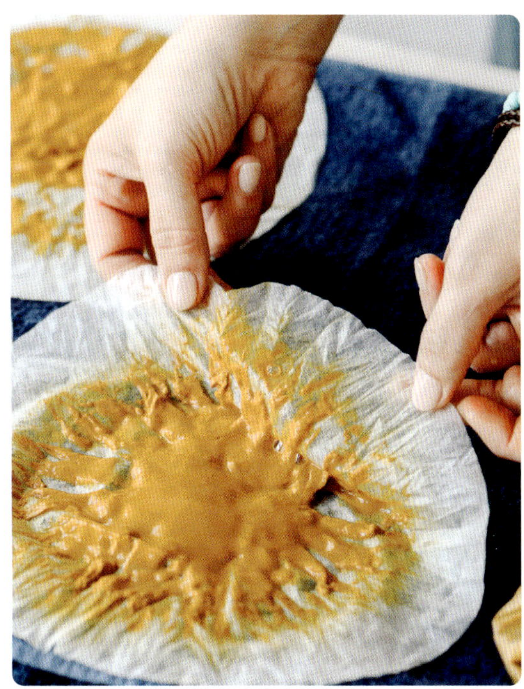

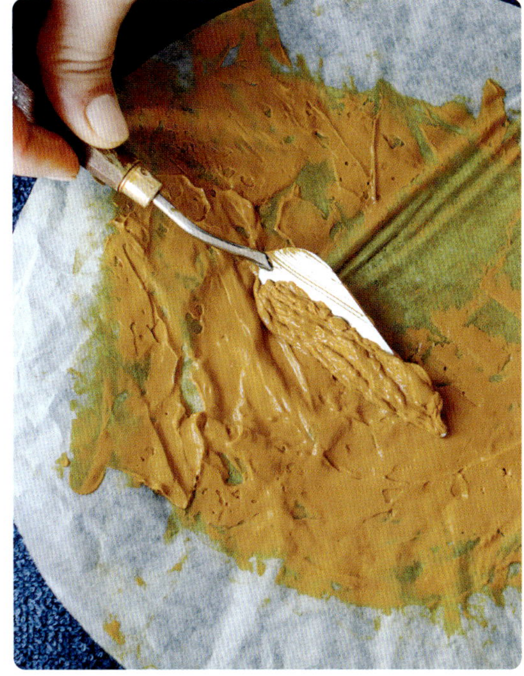

Step 9: Once the water is drained from each filter, carefully lift out the filter and lay it flat on an absorbent towel.

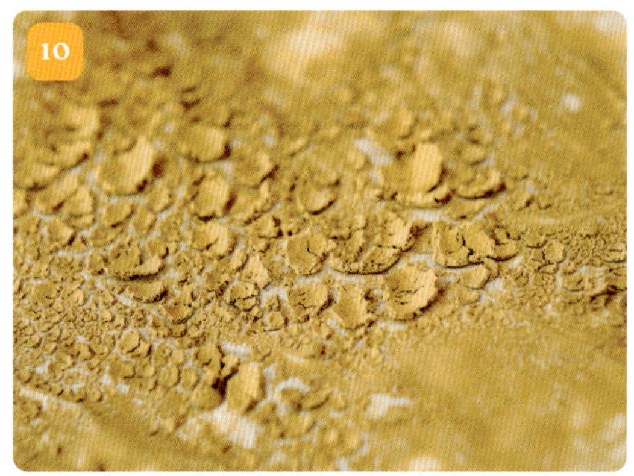

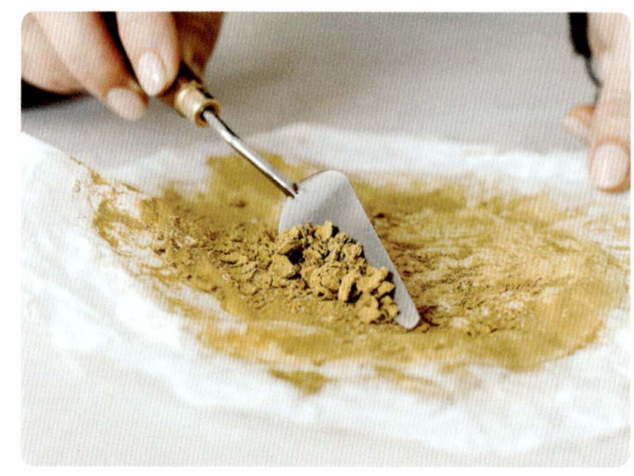

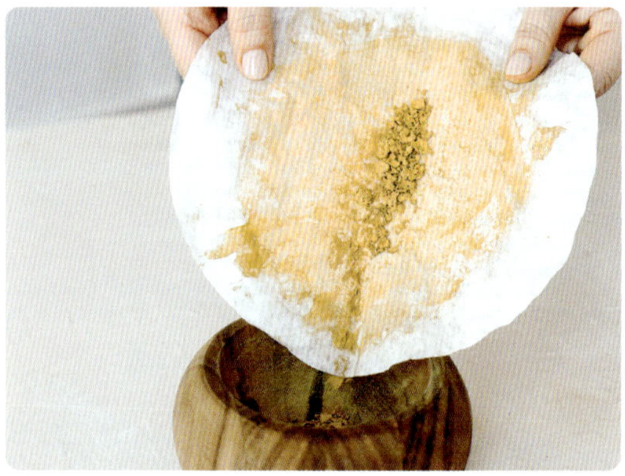

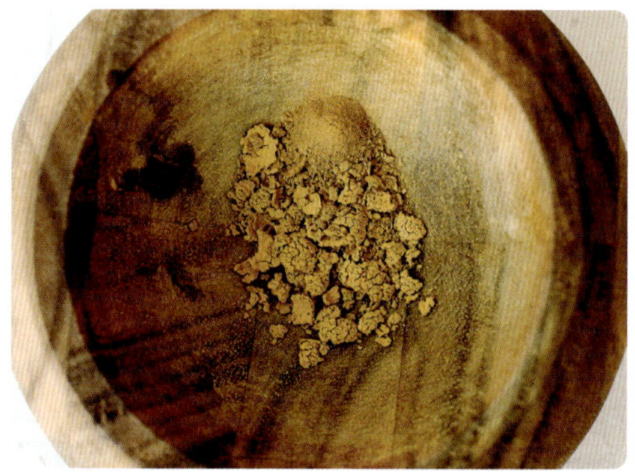

DRYING THE PIGMENT

Your wet pigment is almost ready to be made into watercolor paint! But first, the pigment needs to dry out completely because any remaining moisture can lead to mold growth and spoil the pigment. How quickly it dries depends on the temperature and humidity.

Step 10: Once it's completely dried, wear a dust mask and scrape off the dry pigment using a palette knife. In a mortar and pestle, grind the pigment chunks into a fine powder.

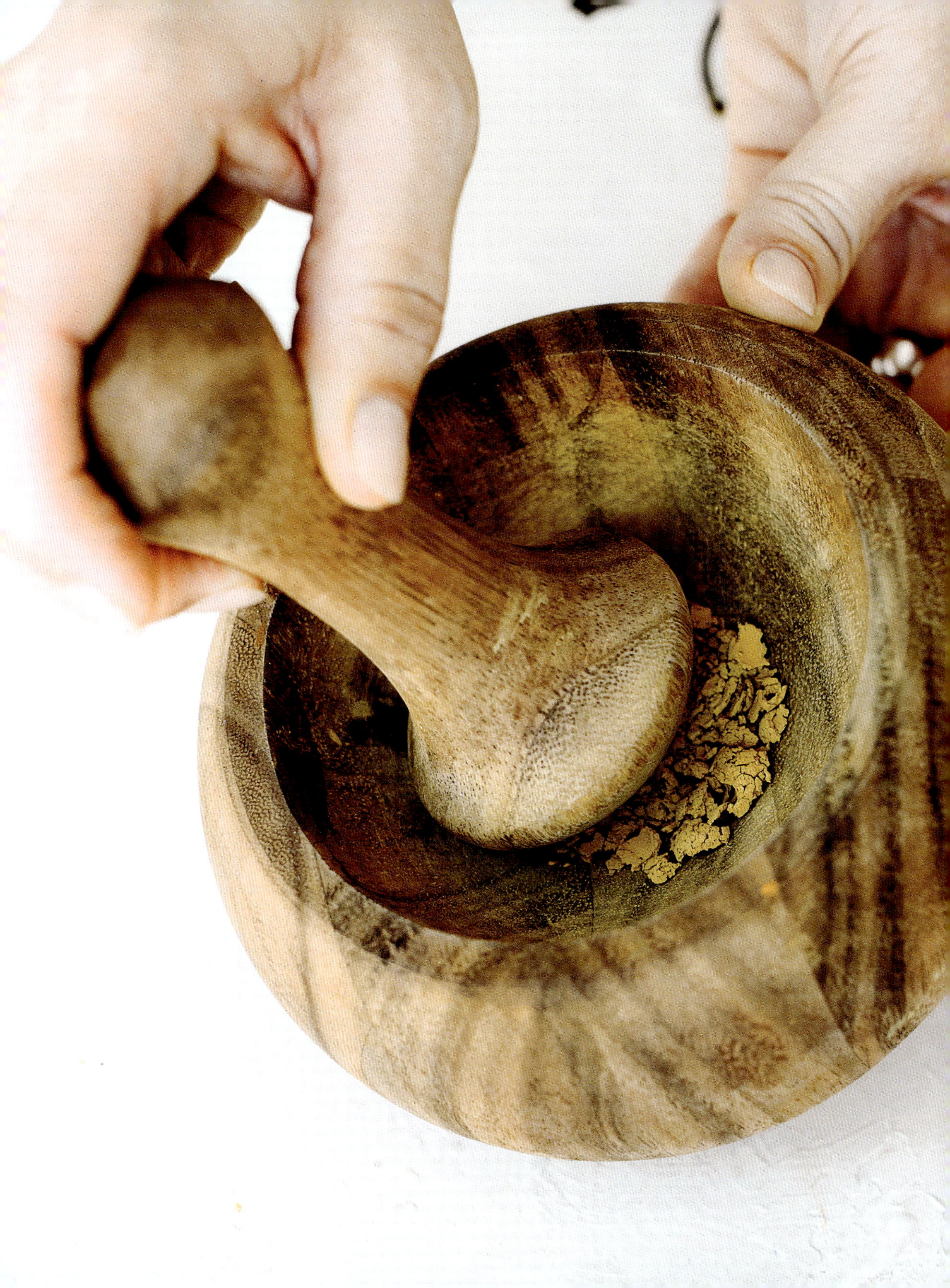

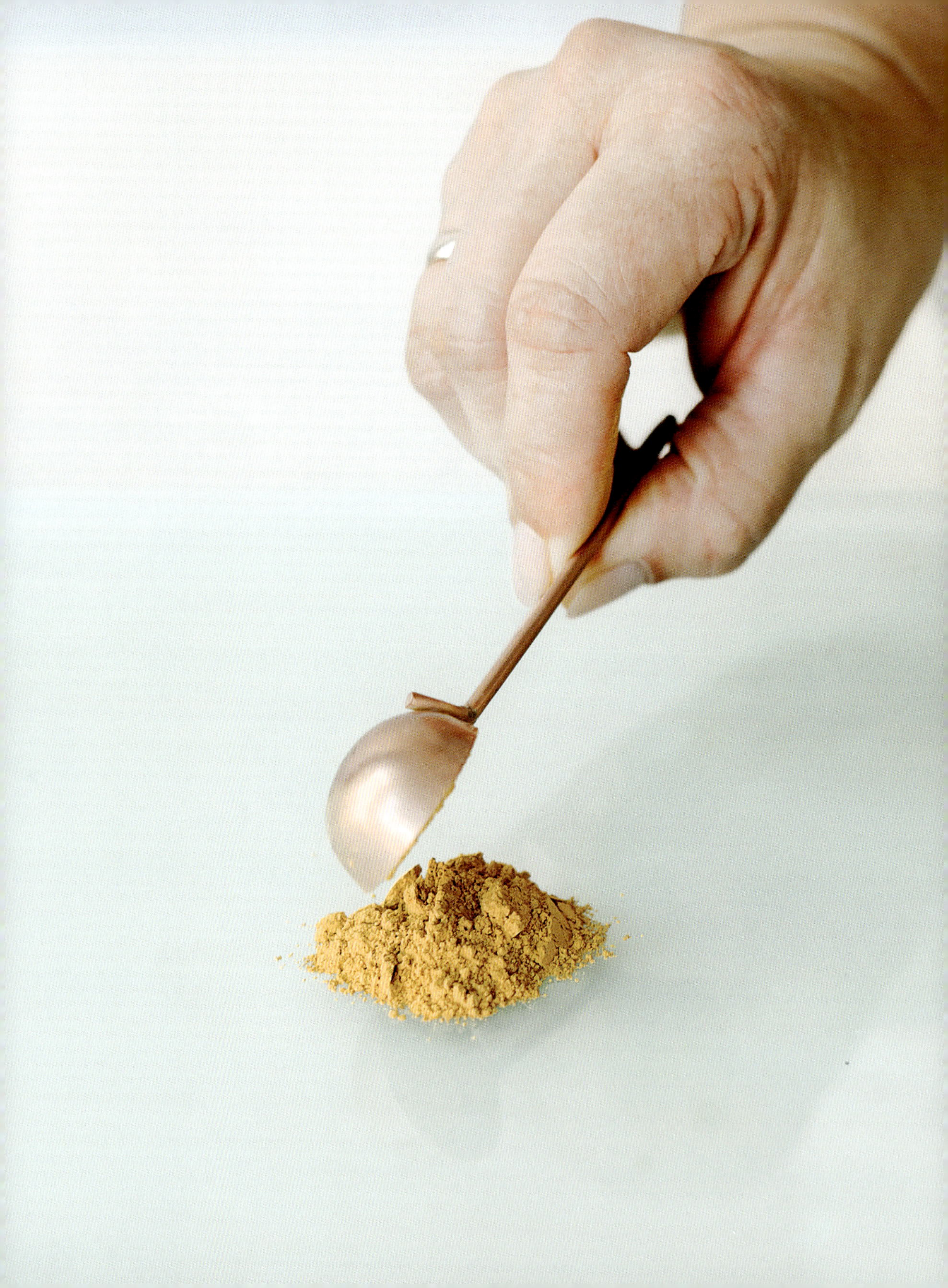

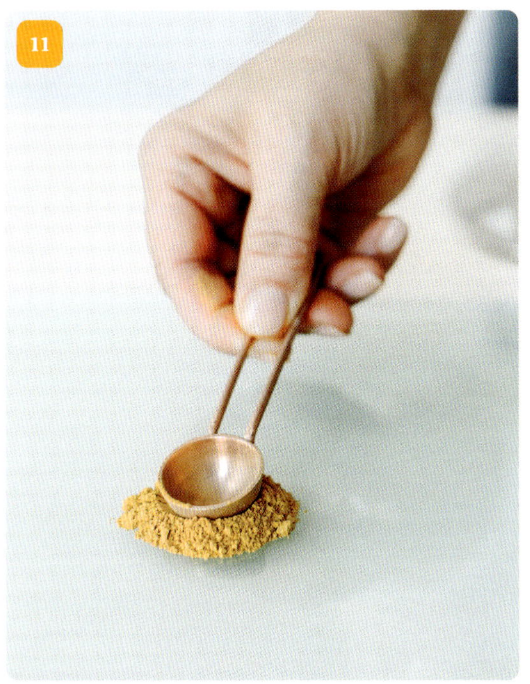

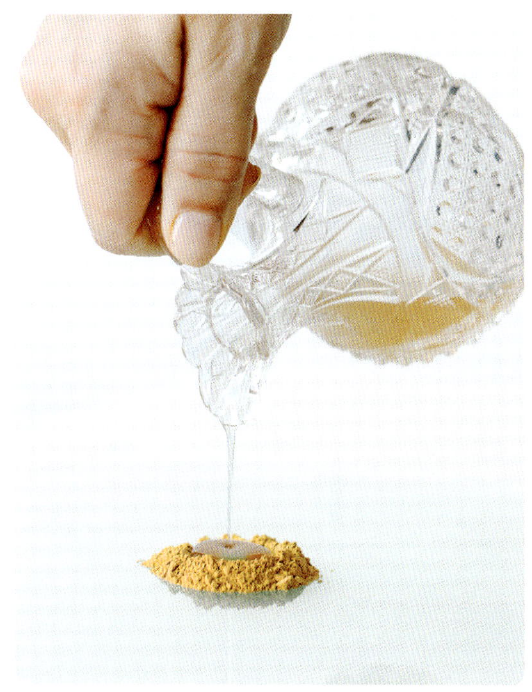

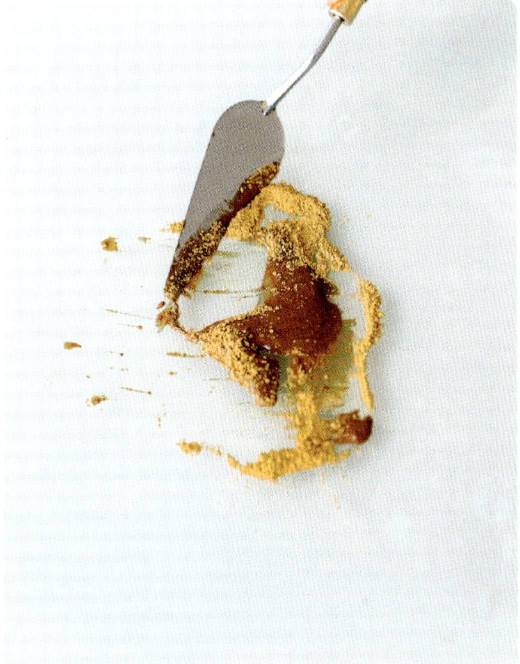

MIXING AND MULLING THE PIGMENT

Mulling is an especially delightful part of the paint-making process. This is when the pigment powder comes to life and essentially, it becomes paint! Mulling is done to grind, mix and suspend the botanical pigment particles within the binder. The watercolor binder helps to adhere the paint to the paper and creates a flowing and smooth consistency.

Step 11: To begin, place a couple of teaspoons (3 to 5 ml) of dried pigment powder onto a smooth glass surface. This is known as a mulling or grinding plate. Drizzle some watercolor binder into the center of the pigment, starting with a 1:1 ratio. Using a palette knife, gently incorporate the pigment into the binder.

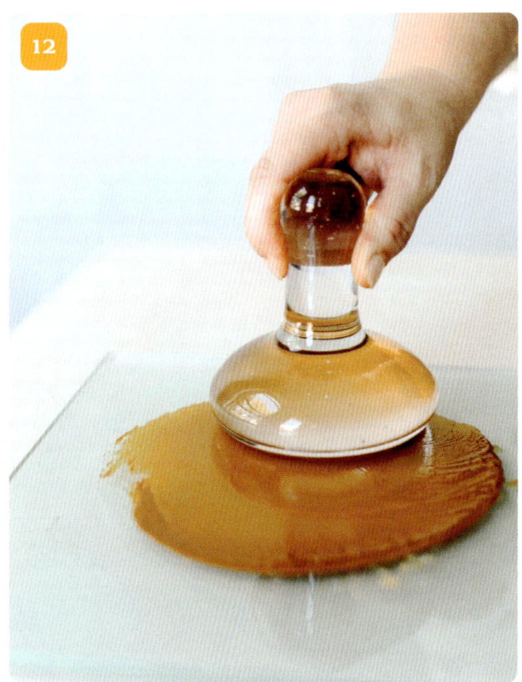

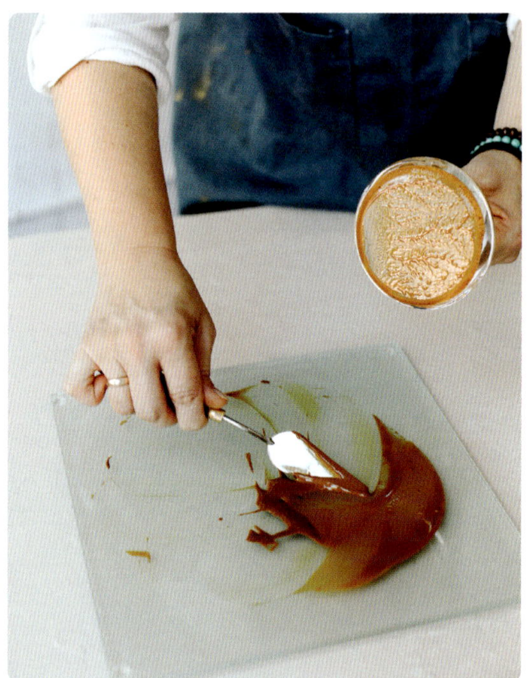

Step 12: Next, applying a gentle amount of pressure, use a glass muller to slowly grind the pigment in circular motions and spread it thinly across the glass. This helps to achieve the finest paint consistency possible. Periodically, use the palette knife to scrape the mixture back to the center, then continue mulling. The final mixed pigment should be glossy and smooth with the consistency of warmed honey: thick but still viscous enough to drip off the point of a palette knife. At any point in the mulling process, if you find your glass surface getting too dry, sprinkling in drops of water is helpful.

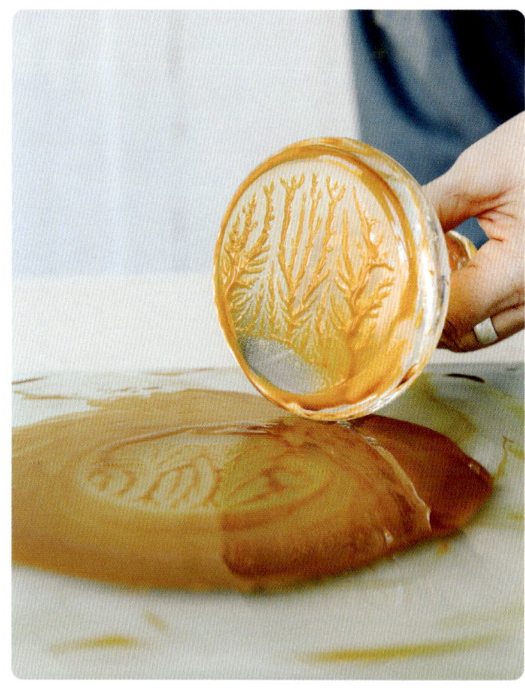

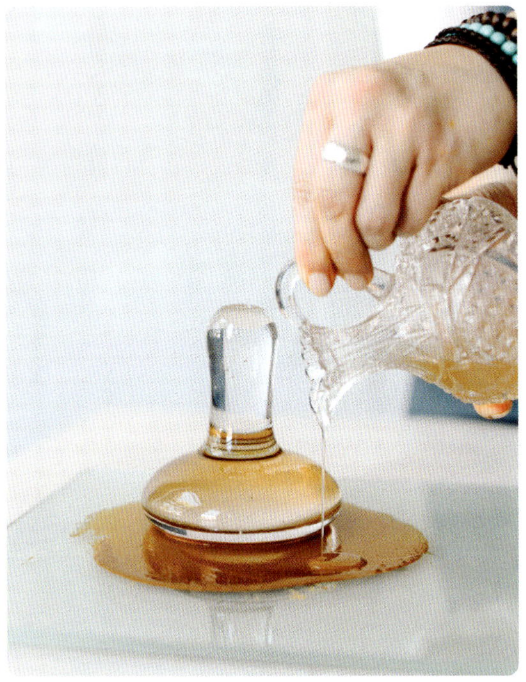

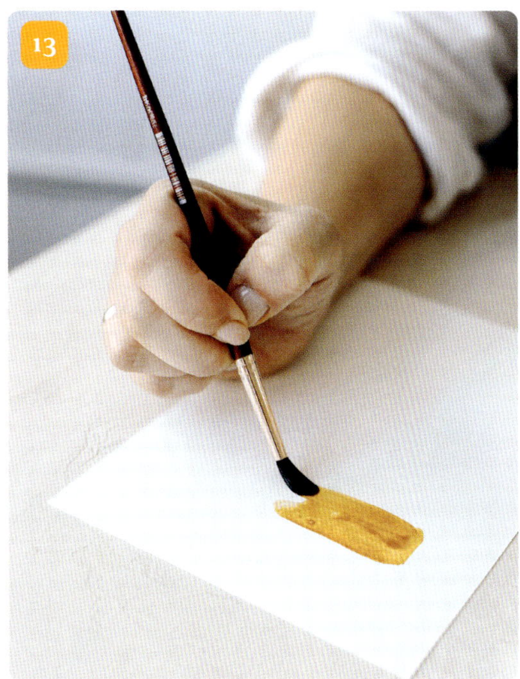

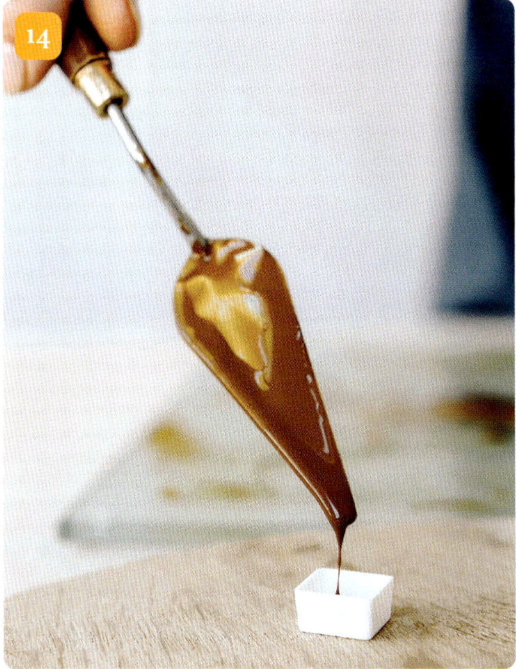

Step 13: Once you have a thoroughly mixed watercolor paint, it is helpful to now test the paint mixture on watercolor paper. When the paint swatch is dry, rub the swatch. If the paint is well adhered to the paper, you've added the right amount of binder. Sometimes you will find that you need to add more pigment, especially if the swatches are too transparent.

Step 14: Once you are satisfied with your mixed watercolor pigment, use a palette knife to scrape the wet paint and drip it into empty watercolor pans. I usually fill two to three pans at a time.

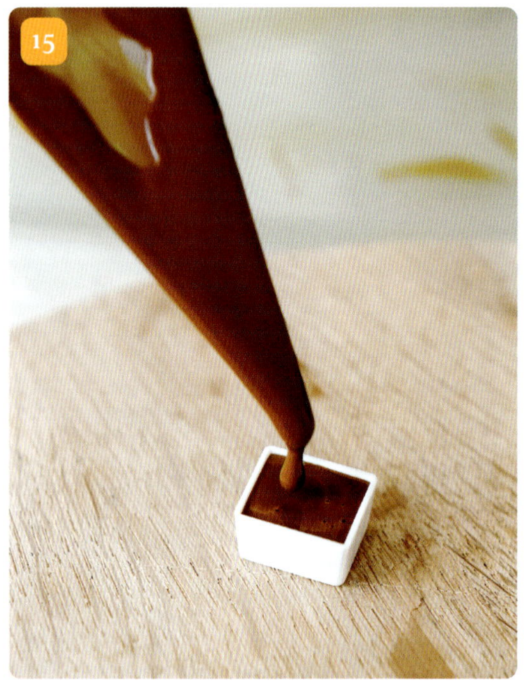

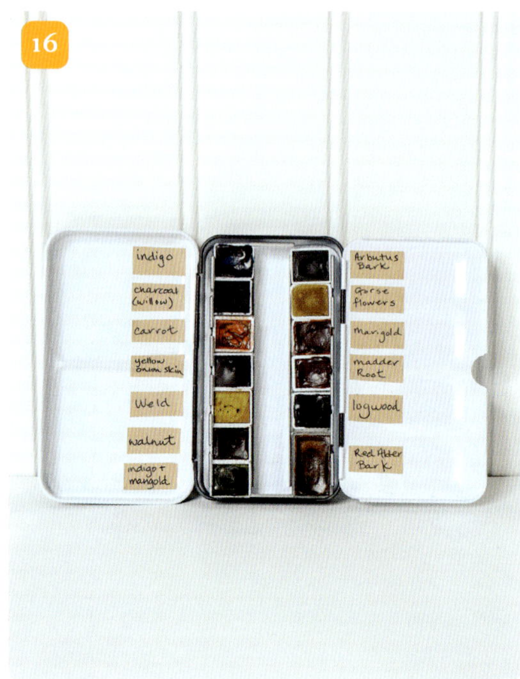

CURING THE PIGMENT

As the paint dries in the watercolor pans, it dehydrates and shrinks considerably! You may be surprised to see how much your paint actually dehydrates; depending on the temperature of the room, the drying process can take several days.

Step 15: Watch your pans over the next few days, and then top them up with more mixed pigment. You may also notice the paint cracking as it dries. Make a note of this and try adding more binder next time. Cracks in the final watercolor "cake" shouldn't interfere with the quality of the paint when using them later on.

Step 16: Lastly, achieving a full pan of dried watercolor typically requires a few top-ups of freshly mixed paint. Eventually, you'll end up with a cake of paint that resembles store-bought traditional watercolors, but with the added satisfaction of knowing you made it yourself!

Natural Watercolor Paint Making

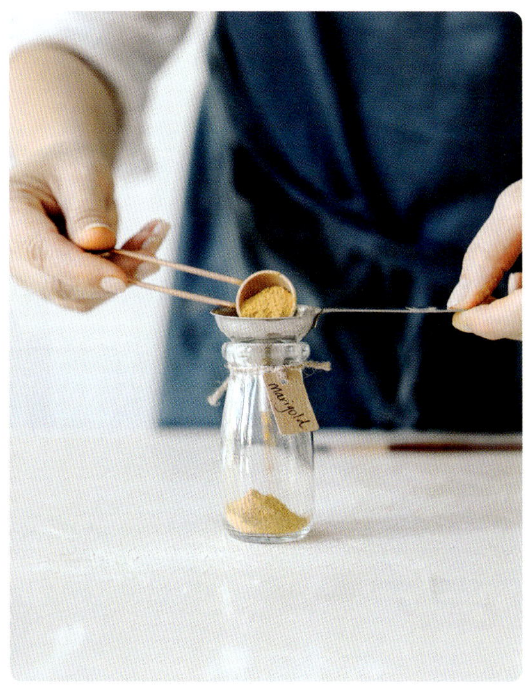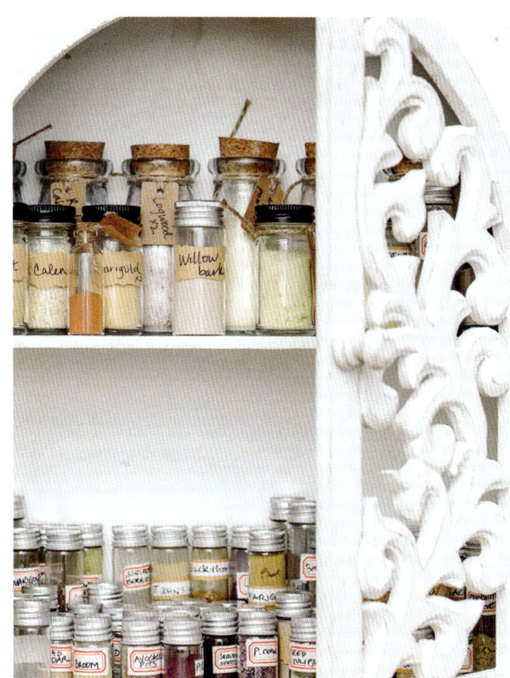

STORING THE PIGMENT

After filling a few watercolor pans, I usually have leftover powdered pigment which I can add to my growing collection of botanical pigments. As long as all the moisture is out of the powder, and they are stored in airtight containers, these dried pigments are shelf-stable and can be mixed with watercolor binder at any point in the future. This is especially handy for when you want to top up watercolor pans or when you want to mix up just enough paint for a specific painting project. Store any powdered pigment in small airtight jars or containers. Having a small funnel to the fill jars is helpful. Label the jars with the date and name of the plant pigment.

Keep in mind, botanical pigments can lose their color vibrancy over time, especially if exposed to strong sunlight, so it is best to store them in a dark place. I discuss the specific lightfastness of each plant color in the paint recipes. My general rule of thumb is to use stored pigments within a few years of making them. I keep an eye on them to see how they age, as each plant pigment has its own unique personality that you'll come to know. Writing your observations in your dye journal is extremely helpful. That said, don't treat your pigment collection too preciously. Use them up! Fully enjoy the experience of painting with your handcrafted colors. And remember, you can always make more! If you're anything like me, you'll be looking for any excuse to get back into the paint lab!

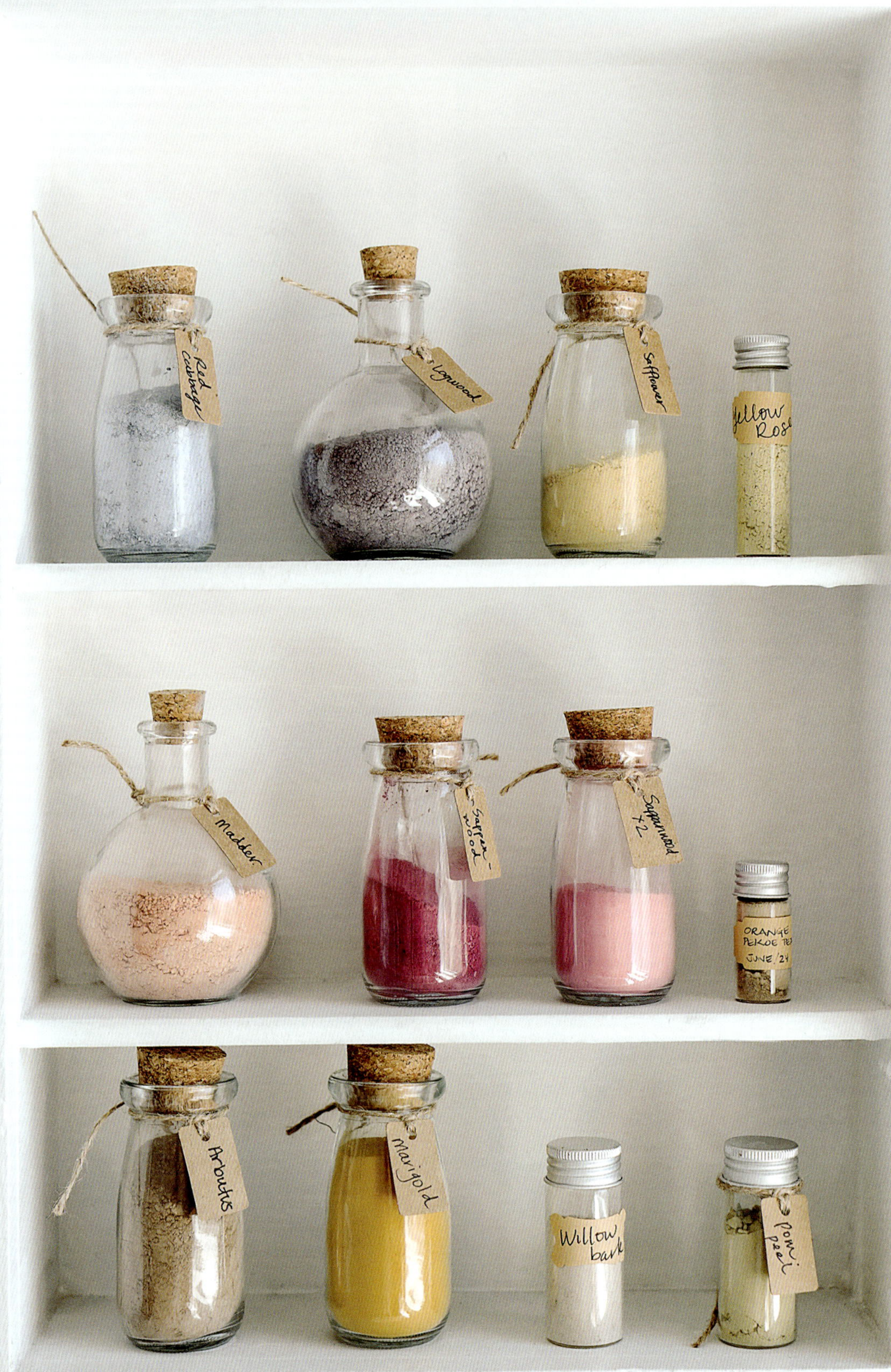
Red Cabbage
Logwood
Safflower
Yellow Rose
Madder
Sappan wood
Sappanwood x2
ORANGE PEKOE TEA JUNE/24
Arbutus
Marigold
Willow bark
Pomi peel

PART 2

THE PAINT RECIPES

The Kitchen

Nature offers us a rich array of colors, and many of the vibrant foods we see on our plates can also serve as sources of pigments for artists! I love experimenting with everyday items, from forgotten vegetables in my fridge to pantry staples and even my tea and spice collections. In my little kitchen, there's hardly anything I haven't tried turning into paint! I affectionately refer to my kitchen as the "paint lab," where I've conducted countless color experiments over the years. In the next section, I'll share some of my favorite paint recipes made from commonly found foods—perhaps they're found in your kitchen too!

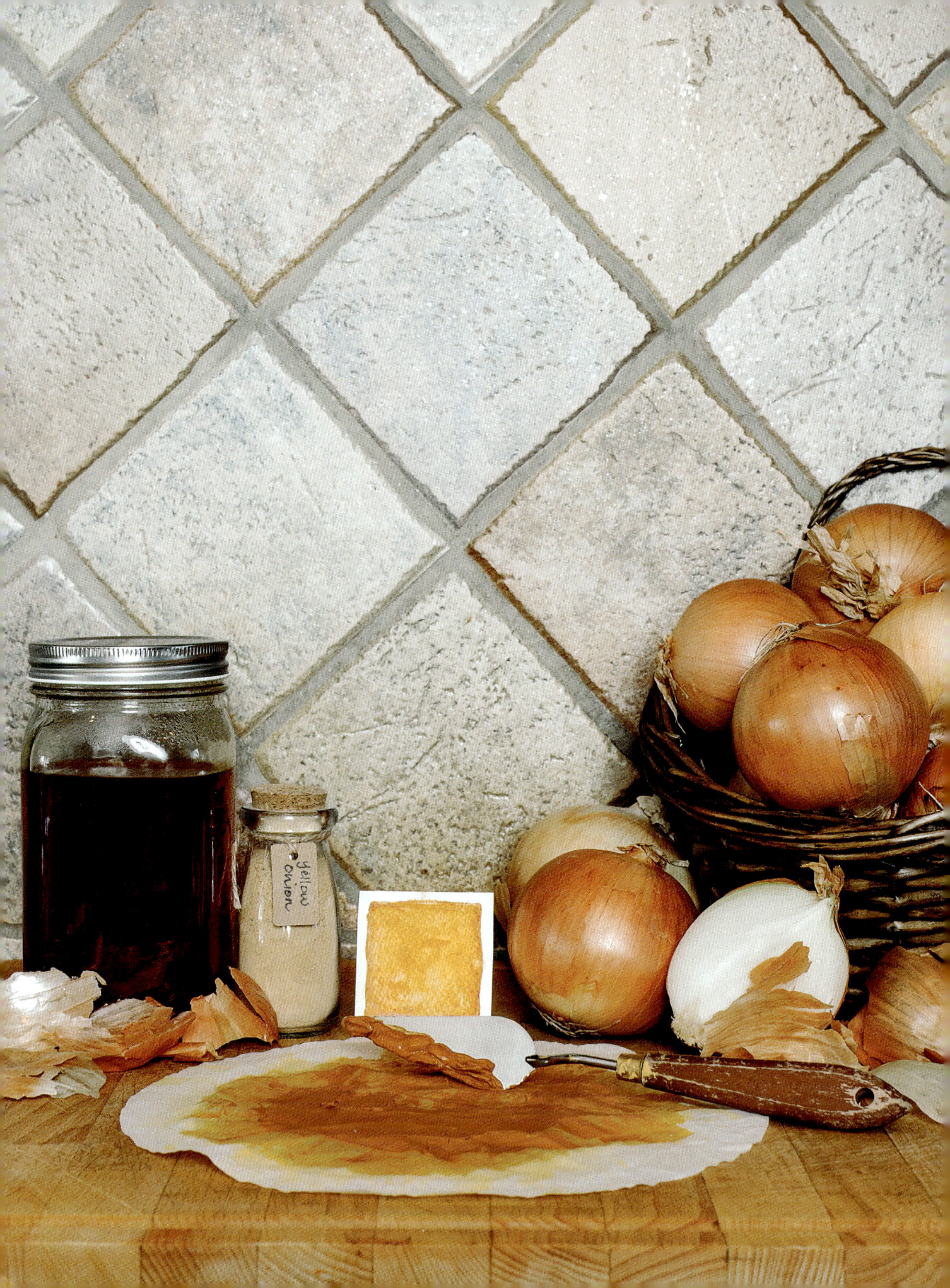

yellow
onion

YELLOW ONION SKINS (GOLD)

The humble yellow onion is a staple ingredient in kitchens around the world. For generations, textile dyers have utilized onion skins to impart beautiful golden hues to yarn and textiles. Yellow onion skins can also serve as an affordable and vibrant source of watercolor pigment. I find great satisfaction in incorporating food waste into my art practice, so when I cook with yellow onions, I always save the papery skins. It doesn't take long to collect enough skins to create a substantial pot of dye. Yellow onion skins yield a lovely golden pigment that reminds me of the ancient earth mineral pigment yellow ochre. Interestingly, the skins can produce a range of colors, from yellows to oranges to browns.

MATERIALS

- *2 cups (20 g) yellow onion skins (packed tightly into measuring cup)*
- *Large stainless-steel dye pot with lid*
- *16 cups (3.8 L) distilled water*
- *Alum*
- *Chalk powder*
- *Watercolor Binder (page 33)*
- *Supplies for the Master Lake Pigment Recipe (page 45)*

Peel and gather only the papery and dry skins from the onions until you have about 2 cups (20 g) of the skins packed tightly into your measuring cup.

Once measured, place the skins in a large pot with 16 cups (3.8 L) of water and cover the pot with a lid. Bring the water to a boil, then reduce the heat to a gentle simmer, stirring occasionally. You'll notice the onion skins releasing their dye quickly!

(continued)

Gently simmer for at least an hour, then remove the pot from the heat. The longer the onion skins soak, the deeper the dye color may become, so you can choose to let them soak overnight or proceed with the next steps. I'm usually too excited to wait!

Once the dye bath has completely cooled, remove the skins with tongs. Proceed with following the instructions of the Master Lake Pigment Recipe starting on page 46, starting with filtering the "tea." I typically end up with around 13 cups (3.1 L) of filtered onion skin liquid. Divide this equally between large canning jars (measuring out 3¼ to 3½ cups [780–840 ml] in each jar).

Prepare the alum and chalk as noted in Step 1 and Step 2 of the Master Lake Pigment Recipe. For this recipe, add 2 teaspoons (10 g) of dissolved alum and 1 teaspoon (3 g) of dissolved chalk to every jar of liquid dye extraction.

After the pigment has settled within the jars, proceed with the washing process. I typically need to wash the onion skin pigment two to three times before the water is clear or mostly clear.

Filter the washed pigment through funnels or sieves lined with paper coffee filters, then allow your onion pigment to dry on the filters.

Once the onion skin pigment has dried, scrape it off the filter and add it to a mortar and pestle. Grind it into a fine powder.

Add a couple of teaspoons (3 to 5 ml) of the dried pigment to a smooth glass surface. Add your watercolor binder in a 1:1 ratio and use a palette knife to combine. Then, use a glass muller to mix the pigment into a paint consistency, following the steps on page 57.

Follow the remaining steps for curing and storing the pigment on pages 60–61, and get ready to paint with a beautiful golden yellow watercolor!

RECIPE REVIEW

Onion skins are undoubtedly one of my favorite botanical ingredients to use, and they're a great option for those new to making lake pigments. They offer a wonderful opportunity to practice, as you're using what would otherwise be thrown into the compost. In other words, the stakes are low if any mistakes happen while learning the lake pigment process. Plus, onion skins yield a generous amount of dye, allowing us to create a stunning golden amber watercolor pigment. If you're curious about red onion skins, I provide a recipe for that on page 71.

RED CABBAGE (BLUE)

This recipe may introduce you to working with anthocyanin pigments, the chemical compounds that give plants, flowers, roots, leaves and berries their red, blue or purple hues. Paint makers are often captivated by these beautiful anthocyanins, only to discover that they can be unpredictable and fickle. Their chemically sensitive nature means that even the smallest changes in pH (the acidity or alkalinity) can affect the outcome, making the process of creating a lake pigment from anthocyanins a bit tricky. Creating lake pigments with red cabbage is an affordable way to practice with these more temperamental natural colors and a great way to use that lonely cabbage that might be wilting at the bottom of your fridge!

MATERIALS

- *5 cups (445 g) chopped raw red cabbage*
- *12 cups (2.9 L) distilled water*
- *Large stainless-steel dye pot with lid*
- *Alum*
- *Chalk powder*
- *Watercolor Binder (page 33)*
- *Supplies for the Master Lake Pigment Recipe (page 45)*

Add the chopped cabbage and distilled water to a large stainless-steel pot and bring it to a boil. Cover the pot with a lid and lower the heat to simmer for about half an hour, or until the cabbage has lost most of its purple color. The water should now be a beautiful shade of purple.

Filter this liquid as explained on page 38 of the Filtering the "Tea" section. You should end up with around 9 cups (2.2 L) of filtered liquid.

(continued)

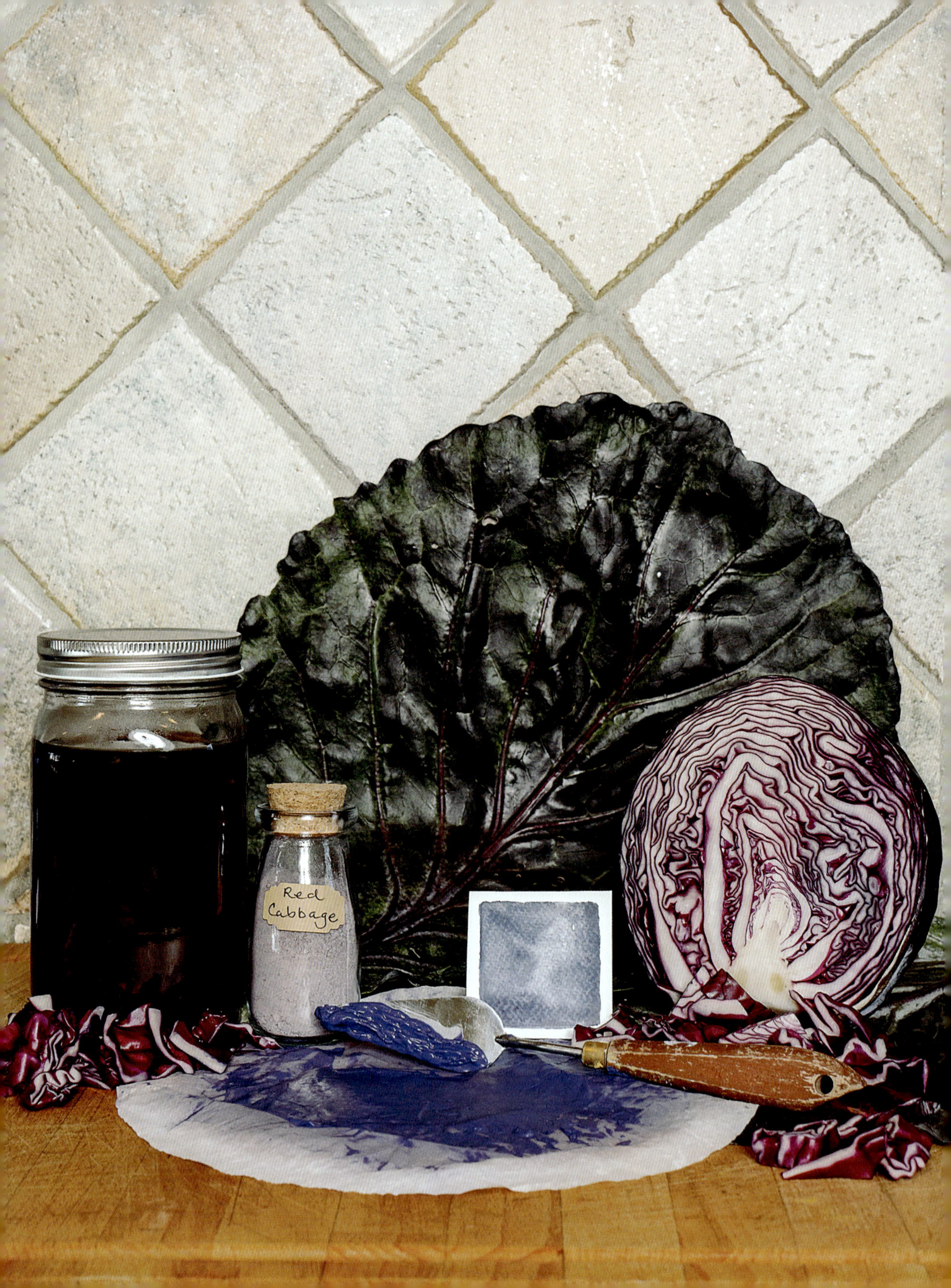

Red
Cabbage

Equally divide the filtered cabbage "tea" in large canning jars. I usually have enough liquid to add around 3 cups (720 ml) to 3¼ cups (780 ml) to each jar.

Next prepare the dissolved alum and chalk as described in the Master Lake Pigment Recipe (page 46). However, for this recipe, you're going to make some adjustments to the measurements. To each jar of red cabbage "tea," do the following:

Add 2½ teaspoons (13 ml) of dissolved alum and gently stir. Notice the color change to a deep purple! Next, dissolve ¾ teaspoon of chalk in a few tablespoons (15 to 30 ml) of hot water to make a smooth slurry. Add to the jar and gently stir. A good amount of fizzing and swirling in the jar indicates a successful chemical reaction. Watch for foam that may spill over and be ready with rags to clean up any mess.

Allow the fizzing to dissipate as the pigment settles to the bottom of the jars. This may take a few hours. The liquid separated from the pigment solids will likely be very dark, making it hard to see the pigment at the bottom of the jar. Place the jars in front of a good light source before proceeding with the washing process described on page 50. I typically repeat this washing process three times.

Proceed by filtering the pigment through sieves or funnels lined with coffee filters. Once this step is completed, carefully place the wet filters on a towel for the moisture to absorb.

You may choose to mix up the wet pigment with your watercolor binder and begin painting right away, or wait for the pigment to dry. This can take a few days. Once the pigment is completely dry, scrape the dried pigment into a mortar and pestle and grind into a fine powder. A reminder that wearing a dust mask is important when working with pigment powders.

As long as there is no moisture left, the powder can be stored in jars and mixed with watercolor binder at any time in the future. Refer to the Master Lake Pigment Recipe (pages 57–61) for more details on mixing, mulling and storing your botanical pigments.

RECIPE REVIEW

Because red cabbage is a low-cost source of color, this recipe offers a low-stakes way to practice paint making with trickier pigments. While it may not be the most lightfast pigment in the realm of botanical colors, I believe it still has a valuable place in your palette. Red cabbage is a fantastic vegetable to explore with children, allowing them to play scientist (or magician!) by modifying the pH to create a rainbow of colors. It's a delight to see how a drop of vinegar can transform a blue-purple pigment into a vibrant pink, or how a sprinkle of baking soda can turn it into a dazzling teal green! This experience beautifully blends science and art into a fun and educational activity. I'll explain in further detail how to modify botanical colors on page 119. Keeping detailed notes and paint swatches in your dye journal is especially valuable when working with chemically sensitive pigments like red cabbage.

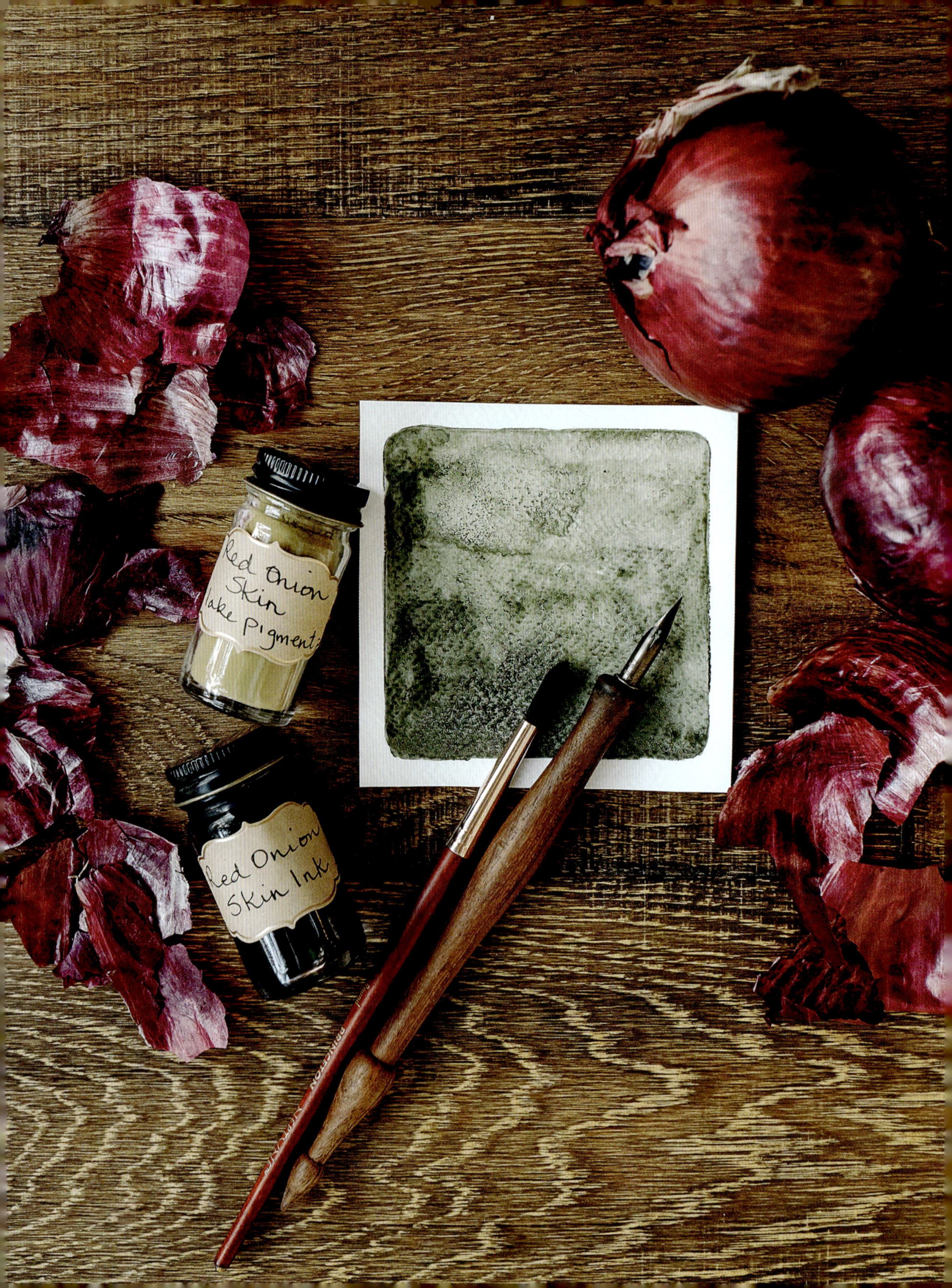

Red Onion
Skin
Lake Pigment
Red Onion
Skin Ink

RED ONION SKINS (GREEN)

Red onion skins are a fantastic source of green pigment—yes, green! The purplish-red skins contain anthocyanin pigments, and when alum is added, the color dramatically shifts to green. This is significant because, despite the abundance of chlorophyll-filled green plants, extracting pure chlorophyll pigment can be quite complicated, and in my experience, chlorophyll greens tend to fade quickly in paintings. That's why I'm sharing the following recipe, which uses the heat reduction method to transform more kitchen food waste into beautiful paint color! This recipe yields a small jar of ink, but it can easily be doubled for a larger batch.

MATERIALS

- *2 cups (20 g) red onion skins (packed tightly into measuring cup)*
- *4 cups (960 ml) distilled water (just enough to cover skins)*
- *Large stainless-steel dye pot*
- *Small stainless-steel saucepan*
- *Heat-resistant silicone spatula*
- *Alum*
- *Gum arabic powder*
- *Clove oil or whole cloves*

Place about 2 cups (20 g) of red onion skins and the distilled water in a large stainless-steel pot. Do **not** cover it with a lid.

Heat by bringing the water to a boil, then reduce it to a low simmer. Heat the mixture for about 30 minutes, stirring often, then turn off the heat and let the skins soak until the extraction is fully cooled.

(continued)

Filter by using a fine mesh sieve and strain the liquid to remove all skins and particles. The volume should be reduced by around 50 percent.

Reduce it further by pouring the liquid into a small clean stainless-steel saucepan and heat on low. As the liquid continues to reduce in volume, the risk of scalding the liquid increases. Watch this step closely and keep stirring with a spatula.

Remove the saucepan from the heat once the liquid is concentrated in color and thicker in consistency. This may take up to 90 minutes to achieve about ⅓ cup (80 ml) of liquid.

While the reduction is still warm, add ¼ teaspoon of alum crystals, and stir until they dissolve. Notice the color shift to a deep maroon. (Once painted on paper, it will dry as green!)

Next, start by adding a ½ teaspoon at a time of gum arabic powder. Mix well until completely dissolved. Test the consistency by painting a test swatch on paper, then allow it to dry. If needed, adjust the thickness by adding more gum arabic and keep notes in your journal to record how much you added.

Stir in 2 drops of clove oil or add two whole cloves for preservation. To store the ink, pour it into a small jar with a tight-fitting lid and store it in a cool, dark place. Inks can last even longer when stored in the fridge. Your ink will show signs of expiration by developing an "off" smell, and if left too long, mold may form. I find that this recipe yields just the right amount to be used up well before that happens.

NOTE: Once botanical inks or watercolors are painted and dry on paper there is no risk of mold. As mentioned on page 21, paintings made with organic pigments will naturally evolve over time. You can find tips on preserving and protecting artworks made with natural pigments on page 135.

RECIPE REVIEW

Creating ink using the heat reduction method is particularly beneficial for delicate botanical pigments. These inks complement your botanical watercolor collection beautifully, allowing you to dip a brush directly into the ink jar for painting. You can also use them with dip or calligraphy pens for writing. Additionally, you can make a lake pigment from red onion skins following the steps outlined in the Yellow Onion Skin (Gold) recipe (page 65). You will be rewarded with a lovely olive-green pigment perfect for mixing into watercolors. However, this book wouldn't be complete without sharing a watercolor-based ink recipe!

ORANGE PEKOE TEA (RUSSET BROWN)

I discovered that my tea collection is a wonderful source of natural paint color. I've experimented with most of the teas on the shelf and I highly recommend making a pigment from your run-of-the-mill black tea. It produces a deep russet brown pigment that is a fantastic addition to your homemade paint palette. Because it is rich in tannins, it is a relatively stable and enduring pigment. This is a very easy recipe to make and it's a perfect rainy-day activity to do in the comfort of your own kitchen. While you're making tea paint, you can brew yourself a cuppa too!

MATERIALS

- *Kettle*
- *7 cups (1.7 L) boiled distilled water*
- *2 (4-cup [1-L]) large canning jars*
- *2 orange pekoe tea bags or black tea bags*
- *Alum*
- *Chalk powder*
- *Watercolor Binder (page 33)*
- *Supplies for the Master Lake Pigment Recipe (page 45)*

Boil a kettle of distilled water. While waiting for the water to boil, prepare two large canning jars by placing one tea bag in each.

Carefully pour 3½ cups (840 ml) of boiling water into each jar and stir. Let the tea bags steep for at least 20 minutes or up to an hour for a richer color. Once steeped and cooled, remove the tea bags.

(continued)

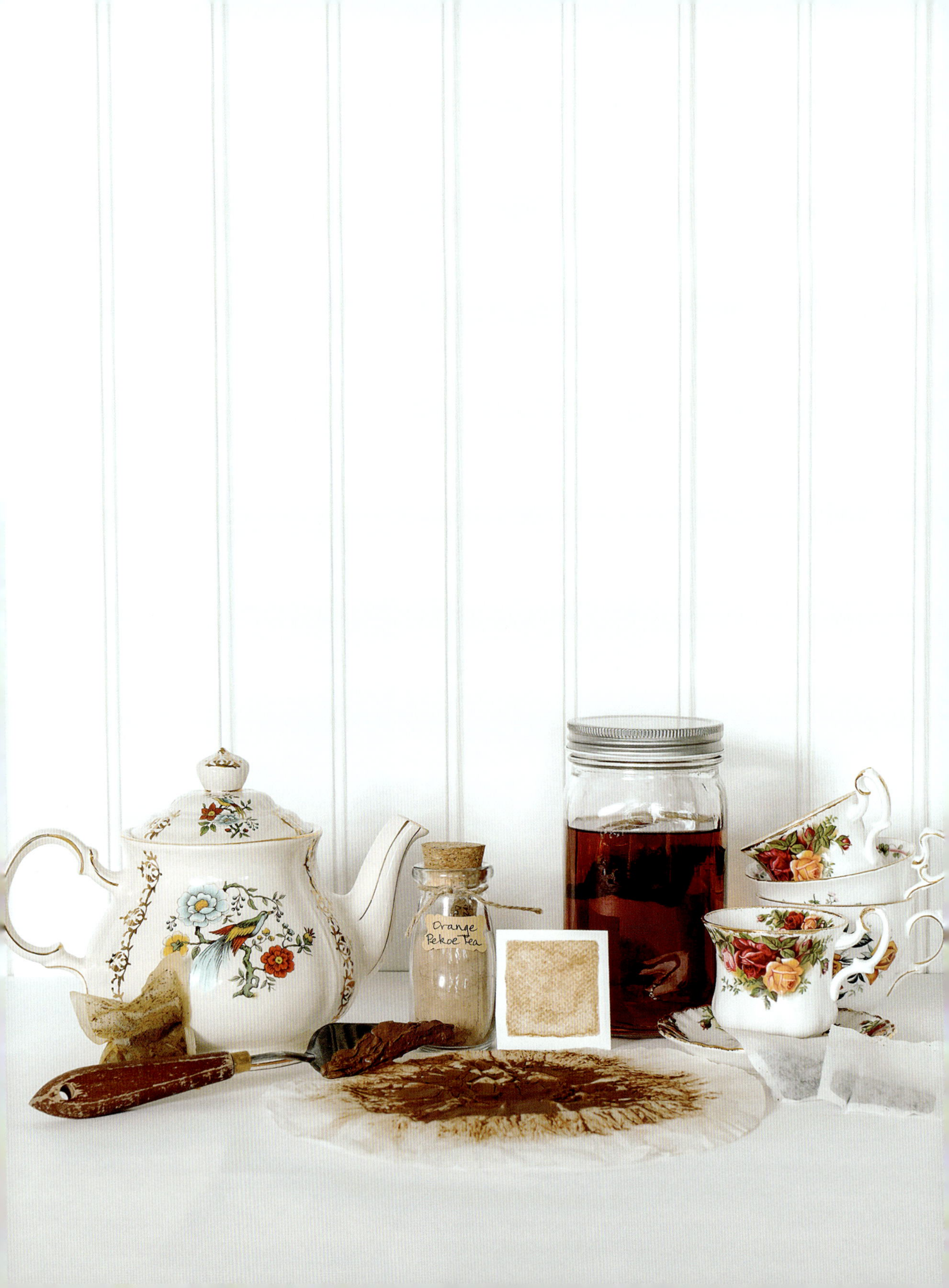

Orange
Pekoe Tea

Dissolve 2 teaspoons (10 g) of alum in a few tablespoons (15–30 ml) of boiling water and add it to the first jar. Create a smooth slurry by completely dissolving 1 teaspoon (3 g) of chalk in a few tablespoons (15–30 ml) of hot water, then add it to the first jar. This looks like you're pouring milk into tea. Repeat this process for the alum and chalk for the second jar of brewed tea.

Once the pigment solids have settled to the bottom of the jars, begin to wash your pigment with fresh water. This recipe typically only requires one or two washes. Review the Master Lake Pigment Recipe on page 50 for more details.

Once the pigment is washed, proceed with filtering it through funnels or sieves lined with coffee filters. When all the pigment is captured in the filters, carefully lay the filters flat on an absorbent towel and wait for the pigment to dry. Placing the filters somewhere warm will speed up the process.

Once the pigment is fully dry, put on a dust mask and scrape the pigment into a mortar and pestle. Grind it into a fine powder, as detailed on page 54. Store in jars with tight-fitting lids.

When you are ready to make watercolor paint, add a couple of teaspoons (3 to 5 ml) of the pigment powder onto a smooth glass surface, then add your homemade watercolor binder in a 1:1 ratio. Using a combination of your palette knife and a glass muller, thoroughly mix until you have a smooth consistency.

It is always a good idea to make test swatches of your paint on watercolor paper and make notes in your dye journal. Once you are satisfied with the appearance, proceed to fill watercolor pans to dry into watercolor cakes as outlined on page 61.

RECIPE REVIEW

My botanical watercolor palette always includes this tannin-rich tea pigment because I appreciate its long-lasting and rich color. An interesting fact about tannin pigments is that they can be darkened by adding iron (or ferrous sulfate). With the extracted pigment made from this recipe, you can make a regular watercolor cake for your paint palette or mix it into beautiful writing ink. I will go into more detail about adding iron to tannin pigments on page 131.

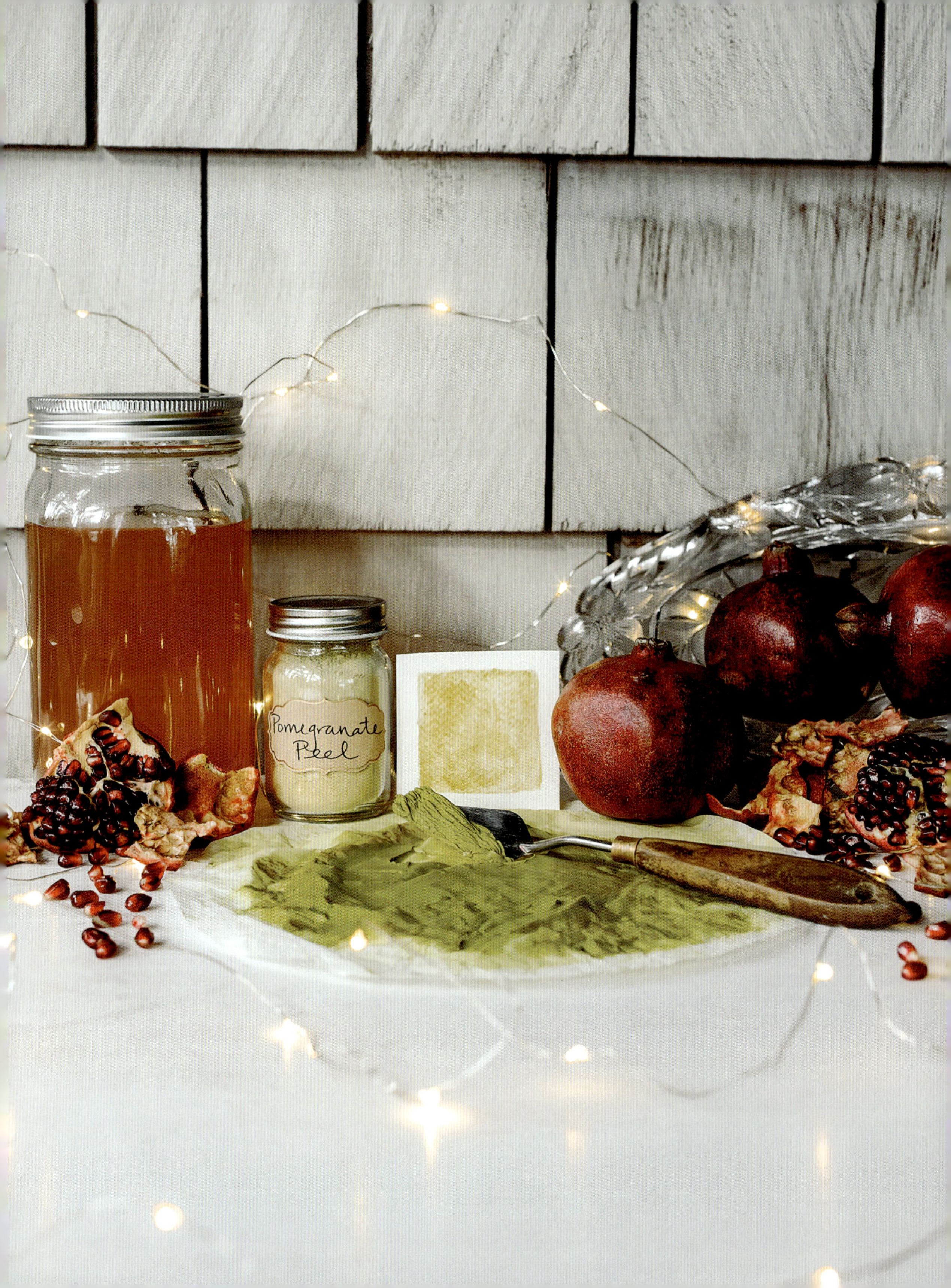
Pomegranate
Peel

POMEGRANATE PEEL (YELLOWY-GREEN)

Pomegranates don't grow in my part of the world. Instead, they make their appearance in grocery stores in the colder months of the year, so I associate pomegranates with being a very special winter holiday treat. I love picking out the seeds and savoring the sweet bursts of juice, but I'm often left with a pile of discarded peels that end up in the compost. When I discovered that pomegranate peels are a popular natural dye for textiles and yarn, I was thrilled! The tannin-rich peels yield a gorgeous golden yellow to yellowy-green pigment, which can also be made into a beautiful watercolor pigment. The resulting color has proven to have very good lightfastness in my paintings.

MATERIALS

- *2 cups (180 g) chopped fresh pomegranate peels*
- *16 cups (3.8 L) distilled water*
- *Large stainless-steel dye pot with lid*
- *Alum*
- *Chalk powder*
- *Watercolor Binder (page 33)*
- *Supplies for the Master Lake Pigment Recipe (page 45)*

Begin by adding about 2 cups (180 g) of chopped fresh pomegranate peels and the distilled water to a large stainless-steel pot. Cover with a lid and bring it to a boil.

(continued)

Once boiling, reduce the heat and gently simmer for at least an hour, stirring occasionally. You'll notice the peels softening and releasing a deep golden, sometimes peachy hue. After simmering, remove the pot from the heat and allow the dye bath to cool completely.

Since the extraction will have fine pulp, thoroughly filter it through a very fine mesh sieve. Repeat this as needed until you have a clear, sediment-free liquid.

This recipe typically yields 9 cups (2.2 L) to 10 cups (2.4 L) of filtered liquid. Divide this liquid into jars, adding between 3 cups (720 ml) to 3½ cups (840 ml) to each. If the extraction is concentrated (less than 3 cups [720 ml] per jar), feel free to add more fresh water to dilute the "tea."

Prepare the alum and chalk as noted in Step 1 and Step 2 on pages 46–48 of the Master Lake Pigment Recipe. For this recipe, add 2 teaspoons (10 ml) of alum (dissolved in hot water) and 1 teaspoon of chalk (mixed into a perfectly smooth, clump-free slurry) to every jar. Watch as the color of the "tea" shifts when the chemicals are added.

Once the pigment solids have settled to the bottom of the jars, wash your pigment with fresh water. This recipe typically only requires one or two washes. Review the Master Lake Pigment Recipe on page 50 for further details.

Proceed with filtering the pomegranate peel pigment through funnels or sieves lined with coffee filters. This process takes a little time. When all the pigment is captured in the filters, lift the filters out and lay them flat on absorbent towels.

Once the pigment has completely dried, wear a dust mask and scrape the pigment into a mortar and pestle. Grind it into a fine powder and store in jars with tight-fitting lids, as outlined on page 54.

When you are ready to paint, add a couple of teaspoons (3 to 5 ml) of the dried pomegranate peel pigment powder to a smooth glass surface. Add your watercolor binder in a 1:1 ratio and using your palette knife and glass muller, mix until you have a smooth consistency. Review the Master Lake Pigment Recipe on pages 57–61 for further details on mixing and storing your pigment.

RECIPE REVIEW

You may be curious about whether you can make paint from the colorful pomegranate seeds, and the answer is yes! However, it's a bit more complex because pomegranate juice is anthocyanin-based. As I've already discussed, working with anthocyanins can be finicky. That said, I've successfully created a beautiful fuchsia-colored watercolor-based ink from pomegranate juice using the heat reduction method, and I've also made a stunning purple using the lake pigment process. While I tend to focus on making paint from the dye-rich peels, I encourage you to experiment with the whole fruit, both the juice and peels.

EXPAND YOUR PAINT PALETTE WITH FOOD GRADE POWDERS

The culinary world has also harnessed botanical colors to naturally color food and drinks. Health food stores market these plant and vegetable powders as "superfoods," and I have been adding these to recipes and to my family's morning smoothies long before I mixed them into paint! The range of vibrant colors that can be achieved from edible sources is extraordinary. In the long run, however, some of these pigments are not overly lightfast. Beet and spinach pigments, for example, are amongst the most fugitive colors I've worked with. Despite their delicate natures, I highly recommend exploring these powders or even the spices in your cupboard.

FOOD GRADE POWDERS

- *Green Spirulina (for green)*
- *Blue Spirulina (for blue)*
- *Butterfly Pea Flower (for blue, violet and pink)*
- *Beet (for magenta or crimson red)*
- *Red Cabbage (for blue, violet and pink)*
- *Hibiscus Flower (for a range of pink and purple)*
- *Turmeric (for yellow)*
- *Carotene (pigment from carrots; for orange)*

MATERIALS

- *Food grade powder of choice*
- *Watercolor Binder (page 33)*
- *Clove oil*
- *Paper coffee filters*
- *Gum arabic powder*

First, test your powder to see how well it dissolves when a few drops of water are added. Some food powders dissolve completely, such as blue spirulina. If this is the case, simply add a couple of teaspoons (5 to 10 ml) of the premade watercolor binder to a teaspoon of the powder. Stir well or mull on your mixing slab to fully combine. Add a drop of clove oil. You can use the paint right away (full strength or diluted with water) or dehydrate for future use in watercolor pans, as described on page 60.

Other food powders may not fully dissolve when liquid is added, such as beet, hibiscus, or turmeric. Instead, they have a gritty texture and need to be filtered to achieve a perfectly sediment-free and useable pigment. If this is the case for the powder you wish to use, start by adding 1 tablespoon (8 g) of the powder to a small bowl. Next, add 3 tablespoons (45 ml) of boiling water and stir to fully combine. Instead of this being a brewed "tea" like in the other lake pigment recipes, this should be thick and concentrated (more like an espresso shot!).

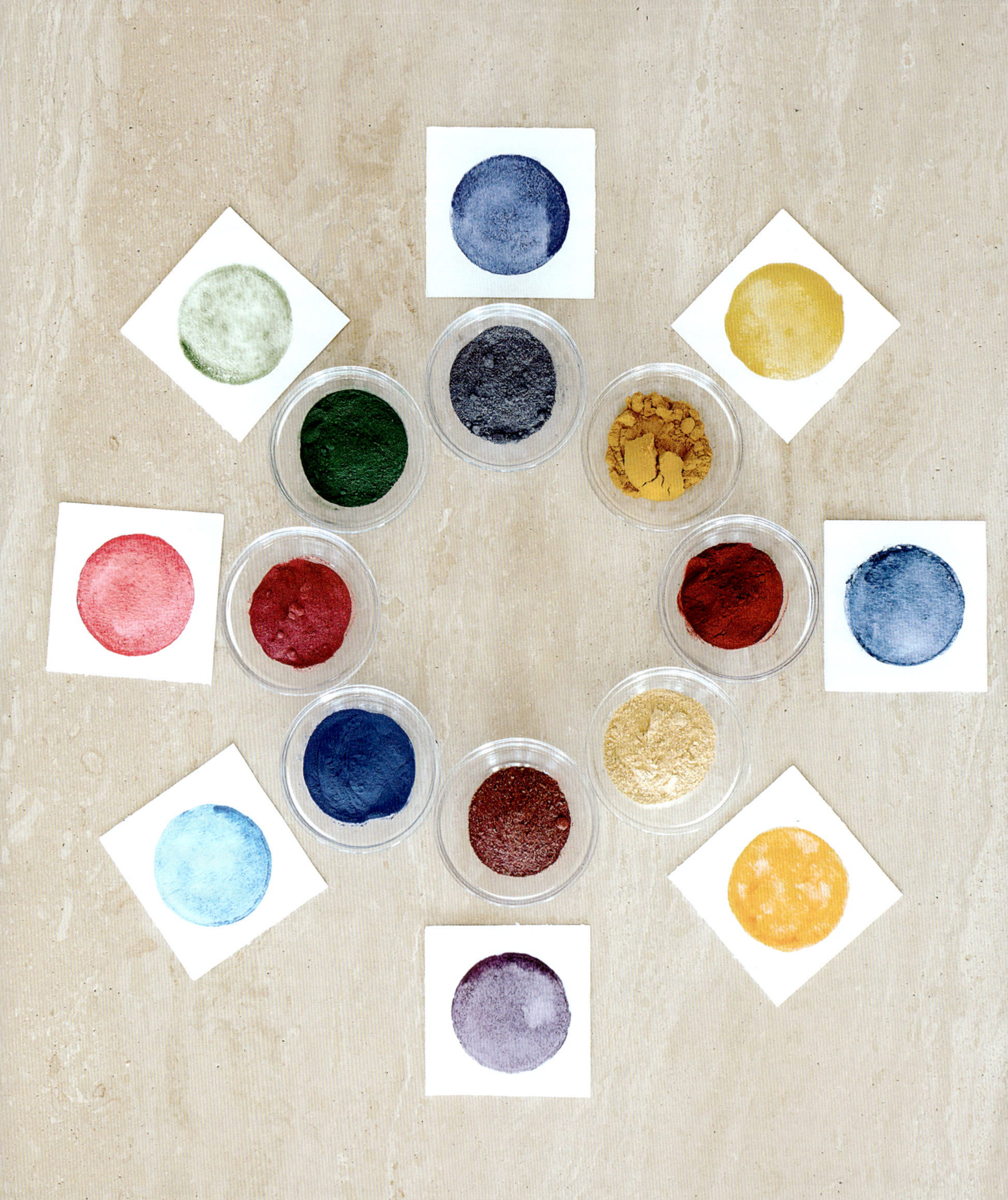

Filter the sediment out by pressing the thick paste through a paper coffee filter. There will now be a small amount of concentrated and colored liquid. To this, add a teaspoon of gum arabic powder and mix until fully dissolved. You are looking for a thick but fluid consistency. Add more gum arabic if necessary. This process is not an exact science. Play around and modify as needed, then note the changes in your journal.

Add a drop of clove oil to the mixture, then pour it into watercolor pans. I will often begin painting with this wet pigment right away. But this wet paint can also be dehydrated into solid water-color cakes for later use.

When filling watercolor pans with your freshly mixed paint, it is important to remember that as the paint dries, it shrinks considerably. A full pan of wet watercolor pigment will likely dry to half of its original volume. To achieve a solid cake of pigment, simply mix up more paint and top up the pans, but only after the first pour is dry. Refer to page 60 of the Master Lake Pigment Recipe for further detail.

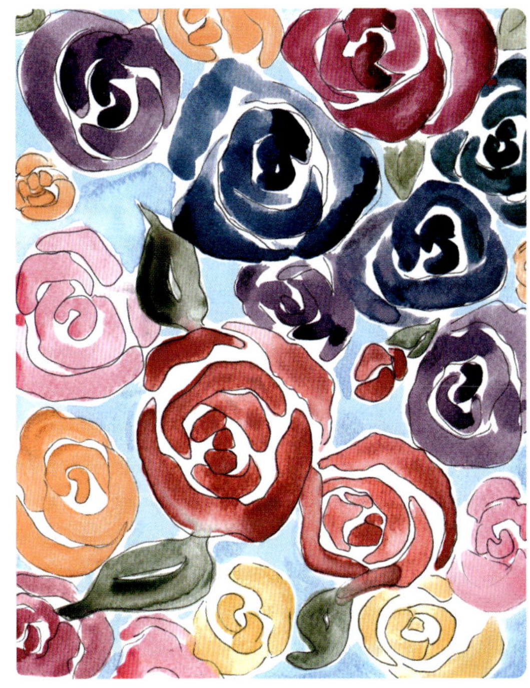

RECIPE REVIEW

Making paint from food grade powders is a great activity for children. I fondly recall my children creating Earth Day paintings using pH sensitive pigments, and this may foster a love for art, science and sustainability all at once. While not everyone will want to work with these powders due to their often-delicate natures, I see their inherent value and beauty. For instance, blue spirulina pigment remains a staple in my watercolor palette. It offers a vibrant and shocking shade of blue that I have yet to find anywhere else in the botanical world.

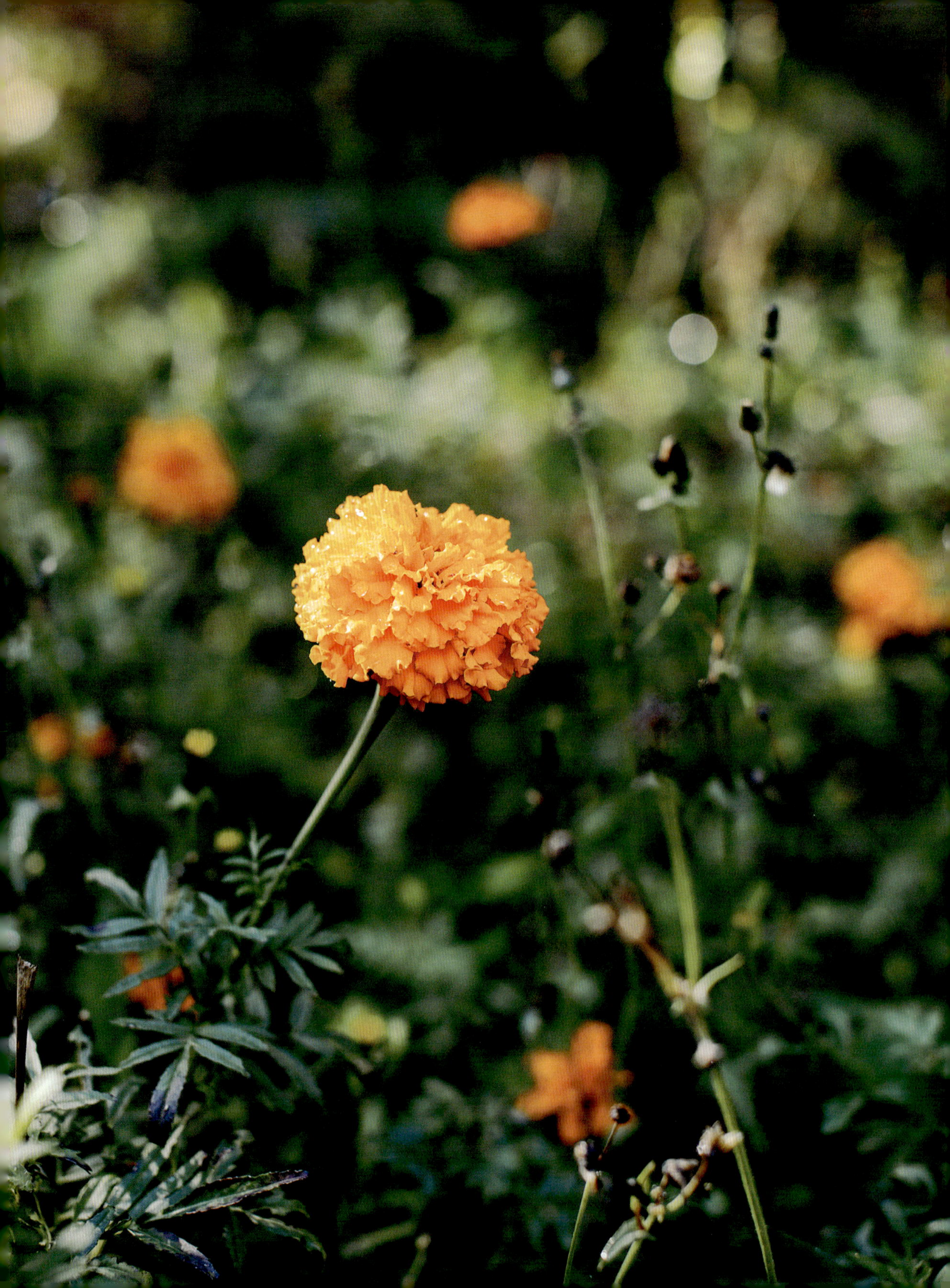

The Garden

Color is everywhere, and it's amazing the amount of color that grows in even the humblest of home gardens. Even plants that are considered pesky "weeds" can also be vibrant sources of color. Many botanical textile dyers and paint makers devote entire sections of their gardens to grow their own dye plants. As you start your exploration, here are two important points to keep in mind: First, always research the toxicity of any plant or flower you plan to use. Sometimes we are surprised to learn that common plants, or specific parts of them, can be problematic. For example, while daffodils are a beloved spring flower, their stems contain toxic sap, so it's wise to keep small children and pets away from your paint-making area. Second, extracting true colors from some flower petals can be quite challenging. I once experimented with red tulips only to end up with a shocking bright green lake pigment! These discoveries and surprises are part of the fun and in the long run, they make us better paint makers.

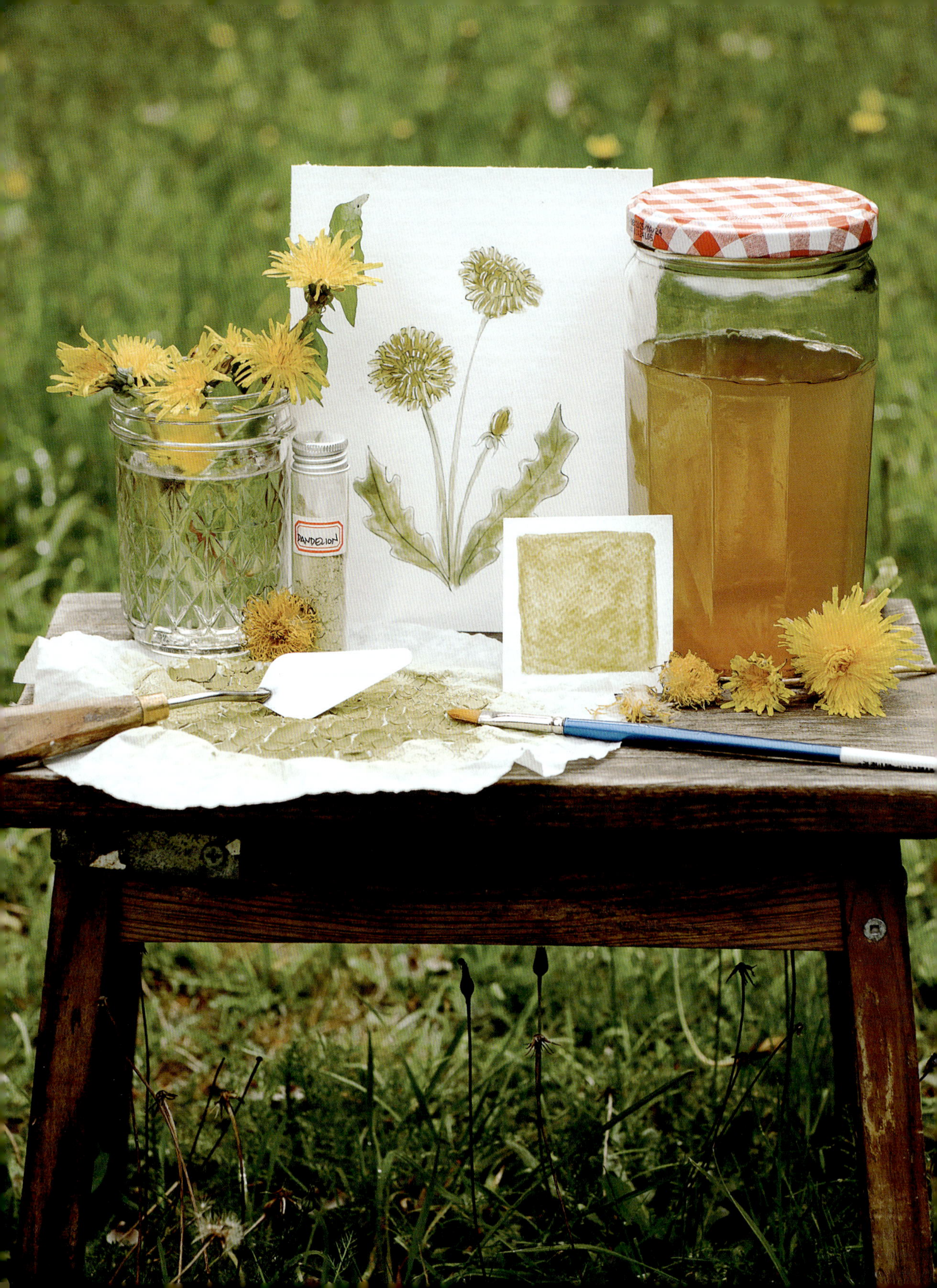

DANDELION

DANDELION (YELLOW)

The dandelion has long been considered a pesky weed by enthusiasts of pristine and manicured front lawns. I, on the other hand, welcome the fluffy and cheerful yellow flowers in my garden because they are the first happy harbingers of spring. Dandelions are a food source for pollinators and humans alike. They are entirely edible, from their flowers and their leaves right down to their roots. They also boast impressive medicinal properties. And as you'll discover, dandelions can even be transformed into a vibrant paint pigment!

MATERIALS

- *2 cups (50 g) fresh dandelion florets/heads (dried dandelion may also be used)*
- *10 cups (2.4 L) boiled water (preferably distilled)*
- *Small stainless-steel saucepan*
- *Blender*
- *Alum*
- *Chalk powder*
- *Supplies for the Master Lake Pigment Recipe (page 45)*

Carefully separate all of the yellow flower petals from the stems, ensuring no green chlorophyll bits make their way into the dye bath. This step is time-consuming but essential for achieving a brighter yellow pigment.

Place the dandelion petals in a stainless-steel saucepan and cover them with the freshly boiled water. Keep the dye bath over very low heat on the stove, avoiding simmering, for at least 1 hour. Stir occasionally. Once the dye bath is well pigmented, remove the saucepan from the heat and allow the extraction to cool completely.

(continued)

Once fully cooled, blend the dye bath liquid (including the dandelion flower petals) in a blender for about 30 seconds, just until the petals are pulverized. Process about 2 cups (480 ml) at a time.

NOTE: I find that a quick blitz in a blender can sometimes help release more pigment from certain plants, especially ones that I don't want to overheat in a dye bath. In future paint-making experiments, you may discover that certain plant pigments can not tolerate heat at all. For example, I have successfully extracted dye from blending flower petals in cold water and skipped the hot water dye bath extraction process entirely. This is another example of experimentation being the key to further developing your paint-making skills!

Filter the blended dandelion liquid thoroughly to remove all organic matter. Since dandelions absorb a lot of water, be sure to squeeze out as much liquid as possible from the flower pulp.

For every 3½ cups (840 ml) of dandelion "tea," add 2 teaspoons (10 ml) of dissolved alum and 1 teaspoon (5 ml) of chalk that has been mixed into a perfectly smooth slurry. This should begin the chemical reaction that causes the dandelion pigment to begin settling to the bottom of the jars. Once the pigment has finished settling, you may move to the remaining steps, including washing, processing, storing and mixing the pigment as described on pages 50 to 60 of the Master Lake Pigment Recipe.

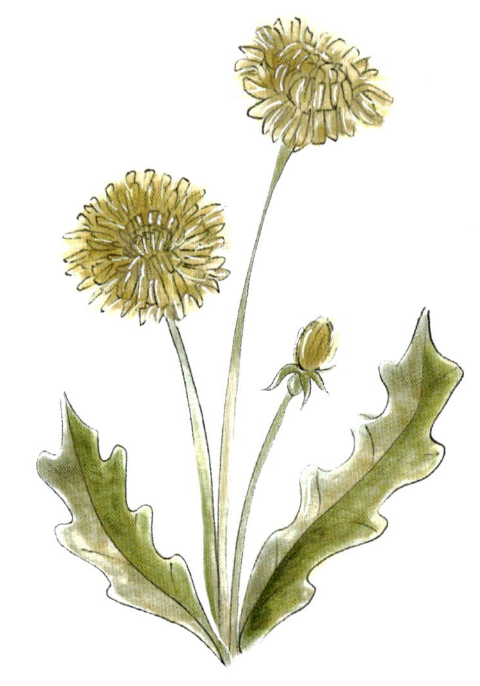

RECIPE REVIEW

Dandelions were my gateway into the world of paint making, reigniting a youthful sense of wonder and delight. Because of this, they hold a special place in my heart, and on my paint palette! While dandelion pigment may not be as long-lasting as some other yellow dye flowers from the garden, it deserves to be celebrated nonetheless. Once you begin working with botanical pigments, you might just find yourself championing the very "weeds" we've been taught to disparage.

MARIGOLD (ORANGE)

If I had to nominate a flower for the best overall flower pigment, marigold would be my first choice. It's relatively easy to extract pigment from and boasts excellent chemical stability, making it a forgiving option for those practicing lake pigment techniques. Thanks to lutein, the carotenoid chemical compound that gives the many varieties of marigolds their orange to red colors, the resulting pigment color is bold and saturated. The added bonus is that it tends to be more lightfast compared to other delicate yellow and orange flower pigments. With so many varieties of marigolds to explore, I enjoy experimenting with new types each year. This recipe can also be adapted for other garden flowers, like calendula or dyer's chamomile, broadening your palette even further.

MATERIALS

- *2 cups (50 g) fresh or dried marigold flower petals (all the green parts removed) or ¼ cup (20 g) dried and ground marigold*
- *16 cups (3.8 L) distilled water*
- *Large stainless-steel dye pot with lid*
- *Alum*
- *Chalk powder*
- *Watercolor Binder (page 33)*
- *Supplies for the Master Lake Pigment Recipe (page 45)*

Add the marigold petals and water to a large stainless-steel pot and cover it with a lid. Simmer gently for 1 hour, stirring often. Afterward, turn off the heat and let the dye bath soak and cool for a couple of hours.

(continued)

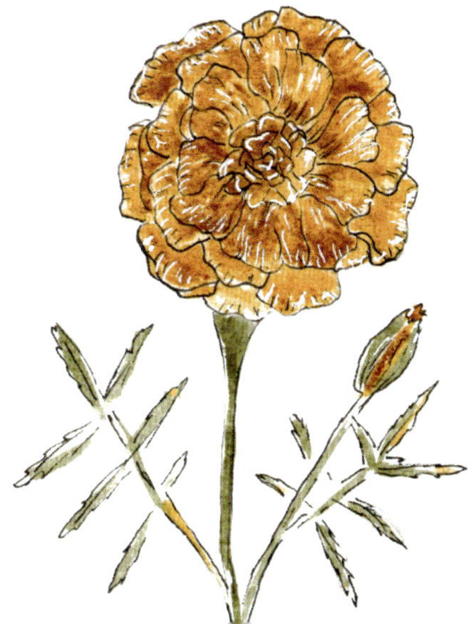

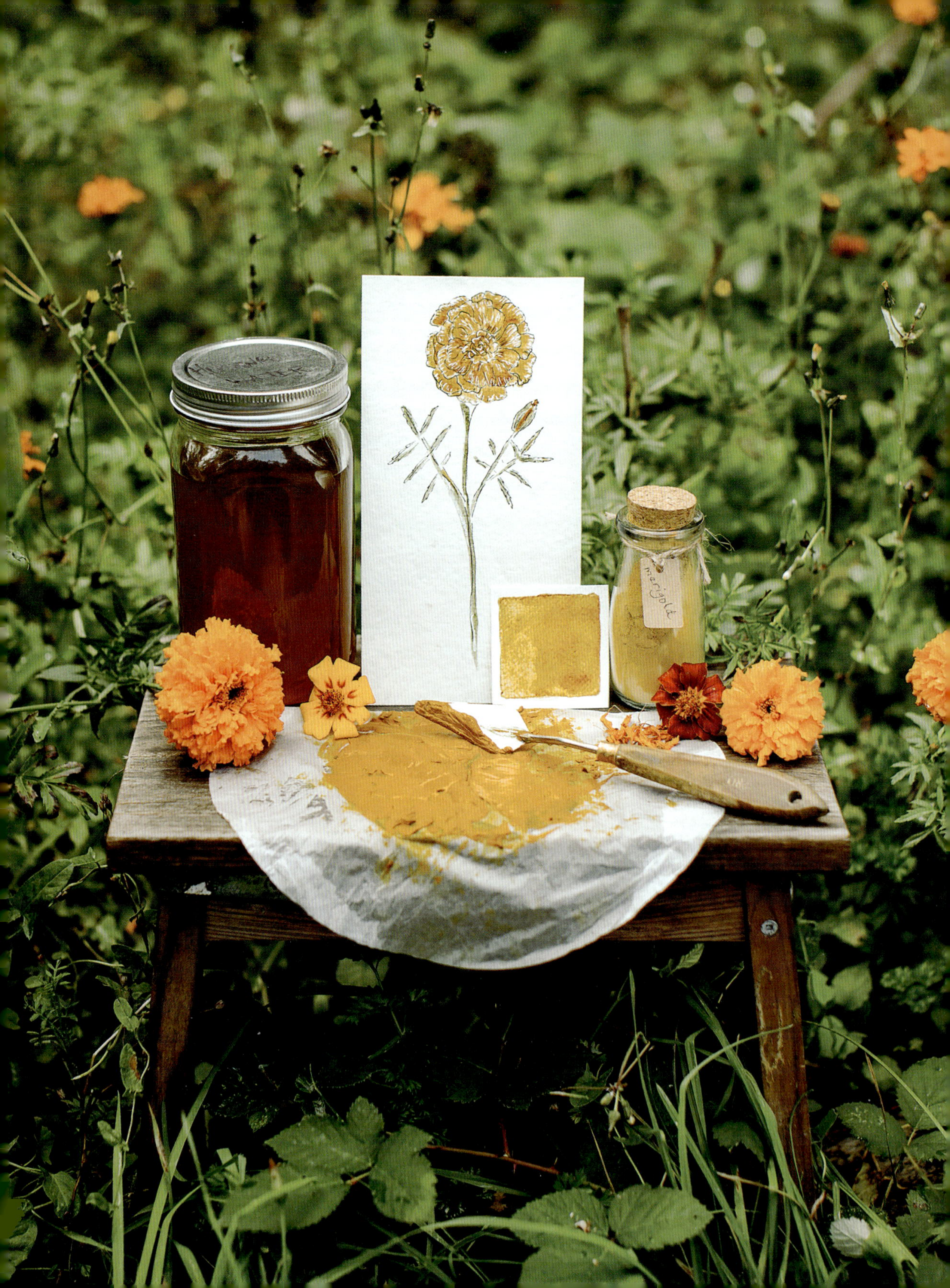

Once cooled, thoroughly filter the marigold "tea" extraction. If you've used ground plant matter, it's crucial to use a very fine mesh sieve and repeat the filtering process until all the sediment is removed.

Divide the strained liquid evenly into four large canning jars. This recipe typically yields around 13 cups (3.1 L) of marigold "tea." Each jar should contain between 3 cups (720 ml) and 3½ cups (840 ml) of liquid. If the liquid is more concentrated, simply add fresh water to dilute it evenly.

To each jar, add 2 teaspoons (10 ml) of dissolved alum and 1 teaspoon (5 ml) of dissolved chalk. Observe the color shift as you add the alum and note it in your journal for future reference.

After the addition of the alum and chalk, the "tea" should begin to fizz and the marigold pigment will settle to the bottom. Once the pigment has finished settling, move to the next step of washing the pigment. Refer to page 50 of the Master Lake Pigment Recipe for detailed instructions on the washing process.

Next, slowly pour the washed marigold pigment through funnels or sieves lined with paper coffee filters. Following the steps outlined in the Master Lake Pigment Recipe on page 53, carefully remove the filters and lay them flat on a towel.

Allow your marigold pigment to fully dry on the filters, then scrape off the pigment using a palette knife. Be sure to wear a dust mask, and add the pigment to a mortar and pestle. Grind the pigment chunks into a fine powder.

Add a couple of teaspoons (3 to 5 ml) of the dried pigment to a smooth glass surface. Add your watercolor binder in a 1:1 ratio and use a palette knife to combine. Then, use a glass muller to mix the pigment into a paint consistency, following the steps on pages 57–58.

Follow the remaining steps of the Master Lake Pigment Recipe on pages 60–61 for curing and storing your marigold pigment.

RECIPE REVIEW

Because I love marigolds so much, they were chosen to be the featured plant in the Master Lake Pigment Recipe chapter (pages 43 to 61) of this book. If you're interested in growing your own dye plants, marigolds are a fantastic choice. Even with limited space, you can harvest a substantial amount of pigment from just a few potted marigold plants. Simply pick off the flower heads as they wilt and dry them. Removing flower dead heads encourages new blossoms, and by the end of the growing season, you'll have a rich supply of golden pigment to use through the colder months.

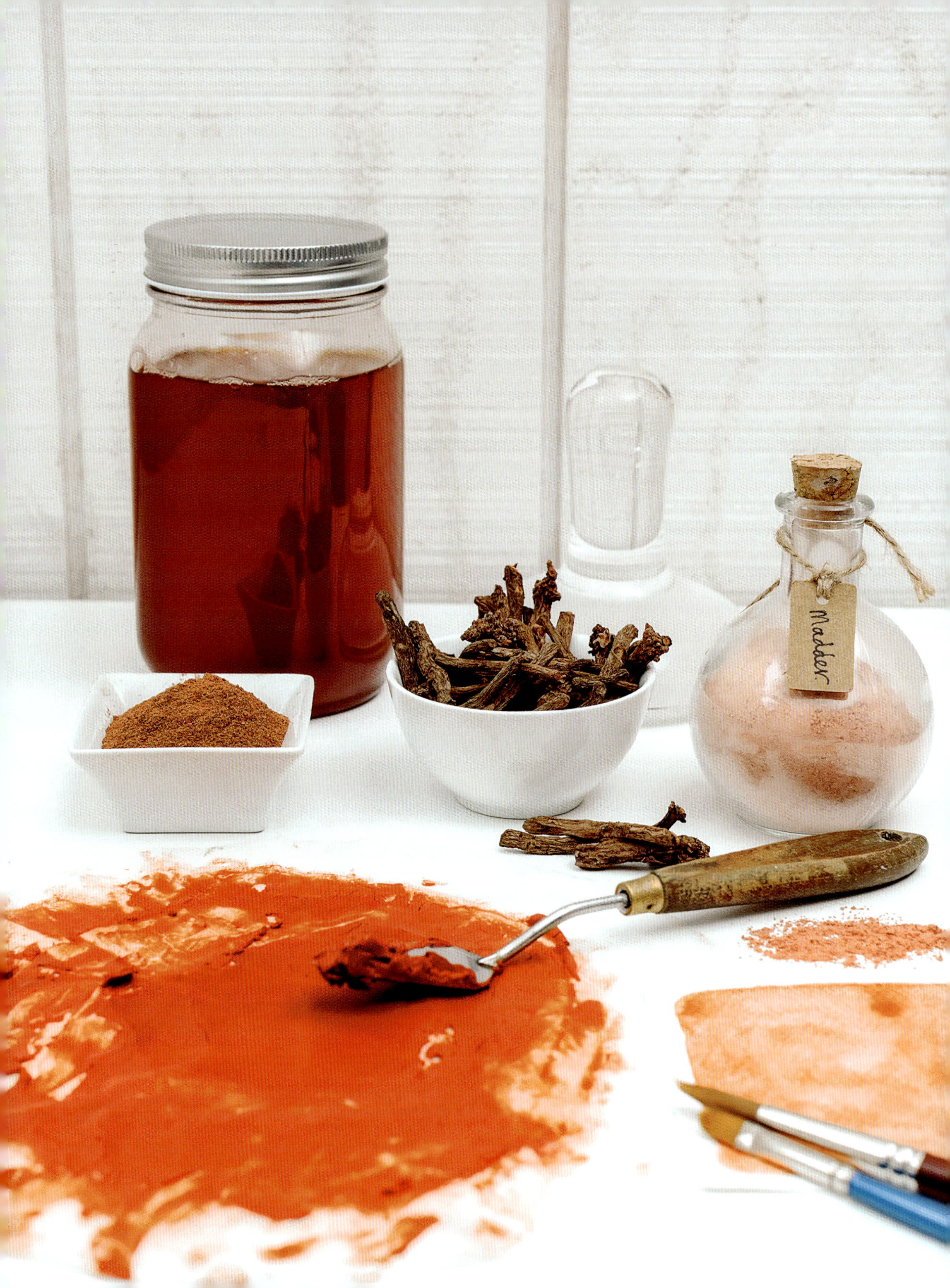
Madder

MADDER ROOT (RED)

Madder root (*Rubia tinctorum*) offers reliable and resilient red dye from a chemical compound called *alizarin*. It can yield a range of shades from crimson to fiery orangey-reds, as well as deeper brown tones like brick red. Botanical sources of true red dyes are hard to find, and so it is not surprising that madder root became an important dye plant throughout history. However, the complex chemical composition of madder can make the process a bit finicky. Achieving the reddest of reds depends heavily on water temperature and pH—higher temperatures can lead to more brownish hues. This recipe requires careful attention to detail, making your dye journal essential for documenting processes, observations and final results. The following recipe outlines how I get the reddest of reds, but keep in mind that working with madder requires a bit of practice and a sense of adventure.

MATERIALS

- *¼ cup (20 g) ground madder root (If using pieces of root, use around 2 cups [100 g], presoaked for 24 hours.)*
- *12 cups (2.9 L) distilled water*
- *Large stainless-steel dye pot with lid*
- *Candy thermometer*
- *Alum*
- *Chalk powder*
- *Watercolor Binder (page 33)*
- *Supplies for the Master Lake Pigment Recipe (page 45)*

SAFETY GEAR

- *Gloves (It is recommended to wear gloves while handling this plant.)*
- *Ventilation during the dye extraction (such as a stove's hood exhaust fan)*
- *Dust mask (Note: It is always a good practice to wear a dust mask when handling all powders.)*

(continued)

Begin by adding the madder root and distilled water to a stainless-steel pot and covering it with a lid. To achieve the brightest shades of red, it's crucial to maintain a water temperature between 120 and 170°F (50 to 80°C). If you don't have a thermometer, just avoid boiling the dye bath.

Gently heat the dye bath for a minimum of 3 hours, then allow it to cool completely. You can also choose to let the madder soak in the dye bath overnight for a deeper extraction.

Thoroughly filter the madder dye extraction. If you're using ground madder, you may need several rounds of filtering through a very fine mesh sieve. For the final filtering, using paper coffee filters can help.

After filtering, this recipe typically yields around 10 cups (2.4 L) of red liquid "tea." Your final amount may vary, which is perfectly fine. Divide the "tea" equally between large canning jars, adding between 3 cups (720 ml) and 3½ cups (840 ml) of madder dye "tea" to each jar.

Add 2 teaspoons (10 ml) of dissolved alum and 1 teaspoon (5 ml) of dissolved chalk to each jar. A chemical reaction should occur and the pigment solids will begin settling to the bottom of the jar. Once the pigment is done settling, you may proceed with the next step: the washing of the pigment described on page 50 of the Master Lake Pigment Recipe.

NOTE: The red liquid removed during the first wash can be processed again to produce lovely pinkish-red hues.

Filter the washed madder root pigment through funnels or sieves lined with paper coffee filters. Once all the washed pigment is filtered, carefully lay the filters flat on an absorbent towel.

Allow the pigment to fully dry. Wearing a dust mask, scrape the dried madder pigment into a mortar and pestle and grind into a fine powder.

To mix into watercolor paint, add a couple of teaspoons (3 to 5 ml) of the powder to a smooth glass surface. Add your watercolor binder in a 1:1 ratio and use a palette knife to combine. Next use a glass muller to mix the pigment into a smooth and fluid consistency, following the steps on page 57.

Follow the remaining steps of the Master Lake Pigment Recipe on pages 60–61 for detailed instructions on curing and storing your madder root pigment.

RECIPE REVIEW

In my early days of making botanical paint, I faced many challenges trying to extract red pigments from various flowers. Madder root has been my answer to achieving a stable botanical red, and I'm thrilled to have it in my paint palette. I now grow madder root in big pots outside my door, and this is especially rewarding. While madder is easy to grow, it does take a few years before the roots are ready to be harvested for dye. Fortunately, madder root, and all the other plants discussed in this book, are readily available in dried form from dye supply stores.

SUNFLOWER SEEDS (DEEP ROSE, GREY, UMBER BROWN)

Sunflowers are amongst the earliest domesticated crops of the Americas. The Hopi people, of what is now known as Arizona, cultivated the Hopi sunflower, which was used as a food and a beautiful source of dark purple to maroon to a bluish-black dye. This color is from the hulls of the seeds, which are full of anthocyanin compounds. The Hopi continue to use this dye to color their exquisite textiles, wool and basketry, and I'm grateful for their traditional knowledge that continues to inspire textile dyers and paint makers alike. I now grow many varieties of sunflowers in my dye garden, including the Hopi sunflower. Before growing my own sunflowers, I made this recipe from any variety of sunflowers with very dark seeds that I found at local farmer's markets.

MATERIALS

- *1 cup (134 g) fresh Hopi sunflower seeds (or any variety of sunflower with dark purple-black hulls)*
- *2½ cups (600 ml) distilled or pH neutral water*
- *Small stainless-steel saucepan*
- *Heat-resistant silicone spatula*

- *Alum*
- *Baking soda or soda ash*
- *Gum arabic powder*
- *Whole cloves*

(continued)

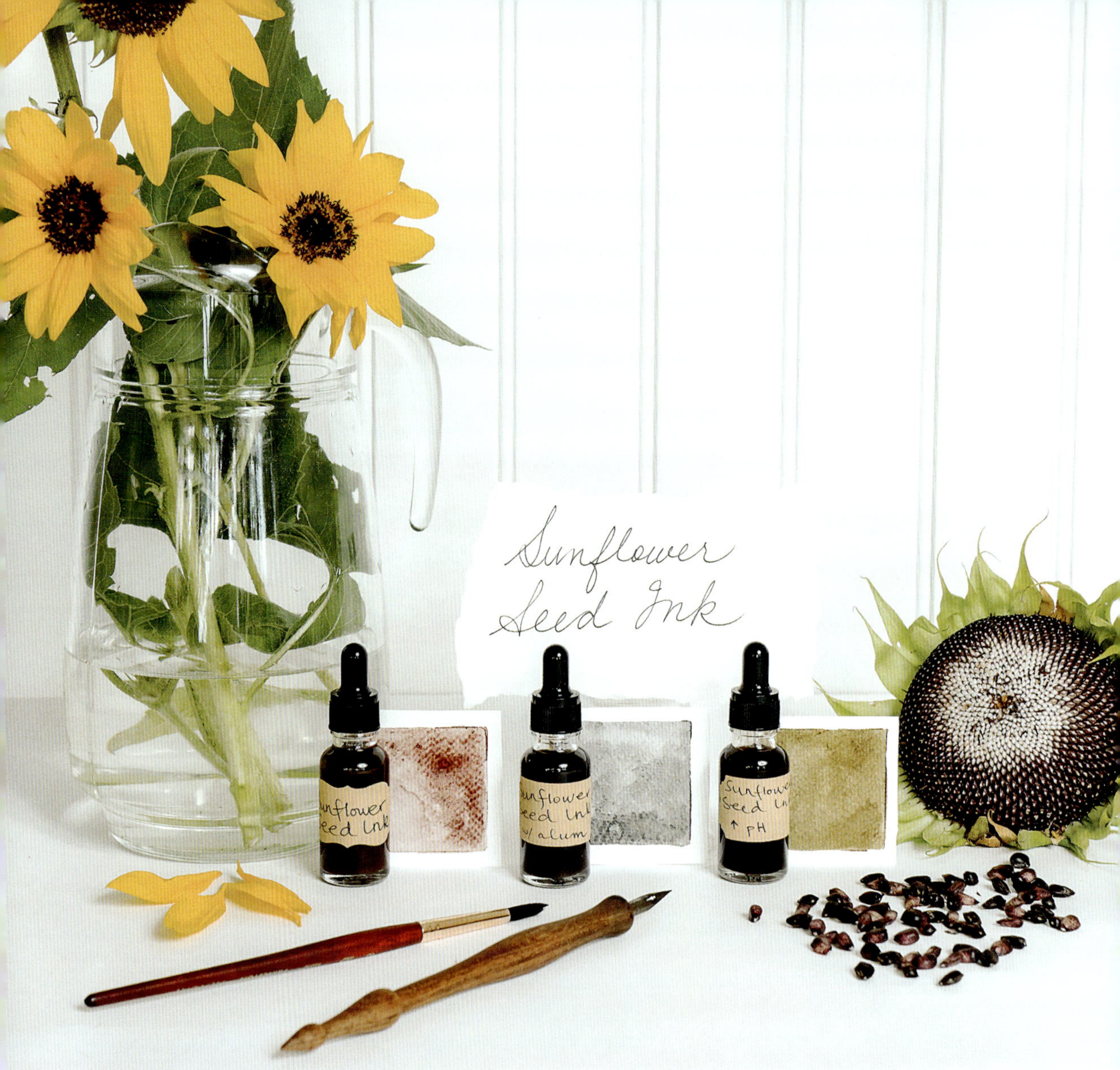

SUNFLOWER SEEDS (DEEP ROSE, GREY, UMBER BROWN) (CONTINUED)

Combine the sunflower seeds and water in a stainless-steel saucepan and heat on medium-high. Do not cover the pot with a lid.

As the water heats, stir continuously with a spatula and watch closely. Once the seeds begin to release their dye, reduce the heat to medium-low to avoid boiling. Keep the pot on low heat for the next hour, stirring often. The liquid should become concentrated in color. Remove the pot from the heat and allow it to cool.

Natural Watercolor Paint Making

Filter the liquid through a fine mesh sieve to remove all of the seeds and particles. Pour the filtered liquid, which should now be about 1½ cups (360 ml), back into a clean saucepan and heat on low without a lid.

Over the next half hour, stir frequently and scrape the bottom of the pot as the liquid reduces and thickens. Swirl the liquid to reincorporate any dye that may have dried on the sides.

The liquid is ready when it has reduced to between ¼ cup (60 ml) and ⅓ cup (80 ml), achieving a thick, syrupy consistency and a rich color. If you notice any sediment, filter it through a fine sieve again.

We are going to make three different colors of ink from this sunflower seed reduction. To do so, divide the thickened liquid into three small bowls and have your dye journal ready to record observations. For each of the three bowls, do the following:

- **Bowl 1**: *No chemical additives will be added. This ink will dry to a more rose hue.*

- **Bowl 2**: *Add a pinch (about ⅛ teaspoon) of alum crystals and stir to dissolve. Notice the color shift to bright purple. Depending on that particular sunflower's unique pigment personality, this ink could dry on the paper as a dark green to dark grey color. This variability is part of the fun!*

- **Bowl 3**: *Add a tiny pinch of an alkali, like baking soda or soda ash. Raising the pH can create a range of colors from earthy greens to browns. Results will vary. This recipe is a wonderful opportunity to play and discover what colors you can create by altering the pH.*

To each mixture, add ½ teaspoon of gum arabic powder at a time, stirring until fully dissolved. Continue adding a pinch at a time until you reach your desired consistency.

Create test swatches and allow them to dry to observe their final colors. Store the ink in small jars with tight-fitting lids and label them accordingly. Add 1 or 2 whole cloves to each jar. If you don't use all of the ink in your art projects shortly after making it, I recommend storing it in the fridge, where it typically lasts a couple of months. Gently shake your watercolor ink before using it.

RECIPE REVIEW

This recipe truly captures the joy and experimental nature of pigment making. There's something magical about watching the color shift as the ink dries on paper. I love that every time I work with sunflower seed dye, the colors are always unique, reflecting the essence of that particular sunflower. Enjoy using a paint brush with your watercolor-based ink, or experiment with writing or drawing using a dip pen or calligraphy pen. May the earthy colors remind you of the warmth of summer and the richness of garden soil. During the dark days of winter, using my summery sunflower seed pigment warms my heart and reminds me that summer will return again.

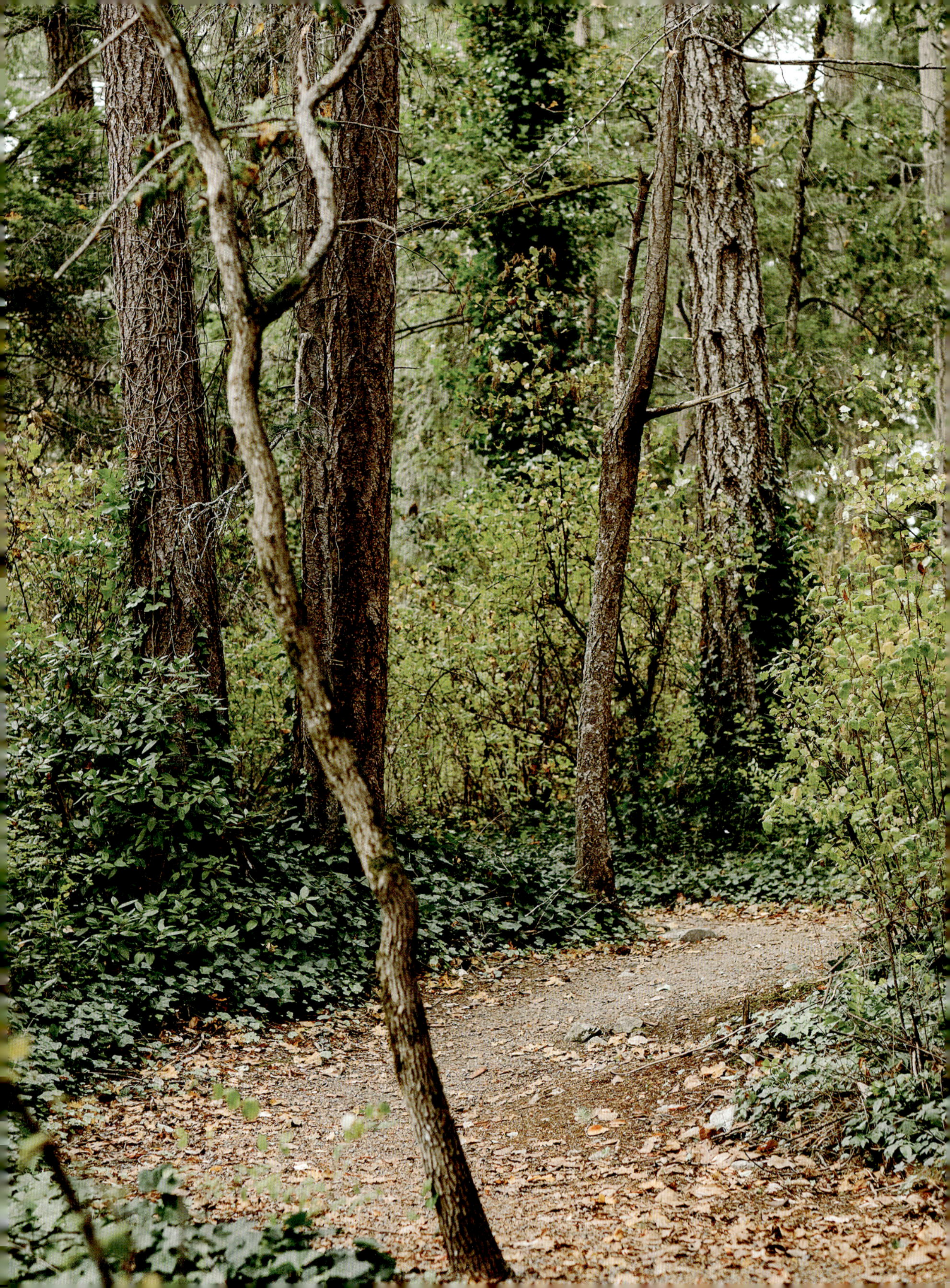

The Wild

Walks in nature offer a wonderful chance to practice mindfulness by paying close attention to the intricate details of plants and the colors of the changing seasons. In the Pacific Northwest, the colder months are often marked by a subdued palette of evergreen greens, along with seemingly infinite shades of brown and gray. Yet, botanical paint making helps me see beyond this typically dreary coastal landscape. Winter presents unique opportunities for color collectors, as storms can dislodge bark, cones, nuts and leaves from trees, scattering them on the ground. In spring and summer, I celebrate the return of the more vibrant wild colors. Paint makers are opportunistic, so keep your eyes open for pigment sources wherever you roam and I encourage you to refer to the set of harvesting guidelines I outline on page 22.

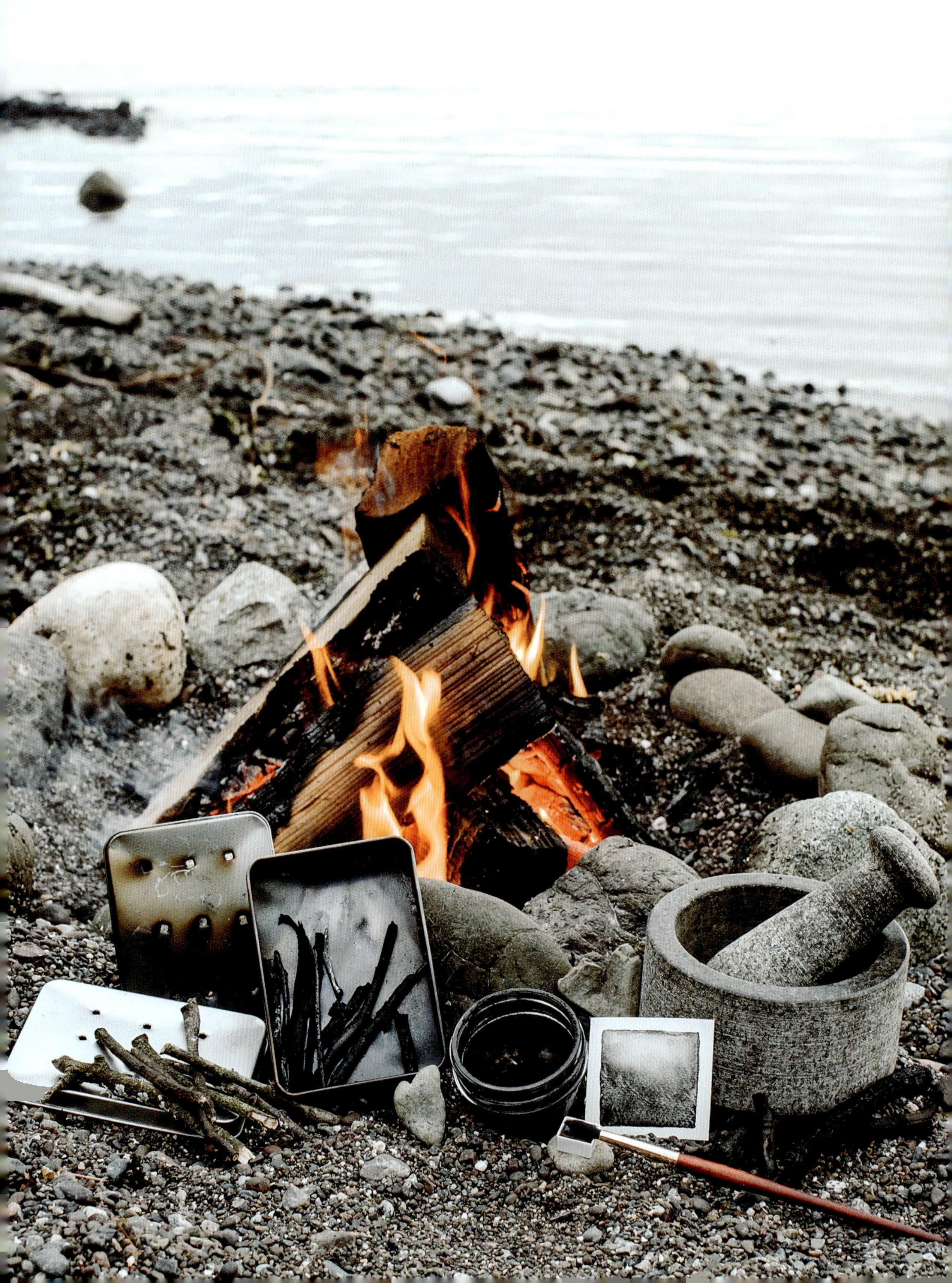

CHARCOAL (BLACK)

This is one of my favorite paints to make because the process invokes old-world charm and autumnal coziness. Traditional sources of charcoal were made from many things, including willow branches, grapevines, animal bones and soot collected from old lamps—but I'm an advocate for using what's readily available and close to home. I have made charcoal with many kinds of tree branches, but where I live, arbutus (Pacific madrone) and willow trees are in abundance, so I can easily collect their branches from the ground. This recipe requires a campfire or a fireplace, but if you don't have access to these, this paint can be made with purchased charcoal powder. Alternatively, you may happen upon charcoal in the wild from old forest fires or lightning-struck trees. Even the charcoal sticks in your drawing stash can be turned into a useable watercolor pigment!

MATERIALS

- *A handful of thin branches or twigs of similar thickness (around the diameter of a pencil)*
- *Nail and hammer*
- *Metal (tin-plated) box or container with a lid*

    To be fireproof, this container should be all metal (no plastic parts). Cookie or biscuit tins or small ALTOIDS® tins work well.

- *Mortar and pestle*
- *Water*
- *Watercolor Binder (page 33)*
- *Spatula*

SAFETY GEAR

- *Work gloves*
- *Heat-resistant oven mitts*
- *Long handled metal tongs*
- *Dust mask*

(continued)

MAKING THE CHARCOAL

Collect twigs and rinse off any dirt and debris. Removing the bark is optional. Wearing protective work gloves, and using a hammer and nail, carefully poke a few ventilation holes in the lid of a tin.

Break the twigs into smaller pieces and place them inside the tin, avoiding overcrowding. Place the lid back on the tin. Wearing heatproof oven mitts and using long tongs, very carefully position the tin in the fire, nestled amongst the hottest coals.

If the fire is sufficiently hot and your twigs are small, 20 minutes should be enough time in the fire. Smoke and vapor escaping from the holes of the lid indicates that carbonization is occurring.

Once again using appropriate safety gear, carefully remove the tin from the fire. Set it aside to cool completely, and only then check the contents. If the sticks are lightweight, black and burnt completely through, they have become carbonized. If there is still uncarbonized wood remaining, return the tin to the fire for more time.

MAKING THE CHARCOAL PAINT

First, put on a dust mask to prevent inhaling fine charcoal particulates. Then place a few pieces of charcoal in the mortar and grind them into a fine powder using the pestle.

Slowly add a few drops of water at a time and continue to grind until you achieve a thick but smooth paste. This takes time (it varies but 5 to 10 minutes to start), but the smoother the paste, the better your paint will be.

Next, add your premade watercolor binder a few drops at a time and continue mixing. Scrape down the sides of the bowl of the mortar with a spatula and continue mixing. The final texture of this mixed pigment will be perfectly smooth (no grit) and glossy. It will be thick but fluid enough to slowly drip off the tip of a palette knife.

At this stage, it's helpful to paint test swatches on paper and let them dry. If the paint hasn't adhered well, add more binder. If there's excess grit, grind the pigment longer. Using a grinding slab and muller can assist with producing a smoother charcoal paint.

Finally, add the mixed charcoal pigment to watercolor pans and set them aside to dry. Alternatively, you can create a thinner watercolor-based ink by adding more liquid watercolor binder. Store all watercolor-based inks in labeled jars with tight-fitting lids and keep them in the fridge to keep them fresh for a couple of months.

Natural Watercolor Paint Making

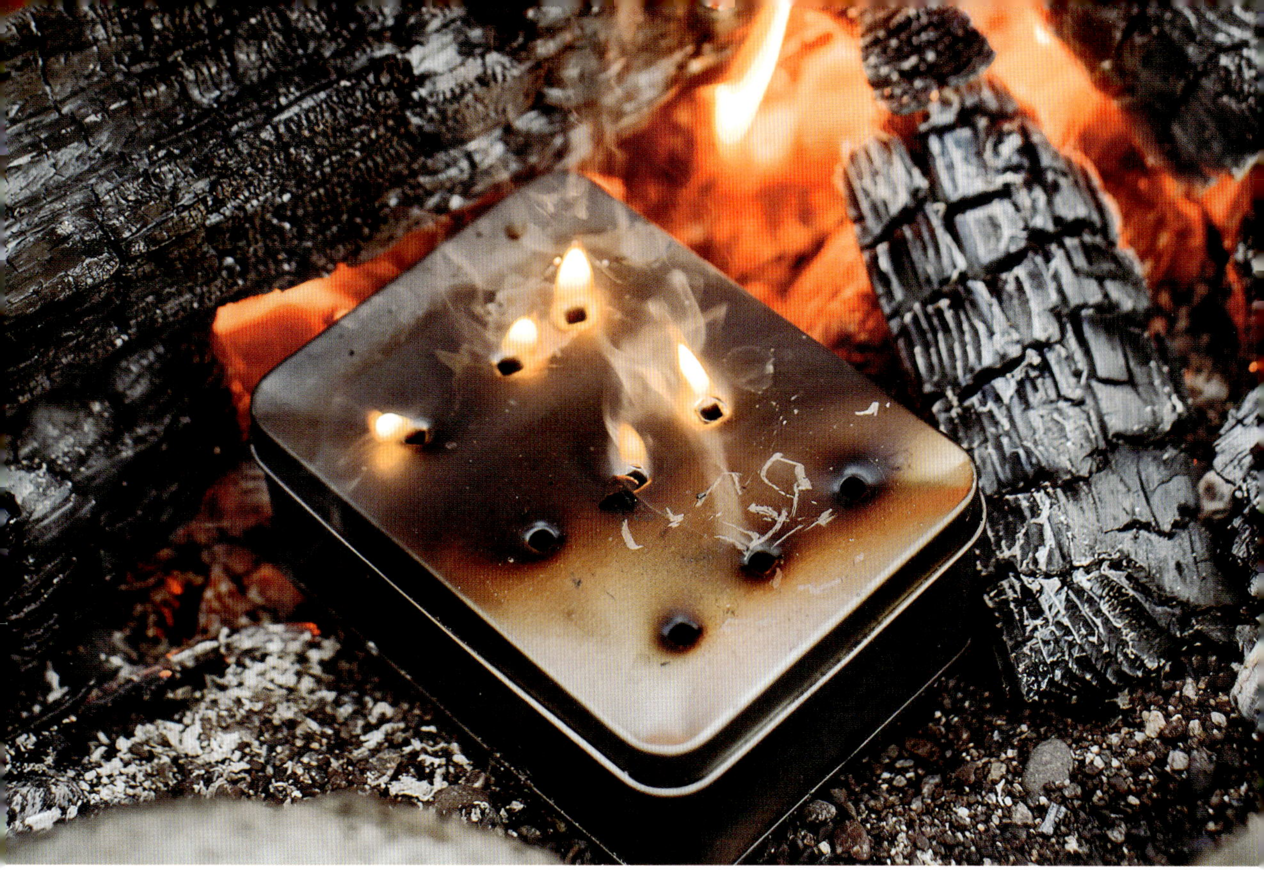

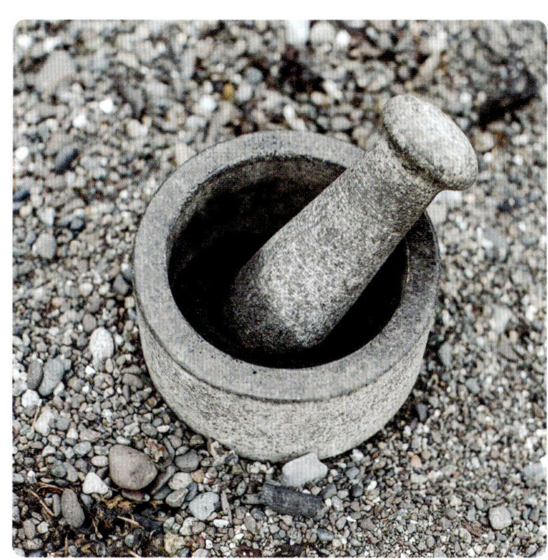

RECIPE REVIEW

Having a high-quality black watercolor pigment is essential for my homemade paint palettes. The process of making charcoal highlights that paint making isn't always an exact science; it often involves testing and modifying to achieve a pigment you're satisfied with. Ultimately, there are no "wrongs" in paint making. It's all about exploring the basic methods so you may find your own path to creating beautiful watercolor pigments that you enjoy using.

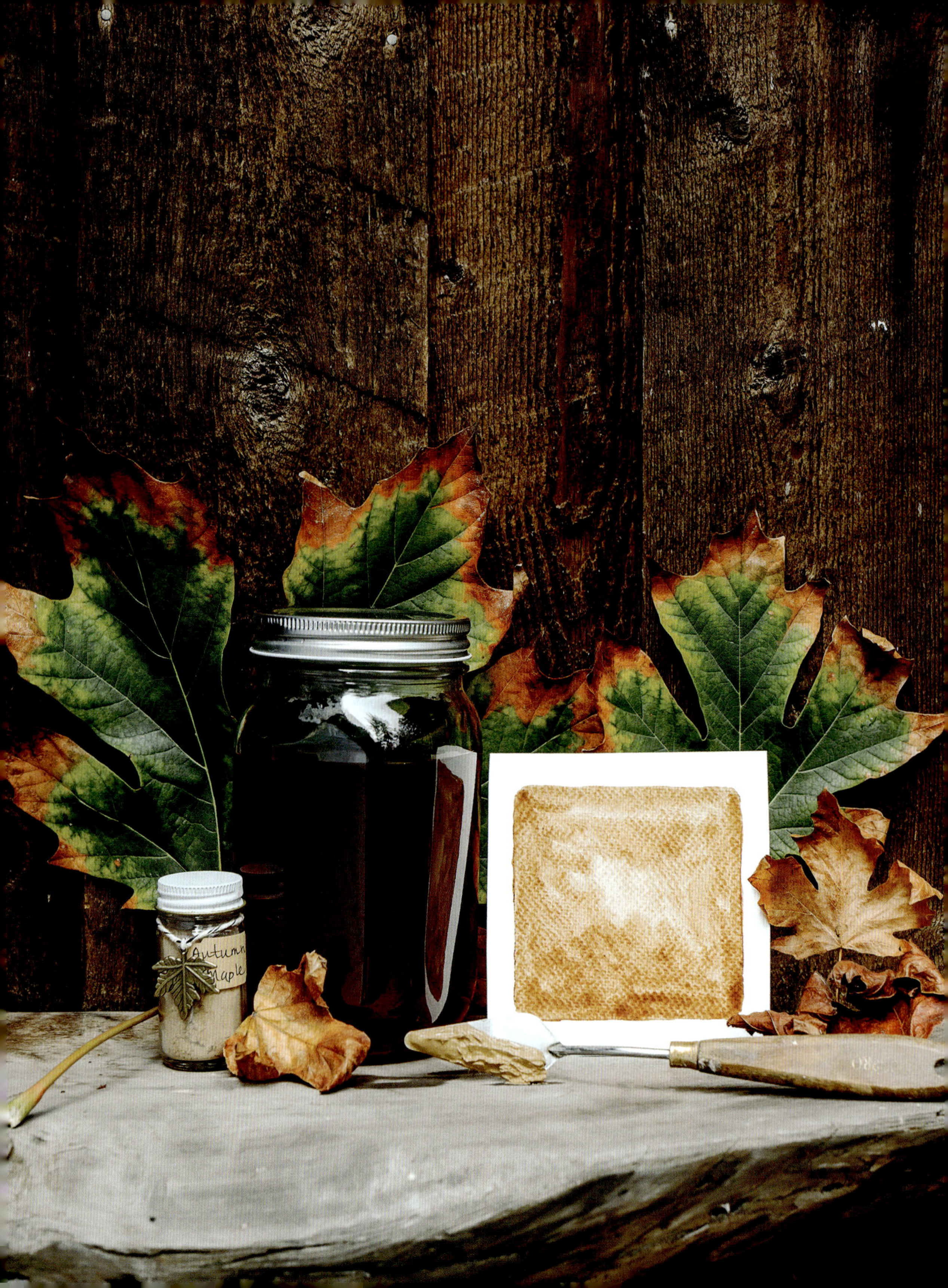

Autumn
Maple

AUTUMN MAPLE LEAVES (GOLDEN BROWN)

Trees are often wonderful sources of color, and I've explored many types of pigments extracted from bark, leaves, wood, cones and nuts. In the autumn, the leaves of deciduous trees lose their green chlorophyll pigment, and this allows for the other pigments in the leaves to be revealed. In October, the Pacific Northwest's forest floor transforms into a carpet of fallen yellow and brown leaves of the bigleaf maple tree. These leaves provide a tannin-rich source of deep brown–colored pigments that have proven to be very resilient and enduring in my artwork. There's a unique kind of satisfaction in wandering through nature, gathering crunchy maple leaves and then returning home to create a batch of maple leaf paint.

MATERIALS

- *8 cups (2 L) dried maple leaves (I measure by stuffing two 4-cup [1-L] large wide-mouth mason jars full of leaves.)*
- *Large stainless-steel dye pot with lid*
- *14 cups (3.4 L) distilled water*
- *Alum*
- *Chalk powder*
- *Watercolor Binder (page 33)*
- *Supplies for the Master Lake Pigment Recipe (page 45)*

(continued)

Add the maple leaves to a stainless-steel pot and cover them with the distilled water. Cover the pot with a lid and heat on medium. I prefer to maintain a moderate heat for an hour or 2, keeping an eye on the dye bath as the leaves release their color. If needed, increase the heat slightly to encourage the extraction. Once you have a richly colored extraction, remove the pot from the heat and allow it to cool completely.

Filter the dye extraction thoroughly to remove all sediment and organic matter, repeating the process until the liquid is perfectly clear as outlined on page 38. This recipe typically yields around 11 cups (2.6 L) of liquid. Divide this equally among three large canning jars, aiming for about 3½ cups (840 ml) in each jar.

To each jar, add 2 teaspoons (10 ml) of dissolved alum and 1 teaspoon (5 ml) of chalk dissolved in a smooth slurry. Watch as the pigment begins to settle to the bottom of the jars.

Once the pigment has finished settling, you may proceed with washing the pigment as outlined on page 50 of the Master Lake Pigment Recipe. Then, slowly pour the washed pigment through funnels or sieves lined with paper coffee filters. Once all the pigment is collected, carefully lay the filters flat on a towel. Allow the pigment to dry completely.

Once the maple leaf pigment is dry, put on a dust mask and, using a palette knife, scrape the pigment into a mortar and pestle. Grind into a fine powder as described on page 54.

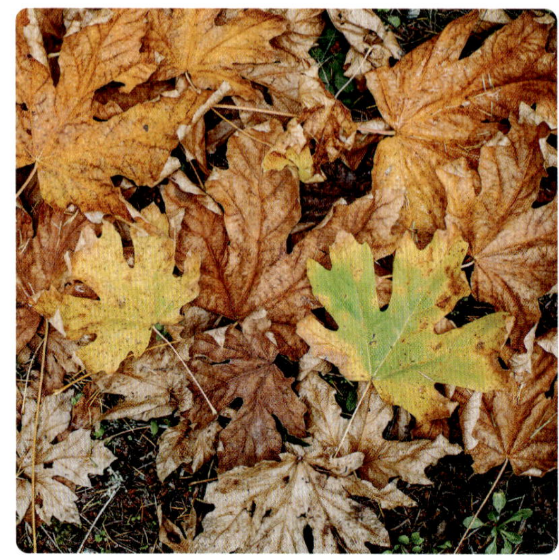

You may now mix this powder with your watercolor binder and fill some watercolor pans. The Master Lake Pigment Recipe on pages 57 to 61 provides further details on mixing, mulling and storing your watercolor paints.

RECIPE REVIEW

You may be wondering if the classic fiery reds, oranges and yellow pigments of other autumn leaves can be captured. I have experimented with some of the more colorful autumn leaves, such as the red leaves of the Japanese maple and the deep maroon leaves of the purple plum tree. These contain the chemically sensitive anthocyanins and as such, it can be a wild ride. Tannin-rich autumn leaves like maple, oak or alder are more reliable pigment options and in time, you, too, will discover your favorites.

Natural Watercolor Paint Making

BLACK WALNUT (DARK BROWN)

The green husks of walnuts have been valued as a rich dye source by many cultures throughout history, and this importance is well deserved. They produce a dark brown dye perfect for dyeing textiles and wool thanks to the powerful tannins and a chemical compound called *juglone*. Just a couple of handfuls of walnut husks provides a lot of dye. Using the lake pigment process, this dye can be turned into pigment powder that can be mixed into a beautiful watercolor paint. I can store the pigment powder for many months and mix it up as I need it. Because this pigment is quite lightfast, I use this paint a lot in my artwork.

MATERIALS

- *Rubber gloves*
- *The husks from about 20 walnuts*

  I collect walnuts when they have fallen to the ground and the husks are green with brown spots. The husks are easy to peel off the nut when they are turning brown.

- *Large stainless-steel dye pot with lid*
- *16 cups (3.8 L) pH neutral or distilled water*
- *Alum*
- *Chalk powder*
- *Watercolor Binder (page 33)*
- *Supplies for the Master Lake Pigment Recipe (page 45)*

(continued)

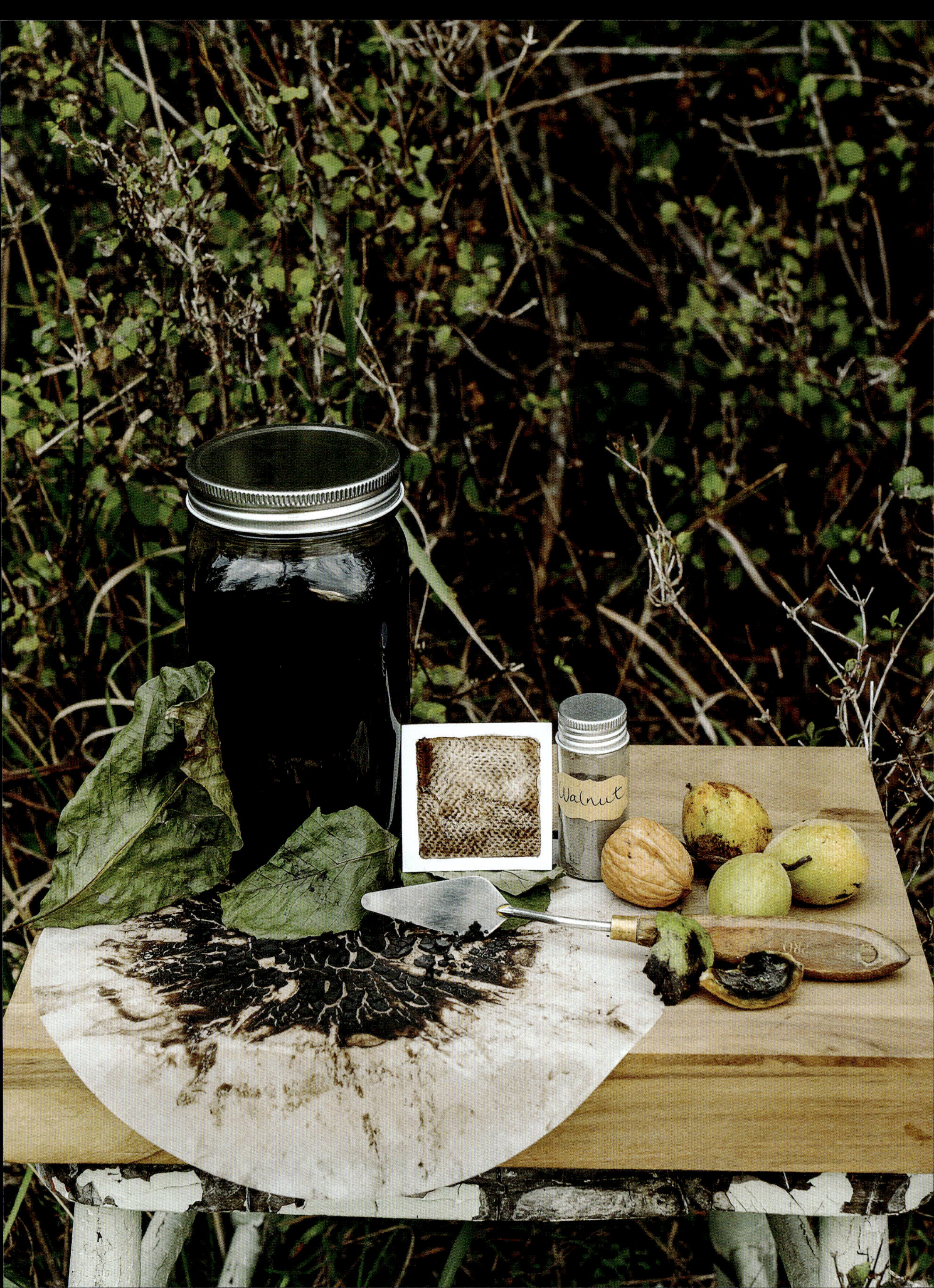
Walnut

BLACK WALNUT (DARK BROWN) (CONTINUED)

Wearing gloves, peel the exterior husks off the walnuts and add them to the stainless-steel dye pot. Black walnut husks are a powerful staining agent, so wear gloves and protect your work surfaces.

Add the water, then cover the pot with a lid. Bring to a boil, then immediately reduce the temperature to a gentle simmer. Continue simmering for an hour or so.

Filter the walnut extraction a few times to ensure all sediment is removed. Pour the filtered walnut "tea" into four large canning jars. The total amount typically yields around 12 cups (2.9 L) to 13 cups (3.1 L). Distribute approximately 3 cups (720 ml) to 3½ cups (840 ml) into each jar. If the liquid is very concentrated (opaque), add about half a cup (120 ml) of fresh water to each jar to dilute it.

To each jar, add 2 teaspoons (10 ml) of alum that has been dissolved in hot water. The liquid may immediately begin precipitating (separating) when the alum is added, and that's okay. Proceed with adding 1 teaspoon (5 ml) of chalk that has been dissolved in hot water and made into a smooth slurry. After both have been added to each jar, wait for the pigment solids to settle.

NOTE: Sometimes, the pigment solids will float to the top. That's okay! During the washing stage, use a turkey baster to siphon the water from the bottom of the jar, instead of the top.

Proceed with washing the walnut pigment as outlined in the Master Lake Pigment Recipe on page 50. I will typically wash walnut pigment two to three times. Slowly pour the washed pigment through funnels or sieves lined with paper coffee filters. Carefully lift the filters out and lay them flat on a towel, allowing the pigment to dry completely.

Once the maple leaf pigment is fully dry, wear a dust mask and use a palette knife to scrape the pigment into a mortar and pestle. Grind it into a fine powder.

At this stage, you can mix a portion of the powder with your watercolor binder and fill a few watercolor pans. For more details on mixing, mulling and proper storage of your watercolor paints, refer to the Master Lake Pigment Recipe on pages 57 to 61.

RECIPE REVIEW

In late September, I start looking for fallen walnuts. Once you know what to look for, walnuts are easy to spot. The familiar brown shells sold in stores are actually encased in a bright green round-to-oblong husk. Black walnut trees are native to North America but have been introduced to other parts of the world, so it is likely you, too, have walnut trees nearby. But if not, you can purchase dried walnut husks through dye suppliers, as they're a popular choice for textile dyers.

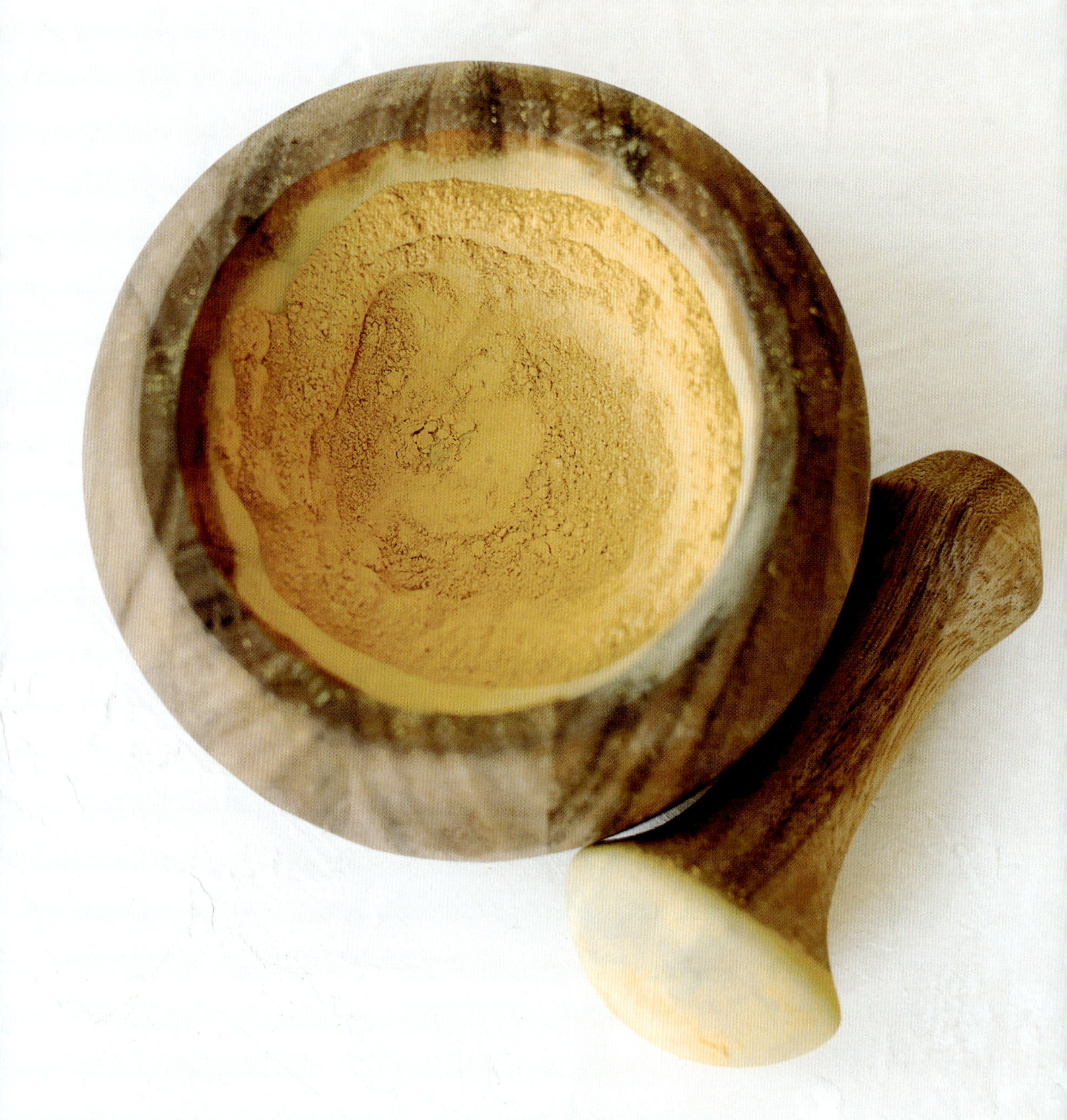

From the Store

Textile dye supply stores sell botanical dye plants from all over the world, and it can be fun to shop for natural colors that may not be locally available to you. And for those of us who do not live in rural settings or cannot get out into nature, nature can come to you! Most stores offer a varied catalog of relatively inexpensive dye plants (when compared to the price of a tube of paint) and they are a wonderful resource to expand your natural watercolor palette. However, it is important that the products you buy are sourced ethically and harvested sustainably from plants or trees that are not endangered. Below are a few recipes using my favorite store-bought dye plants that add some extra pizazz to my homemade natural watercolor collection.

WELD (BRIGHT YELLOW)

Weld (*Reseda luteola*), also known as dyer's rocket, has long been revered by textile dyers for its lightfast properties, as well as for its vibrant, almost neon yellow dye. This color is derived from a flavonoid compound called *luteolin*. Luckily, paint makers can also harness this exceptional dye for our watercolor palettes. I now grow this plant in my dye garden, but for many years, I purchased it regularly in its dried and ground-up form.

MATERIALS

- *⅓ cup (25 g) dried and ground weld (or around 2 cups [30 g] chopped and dried plant pieces, including flowers, leaves and stalk)*
- *12 cups (2.9 L) distilled water*
- *Stainless-steel dye pot with lid*
- *Alum*
- *Chalk powder*
- *Watercolor Binder (page 33)*
- *Supplies for the Master Lake Pigment Recipe (page 45)*

Add the weld and distilled water to a stainless-steel pot, cover it with a lid and bring the dye bath to a boil. Once boiling, reduce the heat to a gentle simmer, stirring occasionally.

Let it simmer for at least an hour. Keep an eye on the color; when the liquid turns a vibrant yellow, remove the pot from the heat and allow it to cool completely.

Filter the weld extraction thoroughly until the liquid is clear and free of sediment. This recipe typically yields about 10 cups (2.4 L) of filtered weld "tea." Regardless of the final amount, divide the liquid equally between three large canning jars, with about 3 cups (720 ml) to 3½ cups (840 ml) in each jar.

To each jar, add 2 teaspoons (10 ml) of dissolved alum and 1 teaspoon (5 ml) of chalk made into a perfectly smooth slurry. This will begin a chemical reaction and the pigment solids will settle to the bottom. Once the weld pigment has finished settling, wash the pigment as outlined on page 50 of the Master Lake Pigment Recipe.

Natural Watercolor Paint Making

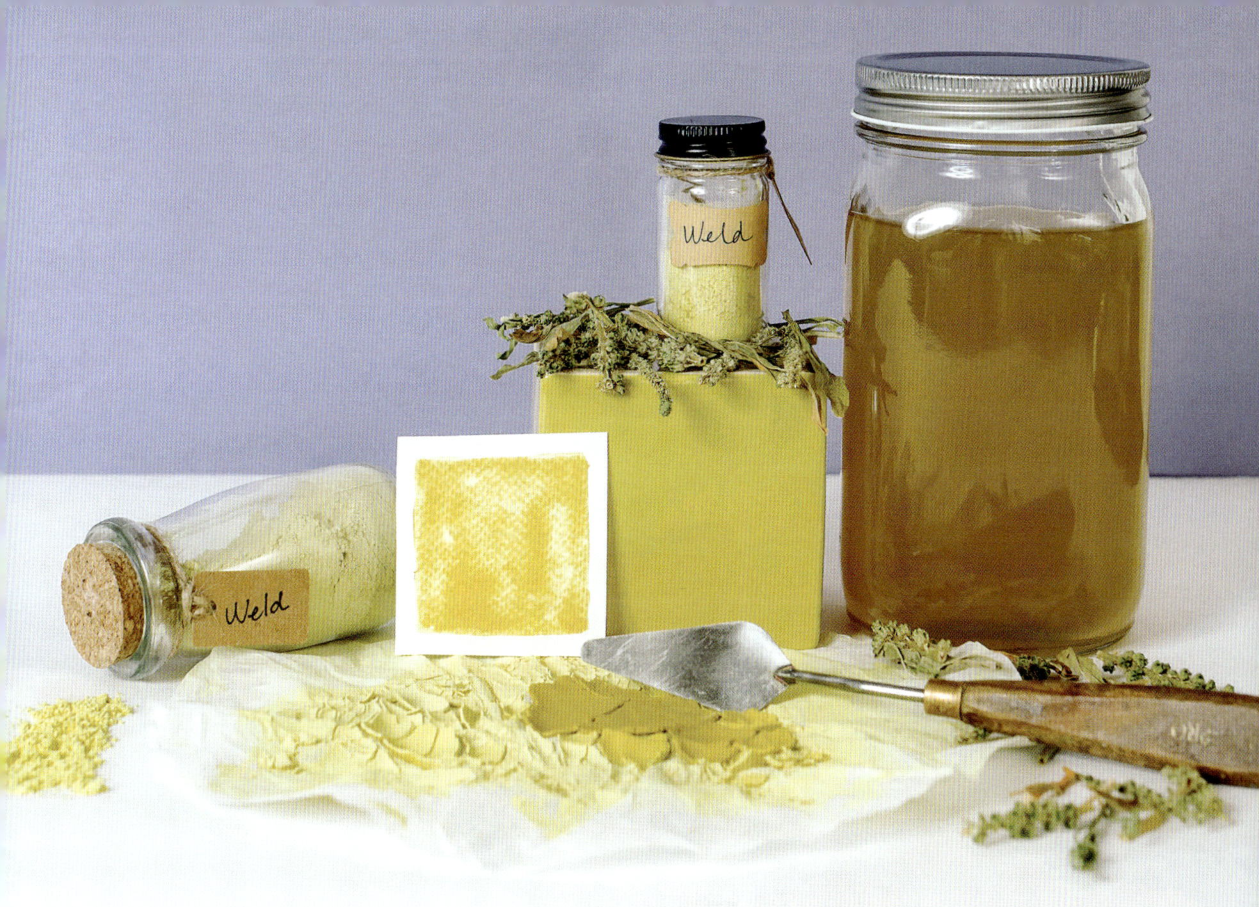

Optional: During the washing stage, save the yellow liquid siphoned out of the jars. You can add this liquid to new jars and repeat the lake pigment process (adding 2 teaspoons [10 ml] of dissolved alum and 1 teaspoon [5 ml] of dissolved chalk) to create a second batch of less vibrantly colored weld pigment.

Follow the remaining steps for mixing, mulling and storing your paint as outlined in the Master Lake Pigment Recipe on pages 57–61.

RECIPE REVIEW

I consider weld to be a botanical primary color, essential for mixing a variety of shades. Its vibrant yellow not only stands out on its own but also plays a key role in creating a decent lightfast botanical green watercolor paint, which I'll detail further on page 125. If you're looking for a super-hero yellow to enhance your watercolor palette, I highly recommend adding this dynamo of a plant to your shopping cart!

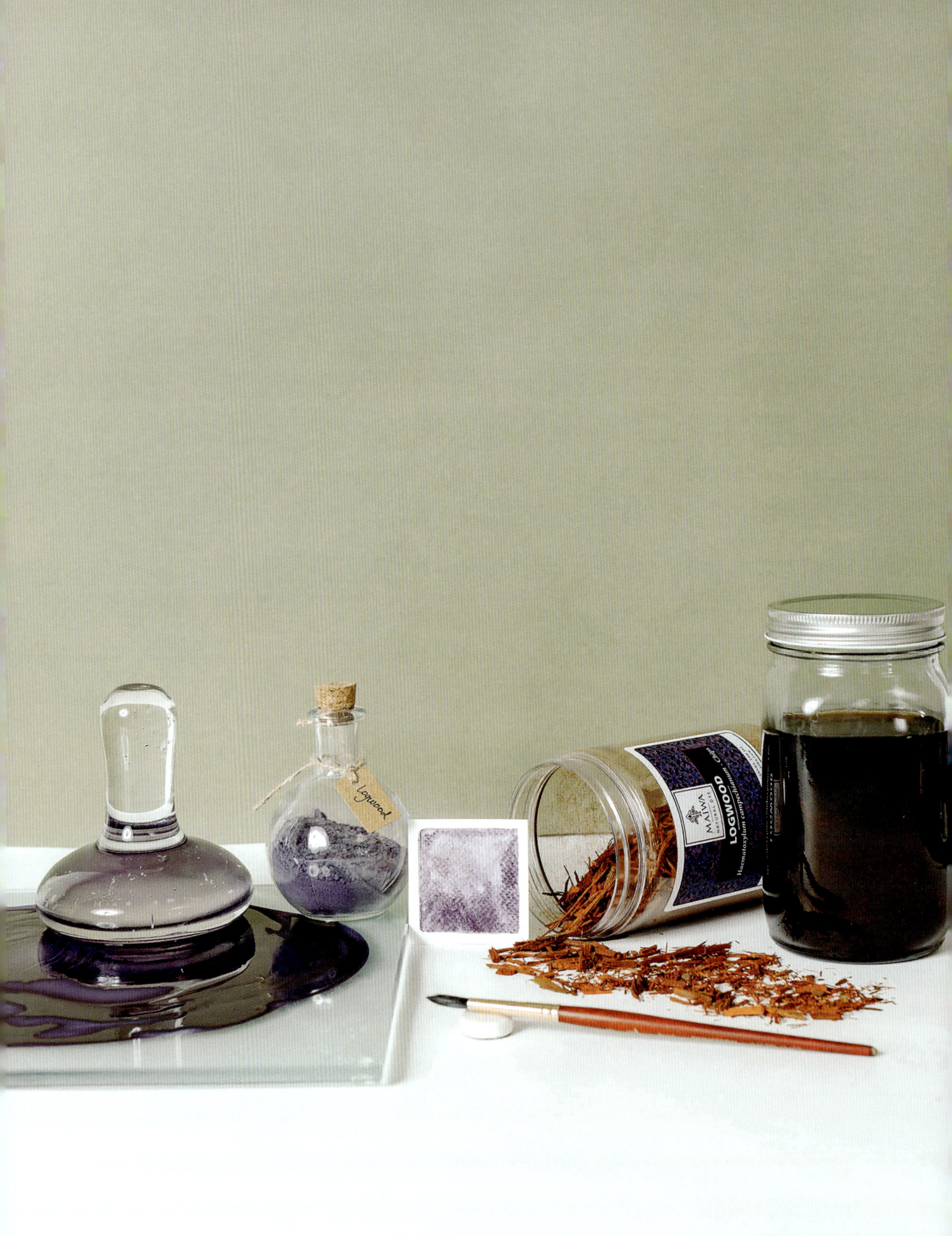

Logwood
MAIWA
NATURAL DYE
LOGWOOD
Haematoxylum campechianum

LOGWOOD (PURPLE)

Logwood is technically part of the legume (pea) family, and the heartwood yields a powerful dark purple dye derived from a pigment compound called *hematoxylin*. Most dye suppliers source logwood from areas where it is grown and harvested sustainably and is not endangered. I buy logwood in the form of wood chips, but it is also sold as a powder. Logwood is extremely pH sensitive, making it somewhat tricky to make consistent purples via the lake pigment process. But it is well worth the effort and the possible learning curve because naturally sourced purples are very hard to capture. In fact, the history of the color purple is fascinating. For a long time purple dye sources were so rare or made scarce by overexploitation that only the most privileged in society wore purple.

MATERIALS

- *¼ cup (15 g) logwood chips*
- *16 cups (3.8 L) distilled (or pH neutral) water*
- *Stainless-steel dye pot*
- *Alum*
- *Chalk powder*
- *Watercolor Binder (page 33)*
- *Supplies for the Master Lake Pigment Recipe (page 45)*

Add about ¼ cup (15 g) of logwood chips and the distilled water to the stainless-steel pot, bring the dye bath to a gentle simmer, then reduce the heat to low, maintaining it just below simmering for 30 to 45 minutes. Logwood dye releases its color quickly, so keep an eye on it. Remove the pot from the heat and let it cool completely or soak it overnight for optimal extraction.

(continued)

Thoroughly filter the logwood "tea," repeating the process until the liquid is completely sediment-free. This recipe typically yields about 13 cups (3.1 L) to 14 cups (3.4 L) of dye. Divide the filtered liquid equally among four large canning jars, adding between 3 cups (720 ml) and 3½ cups (840 ml) to each.

To each jar, add 2 teaspoons (10 ml) of dissolved alum and 2 teaspoons (10 ml) of dissolved chalk. This differs from most recipes but has yielded the best purples for me. Feel free to experiment with different ratios of alum to chalk in each jar and make detailed notes on your observations and color outcomes.

After the addition of alum and chalk, the fizzing chemical reaction should begin. From my experience, logwood pigment takes longer to settle, so letting the jars sit overnight is very helpful. Once you are sure that the pigment has finished settling, you may proceed with washing your beautiful logwood pigment. Then, continue on to drying your pigment and mixing, mulling and storing it as outlined on pages 54 to 61 of the Master Lake Pigment Recipe.

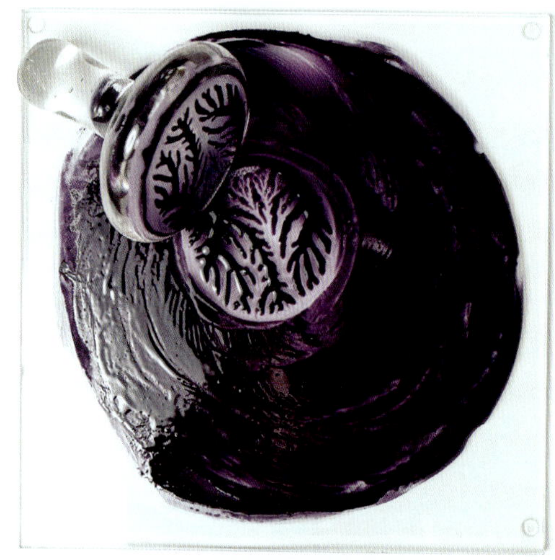

RECIPE REVIEW

In the world of natural dyeing, logwood is popular because it offers that elusive purple dye that can be so hard to find elsewhere in nature. Purple is one of my favorite colors, and despite its somewhat delicate nature, I cannot pass up the opportunity to utilize it to expand the variety of my pigment collection. I hope this recipe helps you create a purple color that you also enjoy painting with, and perhaps you will concoct your own unique logwood recipes to create other beautiful hues and shades of purple.

Natural Watercolor Paint Making

SAPPANWOOD (MAGENTA)

The heartwood of the sappanwood tree, also known as Eastern Brazilwood, contains a colorful compound called *brazilin*, which is widely utilized as a textile dye. It is important to not confuse sappanwood (*Caesalpinia sappan*) with the Brazilwood tree (*Caesalpinia echinata*). The latter has been overharvested and is now considered endangered. Depending on the pH, sappanwood can produce deep reds, bright pinks and oranges, but much like logwood, it is not the most lightfast of the natural dyes. Despite this, the vibrant colors of sappanwood are difficult to resist for paint makers. I have fine-tuned this recipe to make a stunning deep pink pigment, but because sappanwood is chemically sensitive, your color results may vary slightly.

MATERIALS

- *12 cups (2.9 L) distilled or pH neutral water*
- *Stainless-steel dye pot*
- *⅛ cup (10 g) dried and ground sappanwood (a little goes a long way)*
- *Alum*
- *Chalk*
- *Watercolor Binder (page 33)*
- *Supplies for the Master Lake Pigment Recipe (page 45)*

Add the distilled water to the stainless-steel dye pot and stir in the sappanwood. Cover the pot and bring the contents to a gentle simmer, stirring occasionally for about an hour. After an hour, remove the pot from the heat and let the dye cool completely.

(continued)

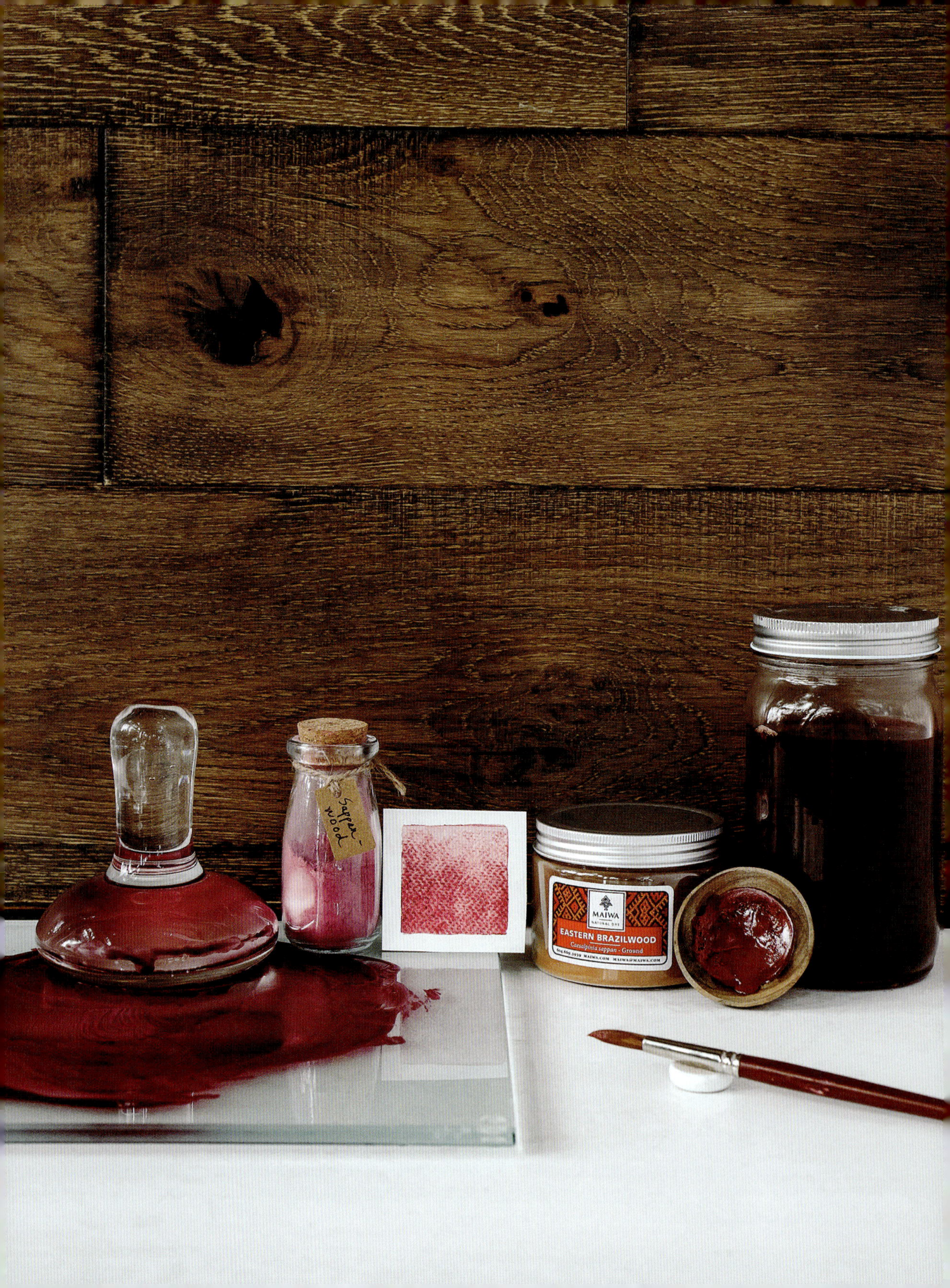
MAIWA
NATURAL DYE
EASTERN BRAZILWOOD
Caesalpinia sappan - Ground
604.669.3939 MAIWA.COM MAIWA@MAIWA.COM

SAPPANWOOD (MAGENTA) (CONTINUED)

Filter the sappanwood "tea" through a fine mesh sieve several times. This usually yields 10 cups (2.4 L) to 11 cups (2.6 L) of filtered liquid; divide it equally among three large glass canning jars.

In each jar, add 2 teaspoons (10 ml) of dissolved alum and 1 teaspoon (5 ml) of chalk mixed into a smooth slurry. After both chemicals have been added, wait for the reaction to begin. The sappanwood pigment solids will begin to settle at the bottom.

NOTE: These measurements can be altered to achieve different hues. In fact, the slightest variation in the amount of alum and/or chalk can alter the final pigment color. Document your results in a dye journal for future reference.

Once the pigment has finished settling, siphon off the colored liquid. This liquid can be added to new jars and the Master Lake Pigment Recipe process can be repeated to extract another round of beautiful pigment, albeit less bold.

Your main jar of gorgeous sappanwood pigment now needs to be washed. Follow the washing instructions on page 50 of the Master Lake Pigment Recipe.

Carefully pour the washed pigment through funnels or sieves lined with coffee filters. Once all your pigment has been captured, lift the wet filters out of the funnels and lay them flat on a towel. When the pigment is completely dry, grind it into a fine powder in a mortar and pestle. Remember to protect your lungs from pigment particles and wear a dust mask.

Lastly, follow the remaining steps of the Master Lake Pigment Recipe on pages 57 to 61 to continue mixing and storing your stunning magenta-colored watercolor paint.

RECIPE REVIEW

Sappanwood is an exotic dye plant that I buy because it creates a beautiful range of unique color opportunities that are not locally available to me. To create more consistency with natural dyes, you can try developing your own recipes by weighing the ingredients instead of measuring by volume. But truth be told, I enjoy the subtle variations that my often intuitive and relaxed methods produce, especially with the more chemically sensitive plants. Whether intentional or accidental, altering the chemistry of sappanwood can lead to exciting and surprising results, producing colors that range from pinks to oranges to ruby reds.

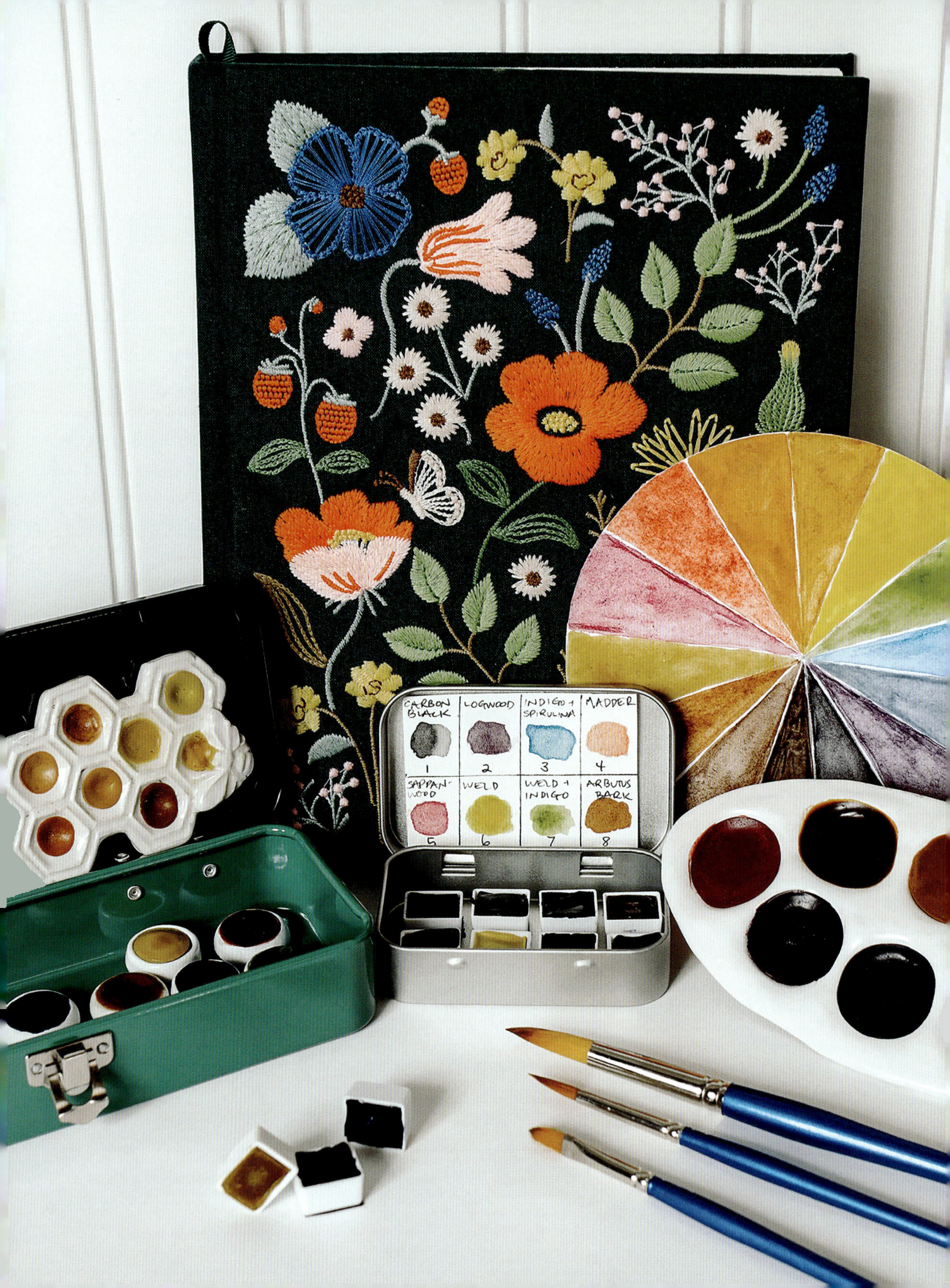

CARBON BLACK
LOGWOOD
INDIGO + SPIRULINA
MADDER
1
2
3
4
SAPPAN WOOD
WELD
WELD + INDIGO
ARBUTUS BARK
5
6
7
8

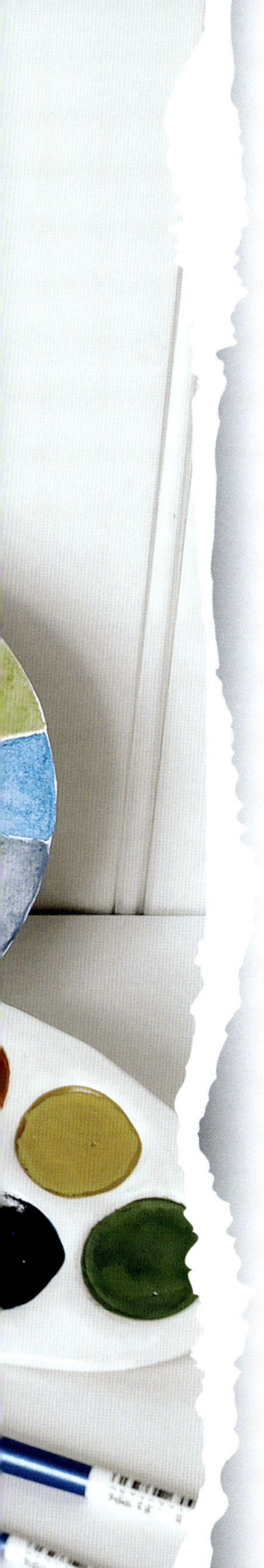

PART 3

USING YOUR PAINTS

Modifying and Mixing Your Color Palette

People are often surprised and impressed to learn that, just like traditional store-bought watercolors, homemade botanical watercolors can also be mixed to create a wide range of new colors. In fact, mixing botanical pigments is particularly exciting because of their unique organic "personalities." It is fascinating to see how the pigment particles blend together, creating vibrant and saturated colors. They often produce beautiful, organic textural effects, like granulation, as the paint dries on the paper. For plant lovers like me, it's truly magical to watch new colors emerge from mixing pigments of various plants, trees, vegetables and flowers and in the process, discover new favorite botanical color blends.

It's important to remember that botanical watercolors won't perform *exactly* like store-bought synthetic pigments. What plant-based pigments may lack in some aspects, like longevity, they more than make up for it with qualities many artists, myself included, cherish—especially their luminosity, "alive-ness" and gentle ecological footprint. Beyond painting with them, mixing these colors and creating color charts are wonderful ways to explore the unique personalities and potential of your homemade pigments.

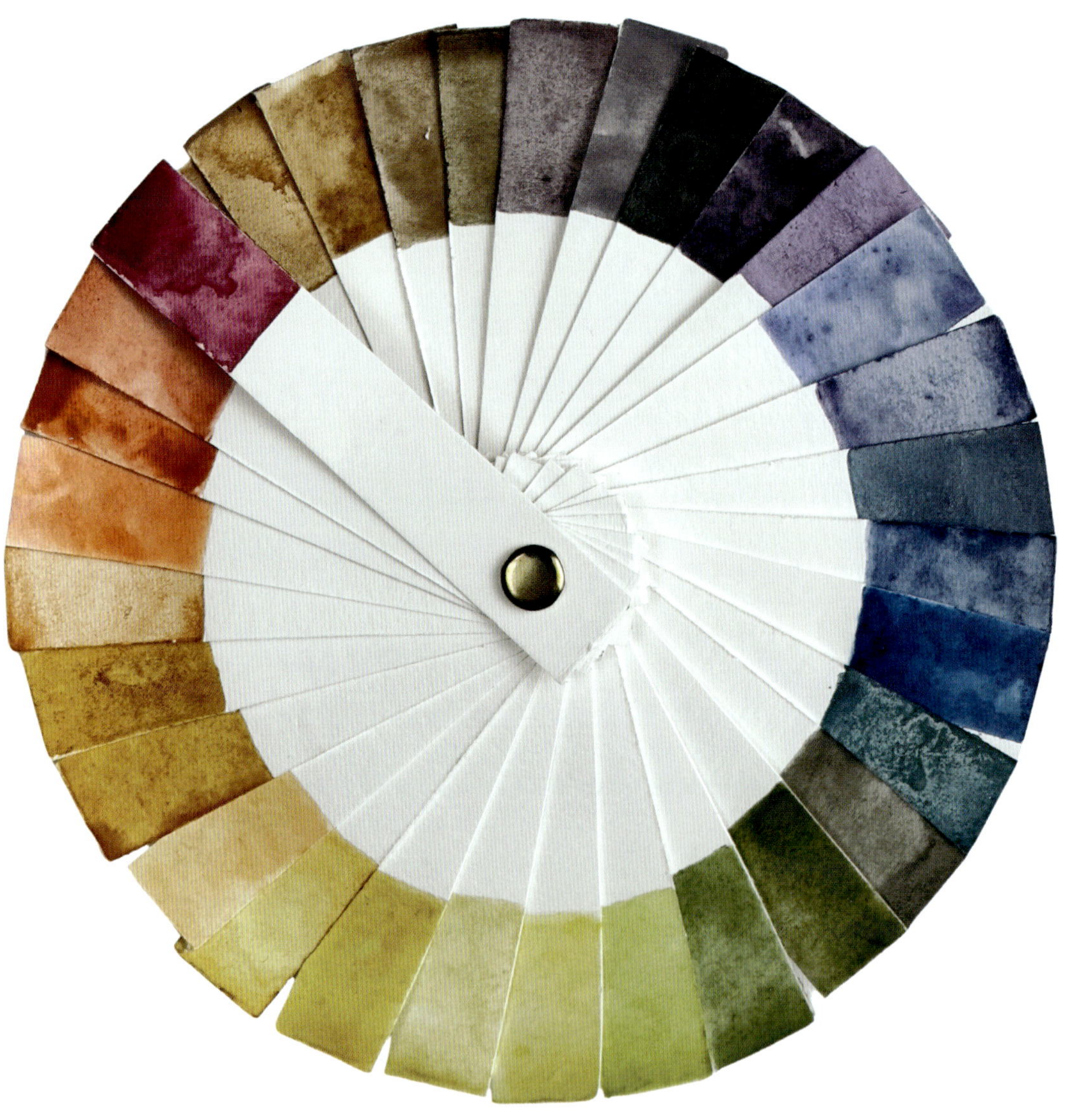

Natural Watercolor Paint Making

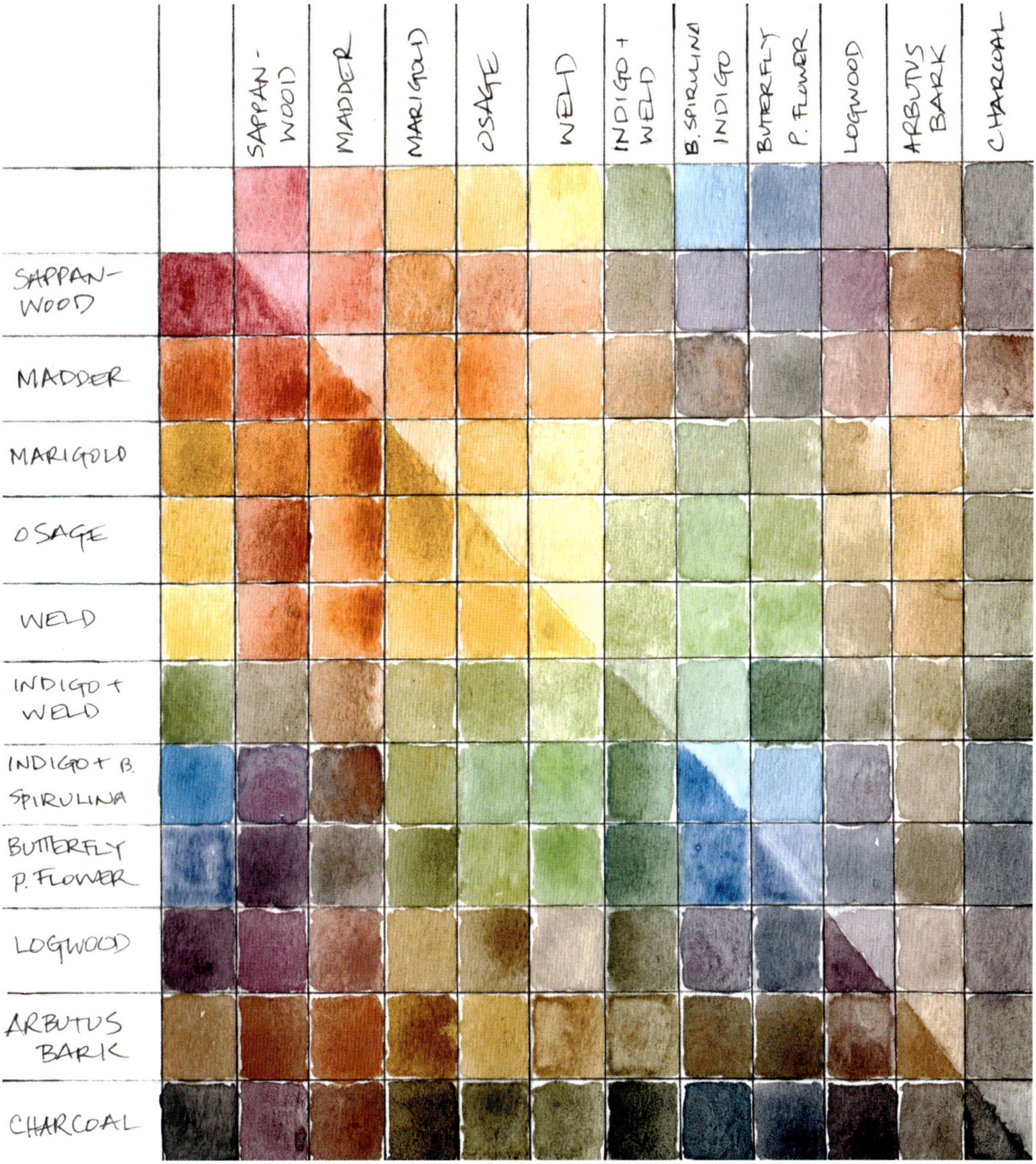
SAPPAN-WOOD
MADDER
MARIGOLD
OSAGE
WELD
INDIGO + WELD
B. SPIRULINA INDIGO
BUTTERFLY P. FLOWER
LOGWOOD
ARBUTUS BARK
CHARCOAL
SAPPAN-WOOD
MADDER
MARIGOLD
OSAGE
WELD
INDIGO + WELD
INDIGO + B. SPIRULINA
BUTTERFLY P. FLOWER
LOGWOOD
ARBUTUS BARK
CHARCOAL

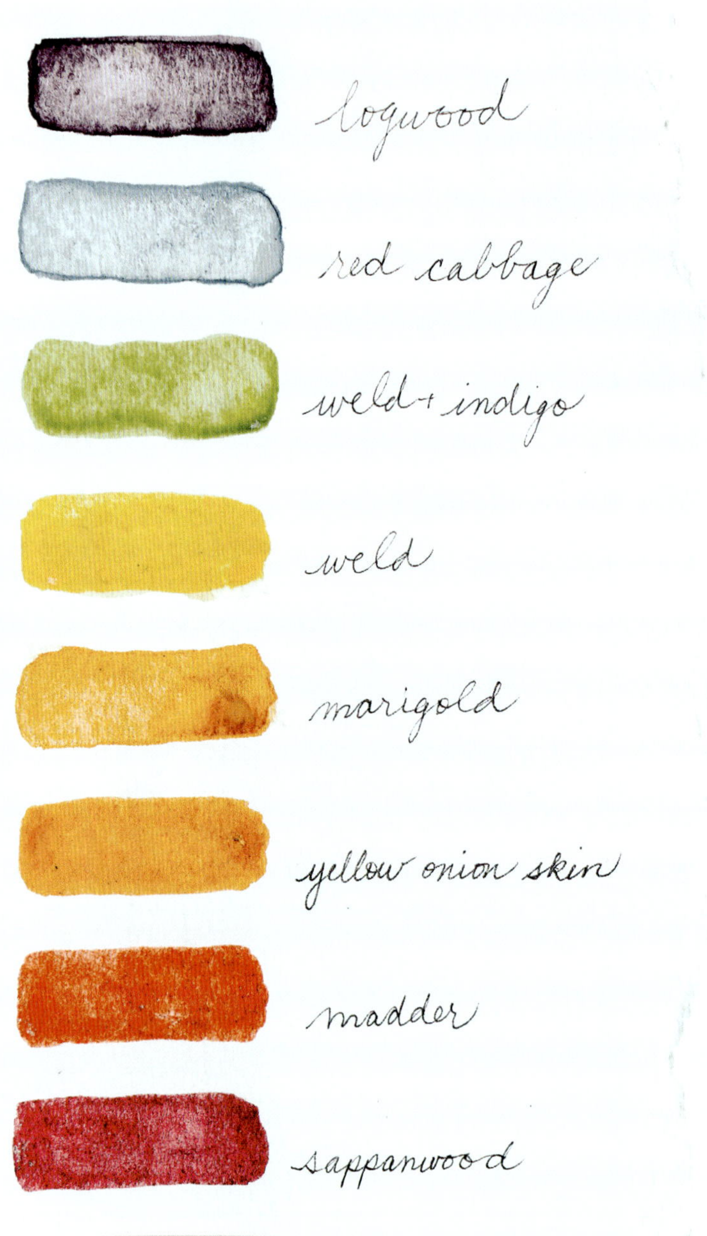

logwood
red cabbage
weld + indigo
weld
marigold
yellow onion skin
madder
sappanwood

MORE WAYS TO MAKE BLUE

Stable and relatively lightfast sources of botanical blue pigments are hard to find. Thankfully nature offers us the chemical compound called *indigotin*. This is traditionally derived from woad and indigo plants, and historically indigo has been a prominent textile dye to create hues ranging from sky blue to dark navy. Because the indigo extraction process is somewhat complicated and therefore beyond the scope of this book, I recommend purchasing indigo extract powder. Extracts are concentrated and dehydrated plant dyes, and are wonderful additions to your pigment collection. Dye extracts can be directly mixed with watercolor binder to make pans of watercolor paint.

MATERIALS

- *Indigo extract powder (I purchase from maiwa.com.)*
- *Blue spirulina powder (optional)*
- *Watercolor Binder (page 33)*
- *Grinding slab*
- *Glass muller*
- *Gum arabic powder (if needed)*

On your grinding slab, start by mixing ¾ teaspoon of indigo extract powder with 2 teaspoons (10 ml) of homemade watercolor binder.

NOTE: For brighter blues, in the mixing stage I will often mix together indigo with blue spirulina powder. I encourage you to explore mixing various ratios of these to discover new and exciting colors for your watercolor palette.

(continued)

Indigo

Indigo and Blue Spirulina

Blue Spirulina

MORE WAYS TO MAKE BLUE
(CONTINUED)

Follow the mixing and mulling instructions on page 57, until your pigment is perfectly smooth. In my experience, indigo powder takes a lot of mulling to fully dissolve. Sprinkling water onto the slab helps the mixing process.

Make a test swatch on paper and allow it to dry. At any point in this process, you may fine-tune the paint by adjusting the ratios of indigo to liquid binder. If your mixture is too watery, you can sprinkle in gum arabic powder to thicken it up.

Add your paint mixture to watercolor pans and allow it to dehydrate as outlined on page 60.

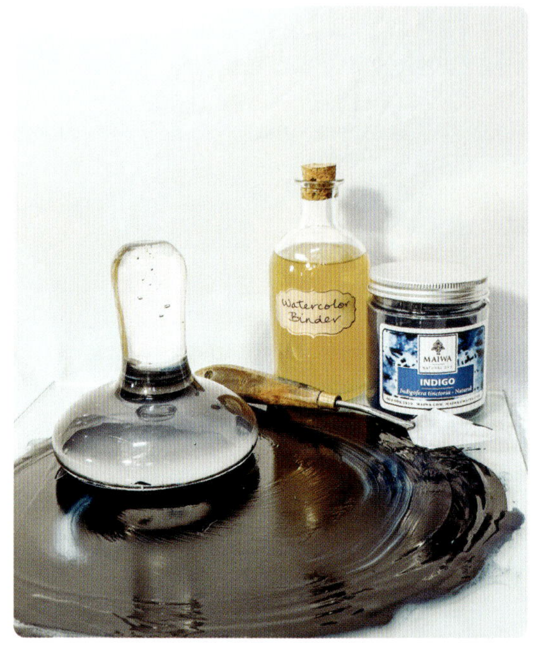

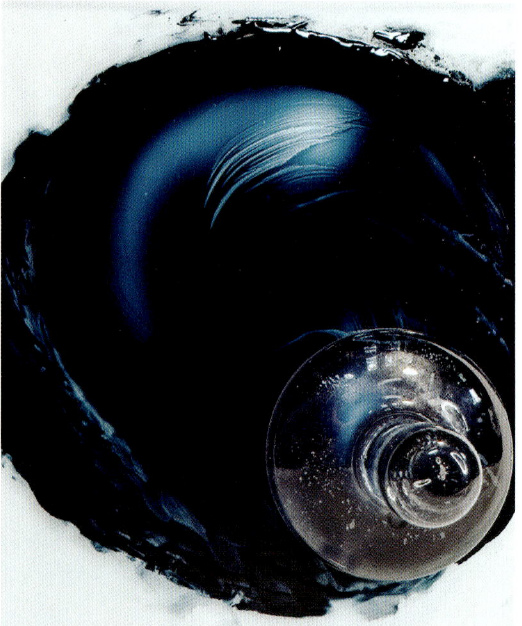

Natural Watercolor Paint Making

MORE WAYS TO MAKE GREEN

Green plants are all around us, and yet it may be surprising to learn that harnessing chlorophyll as a dye for textiles or as a pigment for paint maybe isn't the best use of the plant or our time, due to its complicated extraction process and highly impermanent or "fugitive" nature of the pigment itself when used in textile dyeing or painting applications. Fortunately, there are other ways to create more lightfast and stunning greens for your palette. This is done by simply mixing a yellow botanical pigment you've made from the recipes within this book with indigo extract powder to create . . . a green pigment!

MATERIALS

- *Yellow powdered paint pigment, such as:*
    - *Weld (Bright Yellow) (page 110)*
    - *Pomegranate Peel (Yellowy-Green) (page 77)*
    - *Marigold (Orange) (page 87)*
    - *Yellow Onion Skins (Gold) (page 65)*
- *Indigo extract powder*
- *Watercolor Binder (page 33)*
- *Grinding slab*
- *Glass muller*

(continued)

Indigo and Weld

Indigo and Marigold

On your grinding slab, mix about 1 teaspoon of yellow powdered pigment with a tiny pinch of indigo extract powder. A little indigo goes a long way, as it can easily overpower the yellow.

Add around 2 teaspoons (10 ml) of watercolor binder and mix it together as per the instructions on page 57. Sprinkling water in as needed helps to dissolve the indigo powder and keeps the muller moving smoothly across the slab.

Test your green pigment by making swatches on paper. Adjust the paint by adding more of either the yellow or the indigo pigment.

Pour the wet pigment into watercolor pans and allow it to dehydrate into watercolor paint "cakes" as per instructions on page 60.

NOTE: More olive-green hues can be made by mixing the marigold or the yellow onion skin pigment powder with indigo extract. This book also offers a recipe for a gorgeous green watercolor-based ink in the Red Onion Skins (Green) project (page 71).

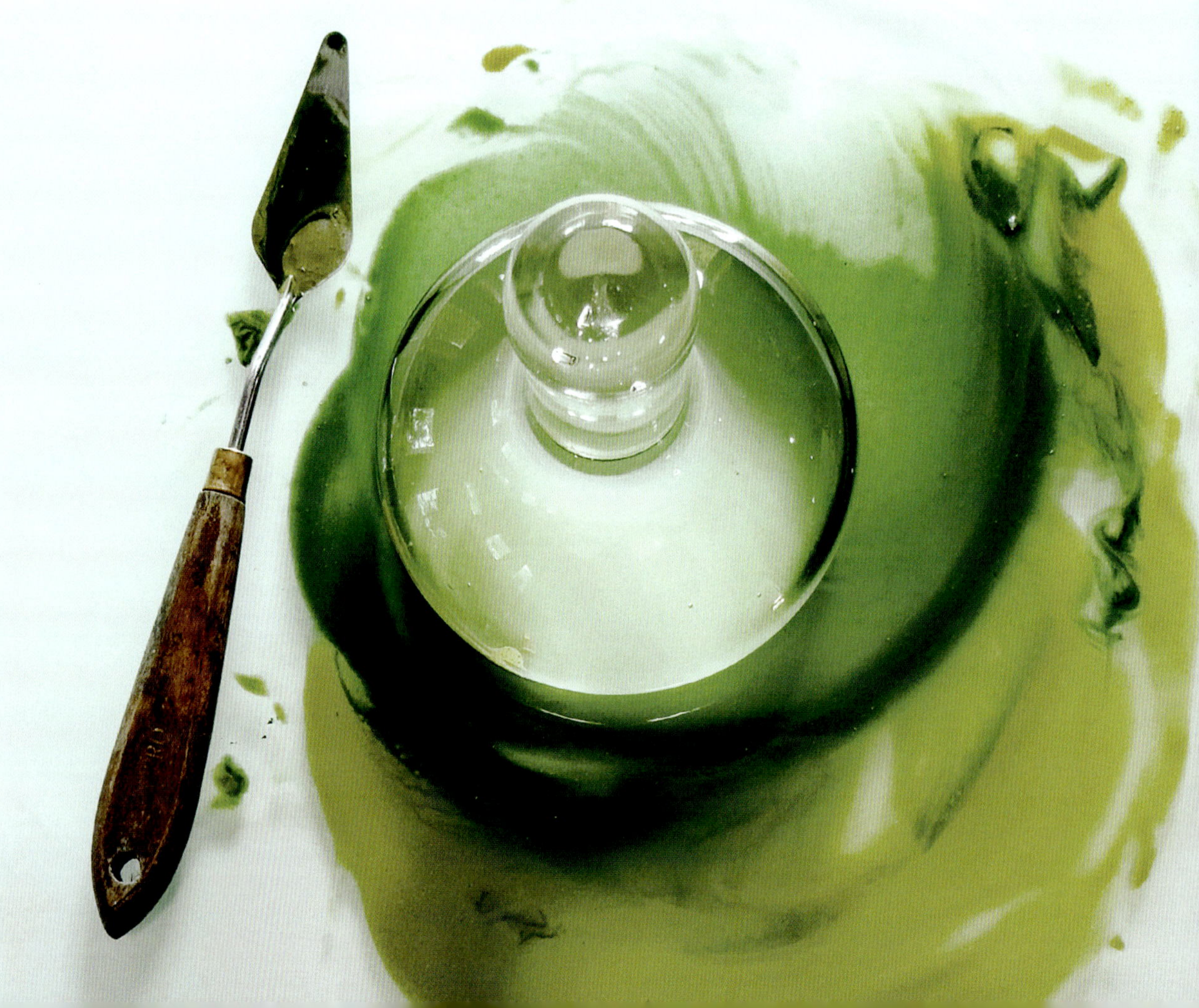

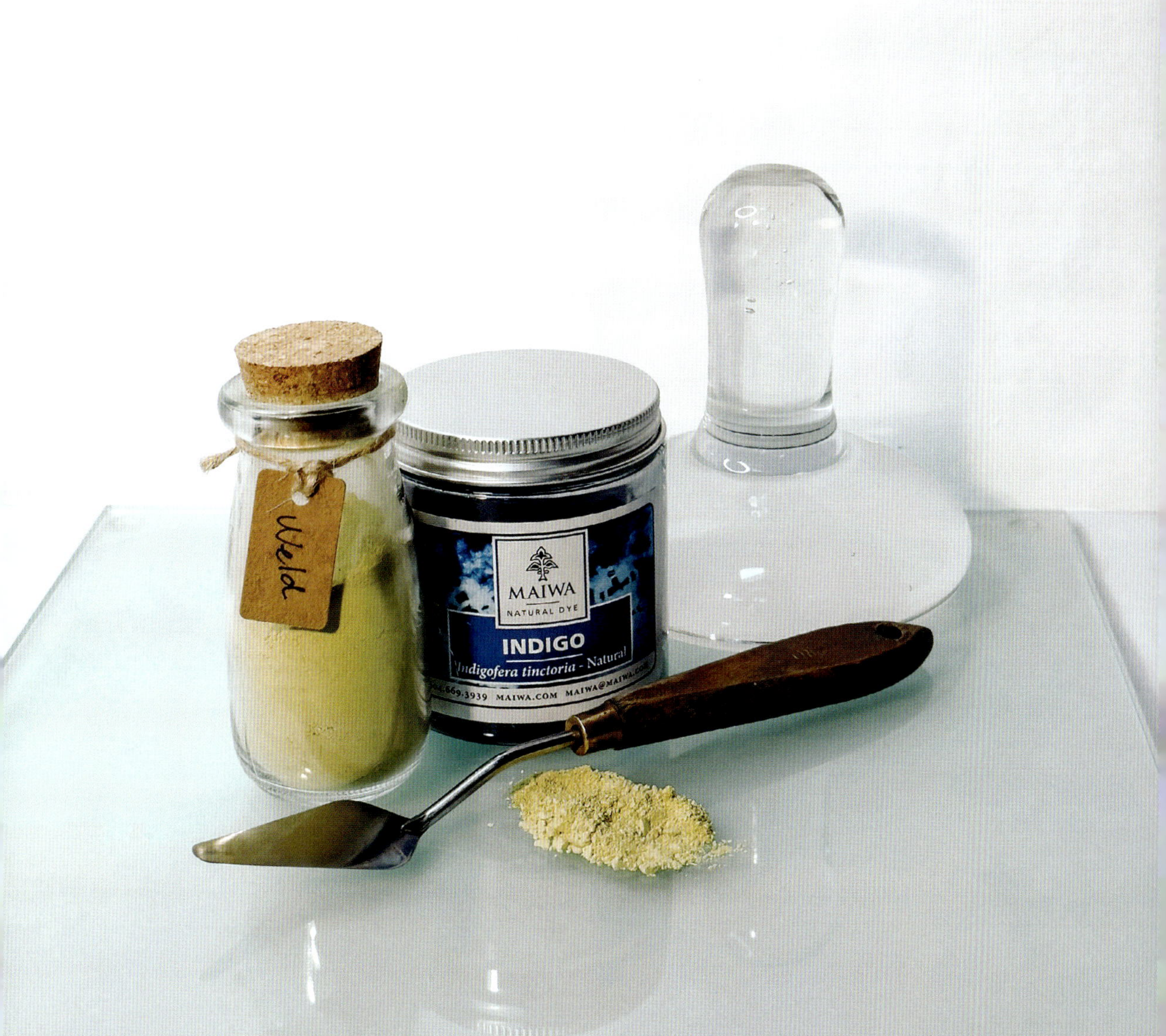

Weld
MAIWA
NATURAL DYE
INDIGO
Indigofera tinctoria - Natural
.669.3939   MAIWA.COM   MAIWA@MAIWA.COM

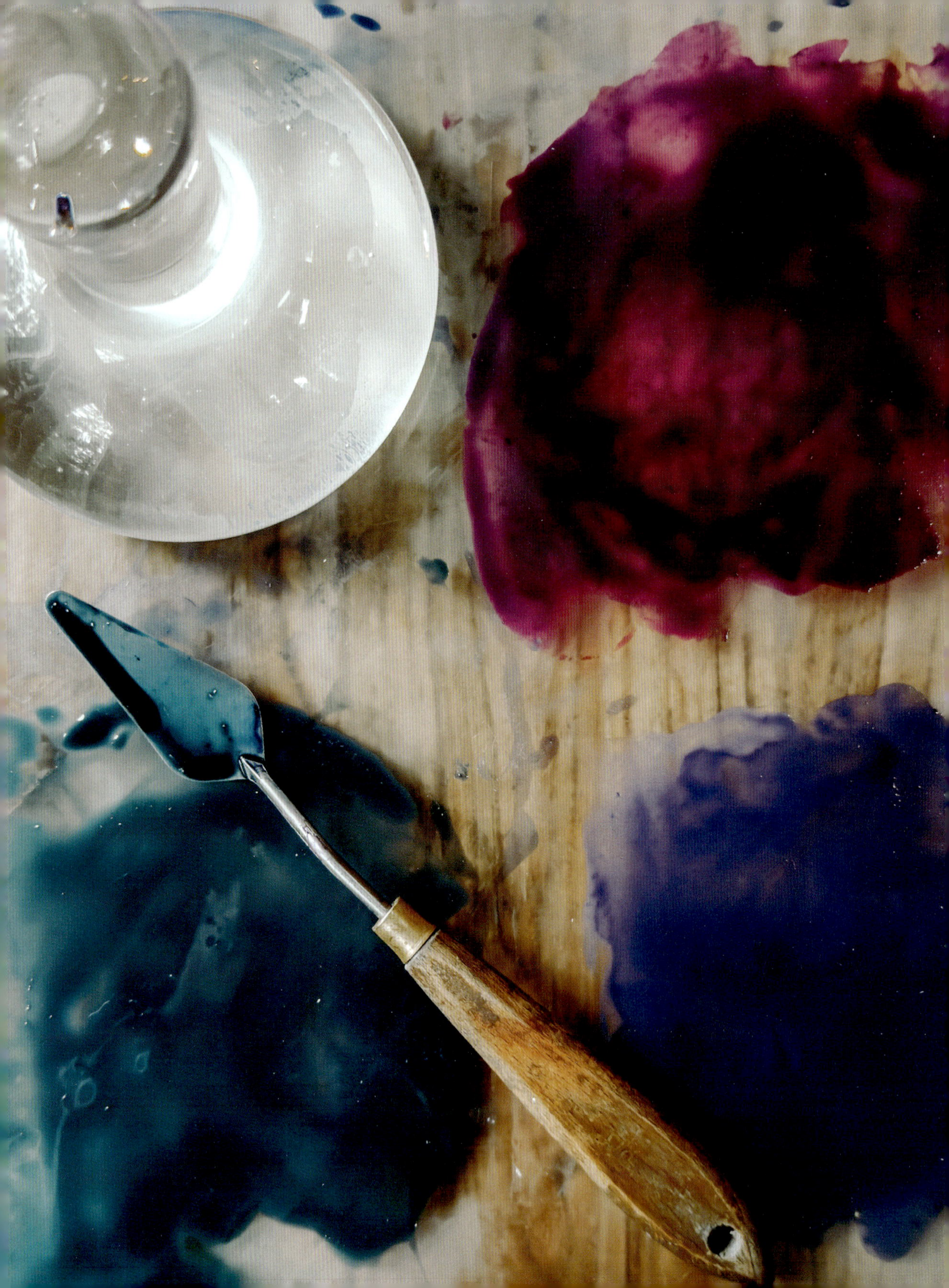

MAKING A RAINBOW OF COLORS FROM RED CABBAGE

The lines between science and art begin to blur when we play with the chemically sensitive botanical pigments, such as the red cabbage pigment made from the recipe on page 67. Due to the presence of anthocyanin chemical compounds, red cabbage is considered a natural "indicator." Essentially what this means is that when the pigment is exposed to changes in pH (acids or bases), the molecules react, transform and, consequently, change color.

THE COLOR CHEMISTRY OF RED CABBAGE

- **Neutral pH (around pH 7):** *With no additives, the pigment is typically blue.*
- **Acidic Conditions (below pH 7):** *When an acid is added, the pigment shifts to purple, then pink.*
- **Basic Conditions (above pH 7):** *When a base is added, the pigment changes to teal and then green.*

MATERIALS

- *Red cabbage pigment powder (page 67)*
- *Watercolor Binder (page 33)*
- *pH Modifiers*

    Acids: Vinegar, lemon juice or citric or tartaric acid crystals

    Bases: Baking soda, soda ash or washing soda
- *pH indicator test strips (optional)*
- *Grinding slab*
- *Glass muller*

On a grinding slab, mix together a couple of teaspoons (3 to 5 ml) of red cabbage powdered pigment with homemade watercolor binder, and mull until a smooth paint pigment is made.

To the mixture, you will add a pH modifier (acid or base) of your choice. Begin by adding a tiny pinch (or drop, if liquid) of the modifier to the wet mixed pigment. Using your palette knife and if need be your muller, mix thoroughly and observe any color changes. Shifts in color usually appear within a few minutes. If the change isn't as noticeable as desired, gradually add more of the modifier, but proceed slowly.

Repeat the above process with fresh batches of red cabbage powdered pigment, experimenting with different amounts of acids and bases to explore the anthocyanin color spectrum.

NOTE: The use of pH test strips can aid in more exact color mixing with pH sensitive pigments, but I prefer to do this more intuitively.

(continued)

MAKING A RAINBOW OF COLORS
FROM RED CABBAGE (CONTINUED)

To prevent cross contamination, it's very important to wash your mixing surface, tools and paint brushes very well between each batch of a pH modified pigment.

When painting with pH modified watercolors, the pigments can react with one another on the paper, which might not always be desirable. However, this interaction can also produce interesting abstract effects that may be welcomed. Just remember that when switching between any modified colors on your palette, use clean paint brushes to avoid cross contamination of your paints.

NOTE: You may also choose to modify the pH of food grade powders, such as butterfly pea flower and hibiscus (described on page 79). I also suggest exploring the pH of sappanwood pigment (recipe on page 115) because it can also have beautiful shifts in color from pink to orange to crimson red through an increase in acidity.

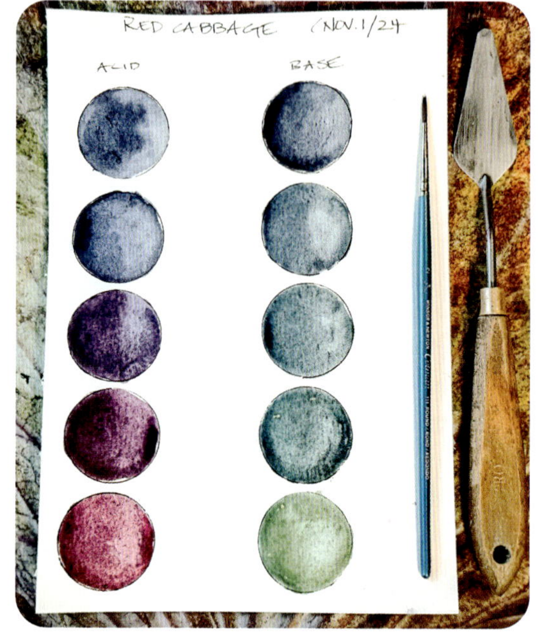

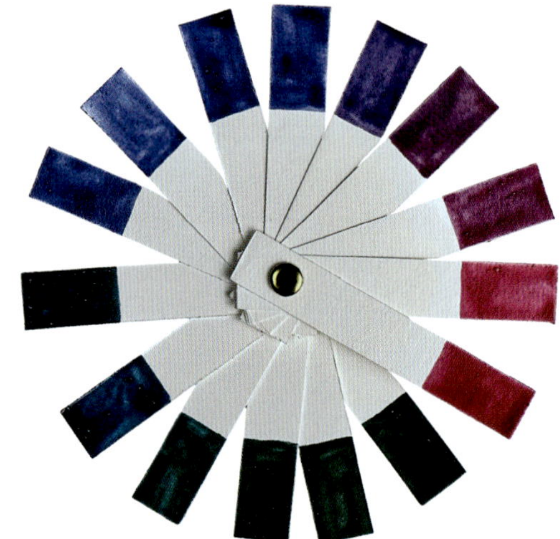

Natural Watercolor Paint Making

USING IRON TO DARKEN TANNIN PIGMENTS

Iron has long been used by natural textile dyers to increase a dye's lightfastness or to modify colors. Many botanical dyes will dull or "sadden" with the addition of iron, particularly those containing tannins. Tannins, which are present in various plants, help protect them from pests and impart an astringent taste found in foods and beverages like black tea and wine. A historically important writing ink (called iron gall ink) is still being made by adding iron to the tannin-rich dye of oak galls.

This book provides watercolor pigment recipes where color is derived from either yellow tannin (pomegranate peel) or brown tannins (tea, maple leaves and black walnut). We can use these pigments with iron to mix up darker, richer versions of themselves.

MATERIALS

- *Powdered paint pigment, such as*
    Orange Pekoe Tea (Russet Brown) (page 73)
    Autumn Maple Leaves (Golden Brown) (page 103)
    Black Walnut (Dark Brown) (page 105)
- *Watercolor Binder (page 33)*
- *Iron (sold as ferrous sulfate crystals from dye supply stores)*
- *Grinding slab*
- *Glass muller*
- *Gloves*

On the grinding slab, mix around a teaspoon of a tannin-based pigment powder with 2 teaspoons (10 ml) of watercolor binder. Mix with a glass muller until it is perfectly smooth as per the mixing instructions on pages 57–58.

Since iron can be a skin irritant, wear gloves. Start by adding a few ferrous sulfate crystals to the wet mixed pigment. A small amount of ferrous sulfate goes a long way since it is a powerful modifier. Mix well to allow the crystals to fully dissolve. I usually wait half an hour to let the color fully shift before adding more iron.

(continued)

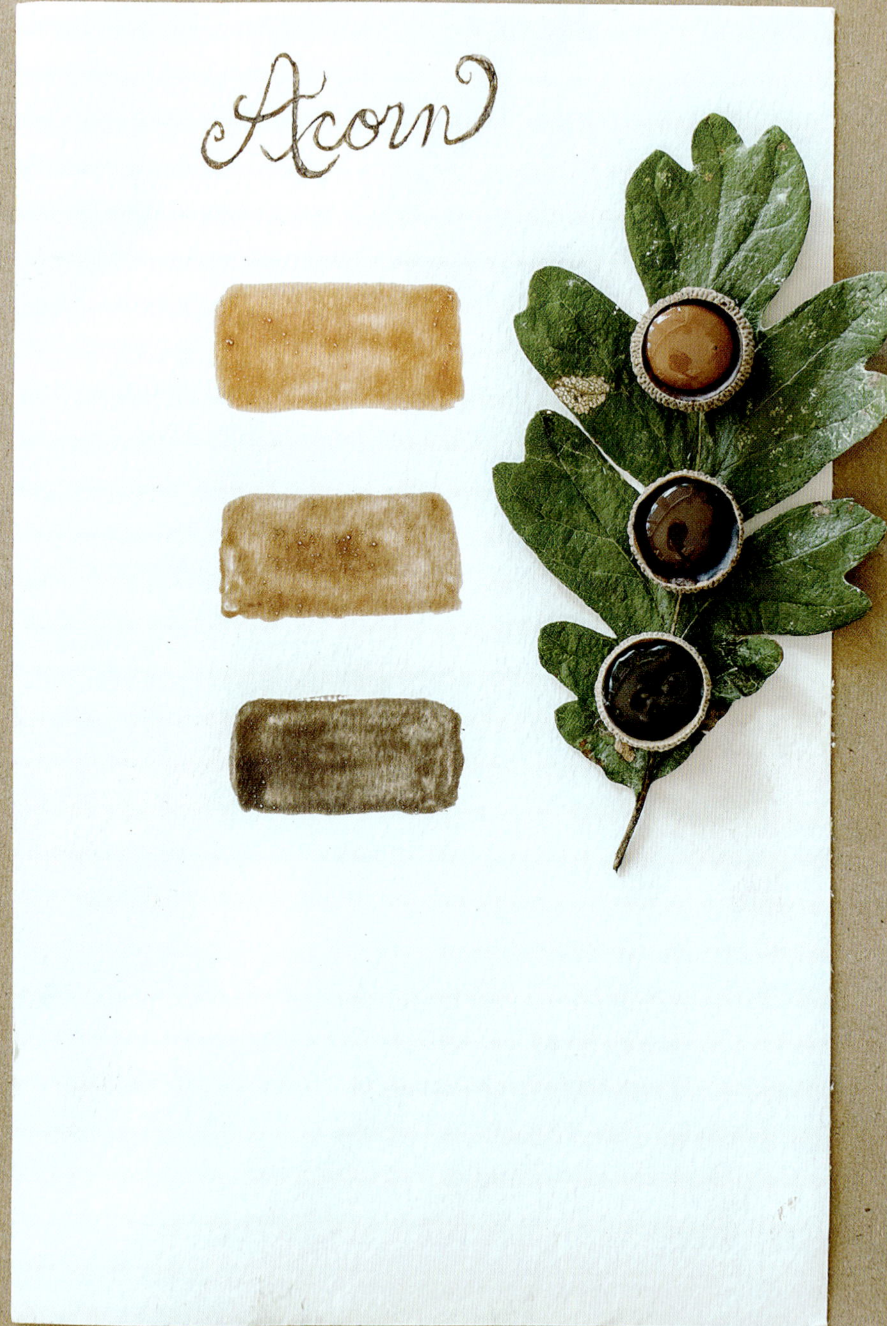
Acorn

Make a test swatch on paper and allow the paint to dry to see the final color develop. To make the paint darker, add a few more iron crystals.

Pour the mixed pigment into watercolor pans and allow it to dry for future use. To create a writing ink, dilute the wet pigment further by adding extra watercolor binder. Add a few drops at a time until a flowing ink-like consistency is achieved. Keep testing your ink on paper using either a brush or a dip pen. Store the ink in jars and keep it refrigerated to extend its shelf life.

It's essential to wash paint brushes and writing nibs thoroughly after each use. Iron can corrode metal calligraphy nibs, so take extra care when using iron-modified pigments. Also, avoid cross contamination on your watercolor palette by keeping iron-modified colors separate from other pigments and wash paint brushes very well. I now have a few paint brushes reserved only for iron-infused pigments.

Lastly, as you explore paint making beyond the recipes of this book, I encourage you to explore other sources of tannin-rich pigments by creating pigments, using the Master Lake Pigment Recipe (page 43), from the shells of acorns, hazelnuts or chestnuts. You may choose to modify these with iron as well.

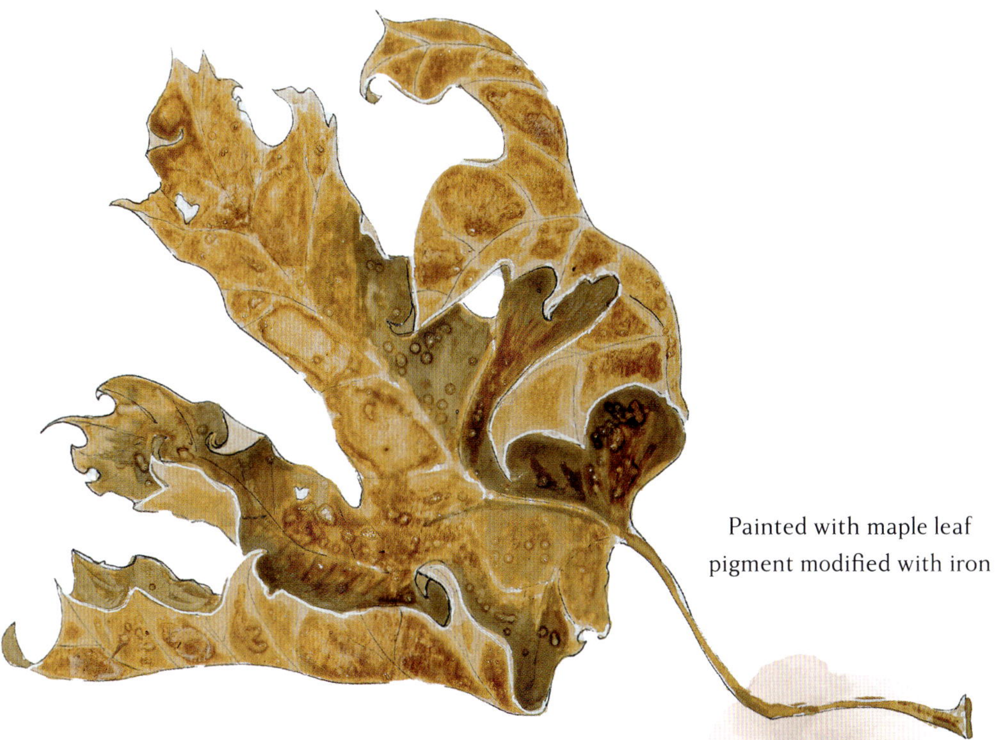

Painted with maple leaf
pigment modified with iron

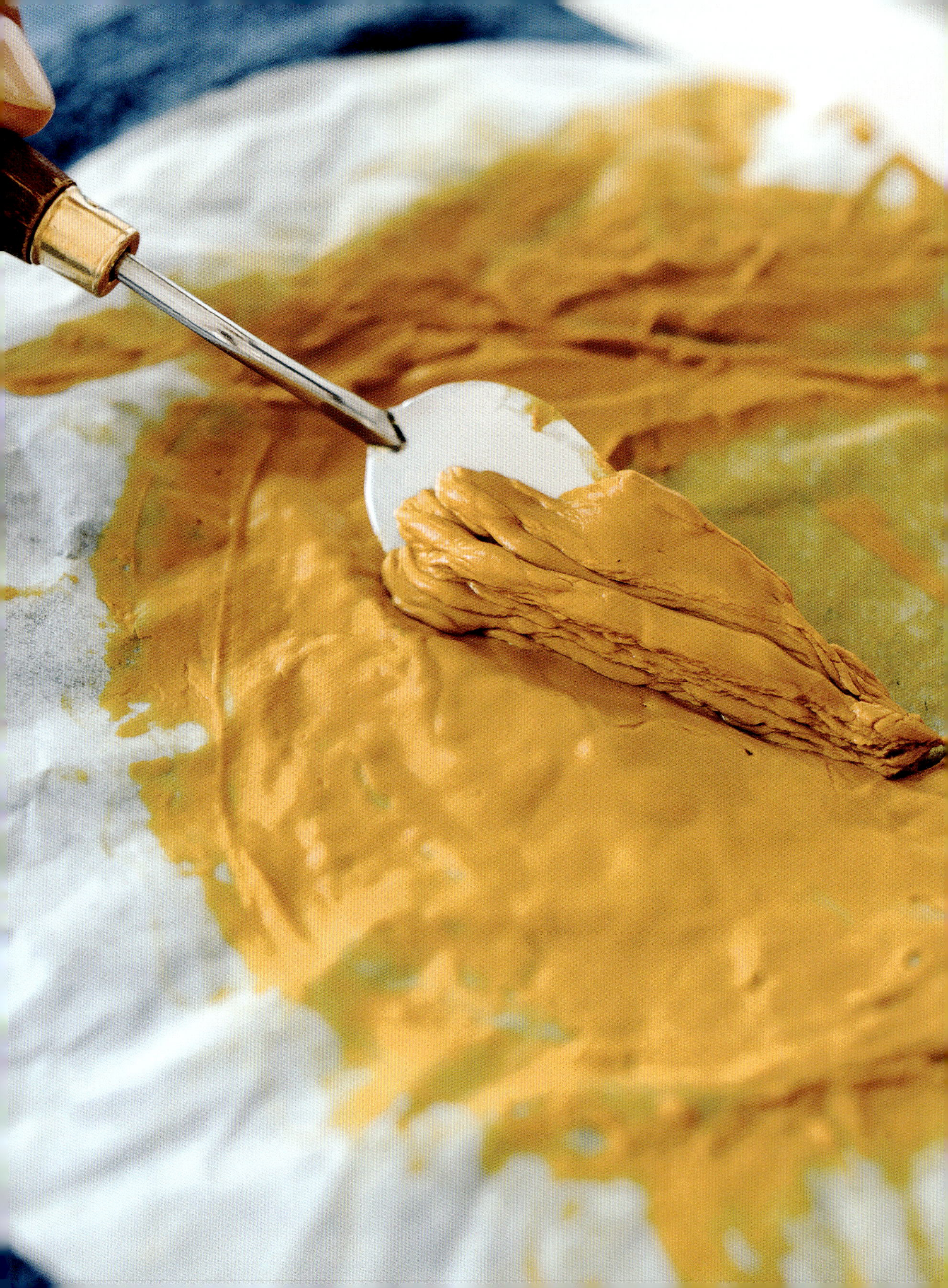

CARING FOR YOUR PAINTS AND PRESERVING YOUR PAINTINGS

I have discussed how each plant pigment has its own unique set of characteristics, and this applies to their varying degrees of lightfastness too. Exposure to light can degrade some pigments more quickly than others. If you plan to sell botanical watercolor paintings, I believe it is important to be upfront about the delicate nature of the pigments used. While it is impossible to make these pigments archival, there are steps that can be taken to help protect and slow the fading process.

- Store all pigment powders and watercolor palettes in a dark place.

- After painting with your watercolors, allow the pans of paint to fully dry out again before putting them away.

- Keep all paintings away from direct sunlight and moisture/humidity. Hang them on walls which receive the least amount of bright light.

- Covering artworks with UV filtering glass may help to slow the rate of fading.

- Sealing paintings (I prefer Jacquard Dorland's Wax Medium) offers protection from the damaging effects of moisture and dirt, which could damage the more delicate botanical pigments.

- Textile artists who use plants to dye yarn and fabric need to pre-treat the fiber with mordants. Mordants are chemicals that work by opening up the pores of the fabric so that the dye can penetrate the fibers and essentially grab hold. This is an important step so that these dyes are as lightfast as possible. A popular mordant in fabric dyeing is alum (the ingredient this book also uses for the Master Lake Pigment Recipe on page 43). Inspired by textile dyers' use of pre-treating fabric, I'm currently experimenting with pre-treating my watercolor paper with an alum mordant. Hopefully, this will help the botanical pigments stick to the fibers of the paper and slow down the rate of fading. Time will tell how effective my experiments are.

- Maintaining a binder full of paint swatches (each labeled with the date) is a wonderful way to document and preserve the paint-making journey. Over time and with more experience, paint makers become more knowledgeable and adept at maximizing a plant's color potential.

- Lastly, and most importantly, if I want my botanical paintings to last forever, I digitally scan or photograph them. These images may be used in other digital art applications, or they can be printed at any time in the future.

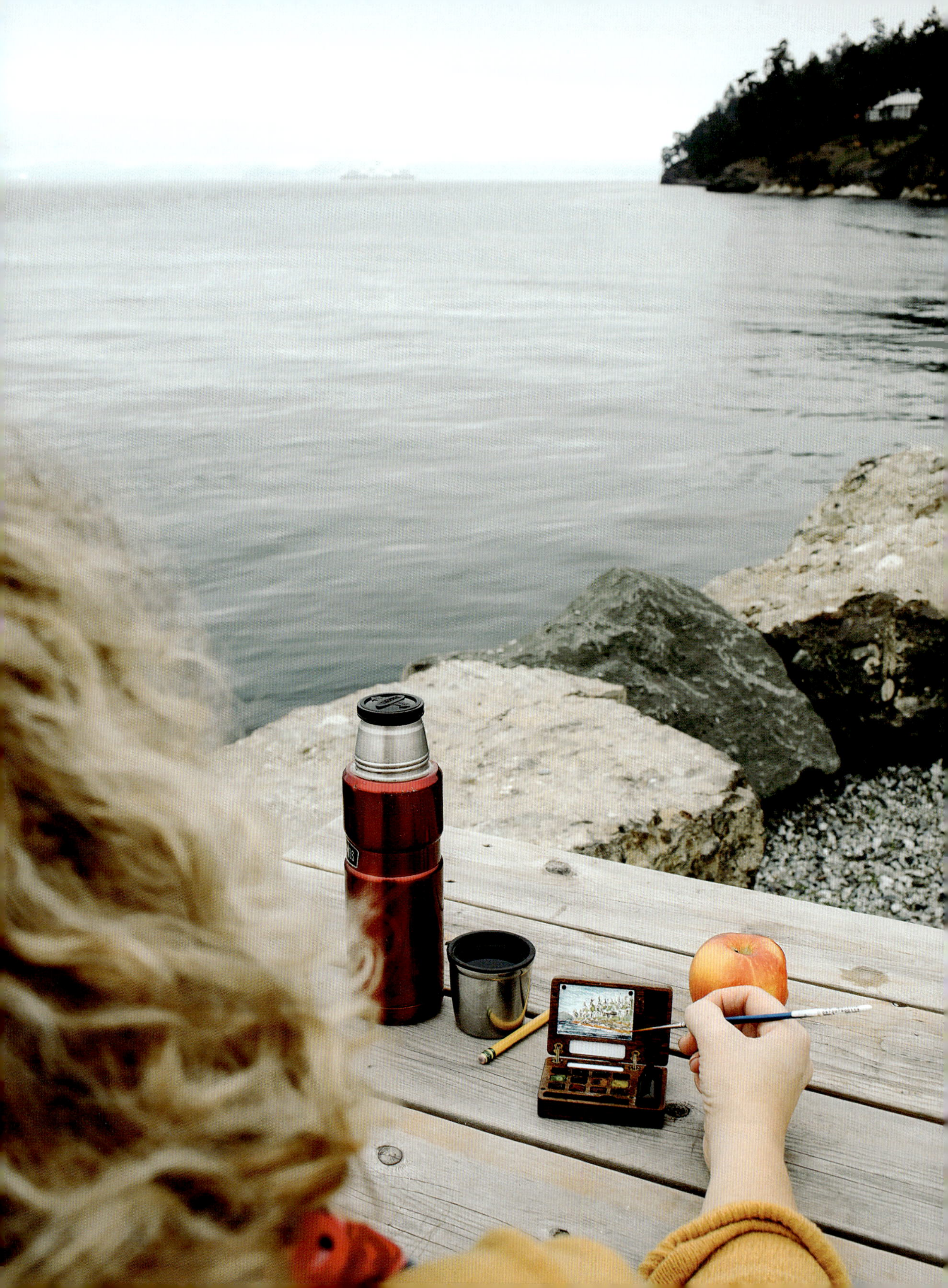

Activities

The color adventures continue after you've mastered the basics of natural paint making. There is a special kind of satisfaction that arises when you start painting with your own handmade watercolors. You'll likely find yourself on a journey of pigment discovery where you'll experiment with meaningful and creative ways to use your paints. In the pages ahead, I share activities that have brought me joy and deepened my connection to botanical colors—and to nature itself. My hope is that I may inspire you to further explore, create and cultivate your own meaningful relationship with the natural world and the rich, vibrant world of natural pigments. But mostly, I hope you have lots of fun!

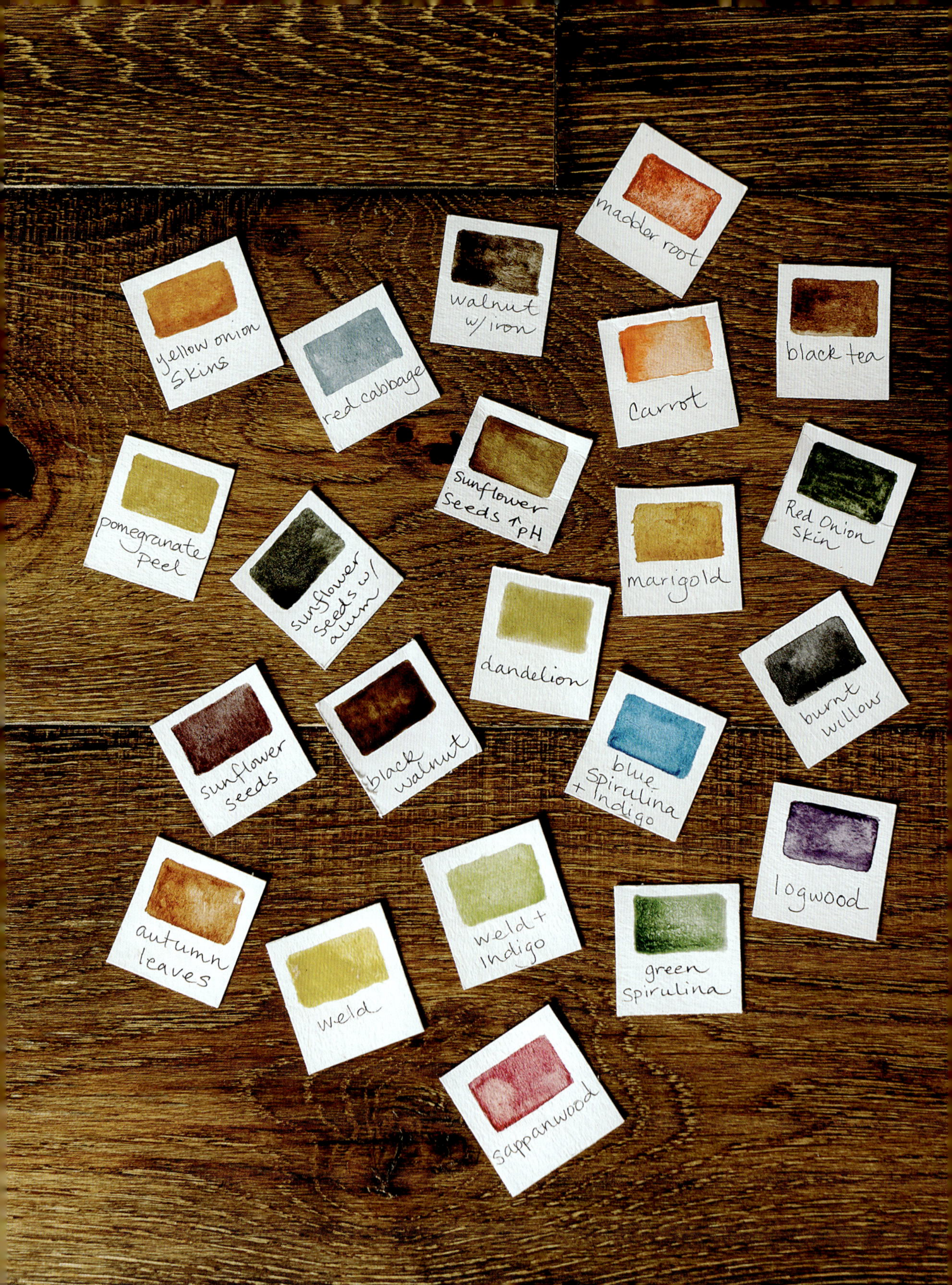

madder root
walnut w/iron
yellow onion skins
red cabbage
Carrot
black tea
sunflower seeds ↑PH
pomegranate peel
marigold
Red Onion Skin
sunflower seeds w/ alum
dandelion
burnt willow
sunflower seeds
black walnut
blue Spirulina + Indigo
logwood
autumn leaves
weld + Indigo
green Spirulina
weld
sappanwood

CURATING COLORS: CREATING PERSONALIZED PALETTES AND PIGMENT COLLECTIONS

Creating watercolor palettes that represent local trees, the changing seasons and your own homegrown plants and flowers, can be deeply gratifying. Each paint captures the beauty of a particular plant, and it also conjures the memory of the journey it took to make that particular color. In fact, watercolor palettes are much like color diaries. Each color is a story. Your stories may begin with a walk in the forest, a basket of walnuts collected from a friend's backyard or maybe the sunflowers you find at a roadside farm stand. Other colors on your palette may represent the hours you spend in your garden, sowing seeds and growing and tending flowers in shades of yellow, gold and purple. Later, when you paint with these handcrafted watercolors and as the brush glides over the paper, the memories rise to the surface again. There are so many color stories waiting to be written, or . . . painted!

It can be fun to build different themed palettes, add your own creative flair to palettes by using unique artisan-made paint palettes or upcycle common household items like bottle caps or other small containers such as tiny jam jars. Curating your homemade paints can be an art form in itself. I have cabinets full of jars of colorful powdered pigments, and these collections remind me of an old-world apothecary. Every stage of natural paint making reveals its own beauty.

While this book provides recipes for a full spectrum of botanical color, I suggest starting simple by building a palette with the primary colors: red, blue and yellow pigments. With just a few pigments, you can mix up additional colors. For red, the Madder Root (page 91) is a great option. For yellow, the Weld (page 110) is perfect. For blue, blue spirulina (page 79) and indigo extract (page 123) are excellent choices.

Adding a secondary color like an orange pigment to your palette is a bonus. The pigment of Marigold (page 87) or Yellow Onion Skins (page 65) are both must-haves for my palette. This book also provides some great options for the color green (see the recipe for Red Onion Skins on page 71). You will have a lot of color possibilities!

Creating earthier colors to include in your botanical watercolor palette is also lovely. The tannin-rich pigment recipes (page 131) are good ways to add depth and richness, as is making a Charcoal (Black) paint (page 99).

Having said all this, it's often enough to use just one homemade color to create meaningful works of art. You will soon discover what plant color calls to you and hopefully you will find this color journey as heartwarming as I have.

PLEIN AIR PAINTING IN NATURE

Plein air refers to the practice of painting outdoors. There is something very nourishing about painting in nature, and naturally, I highly recommend packing your homemade watercolor paints! These outings are best when kept simple. What works for me is packing up the tiniest travel art kit consisting of a small watercolor palette, maybe four or five pans of homemade watercolors within an old ALTOIDS tin, along with a small pad of paper, a couple paint brushes, a little container of water and a few other drawing basics. On cooler days, I pack a thermos with a hot drink, then head outside to find somewhere to sit, sketch and paint. When I travel to more urban settings, I enjoy finding places to sit and observe, and find things that catch my eye to sketch then paint.

Many artists can feel burdened by the pressure to create only "good" art, or perhaps get caught in creating to please others. These plein air outings can provide freedom from the pressures we may feel in our studios, and we can simply create for creativity's sake. The point is to simply step away from our daily lives and immerse ourselves in playful forms of creativity which, for many creative souls, is essential for our overall well-being. Additionally, time spent outside is a simple yet powerful form of self-care. Plein air painting is especially enriching when we use our hand-crafted watercolors.

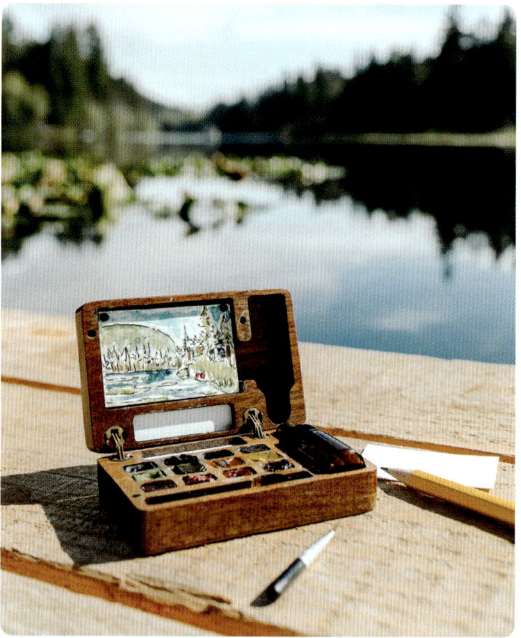

Natural Watercolor Paint Making

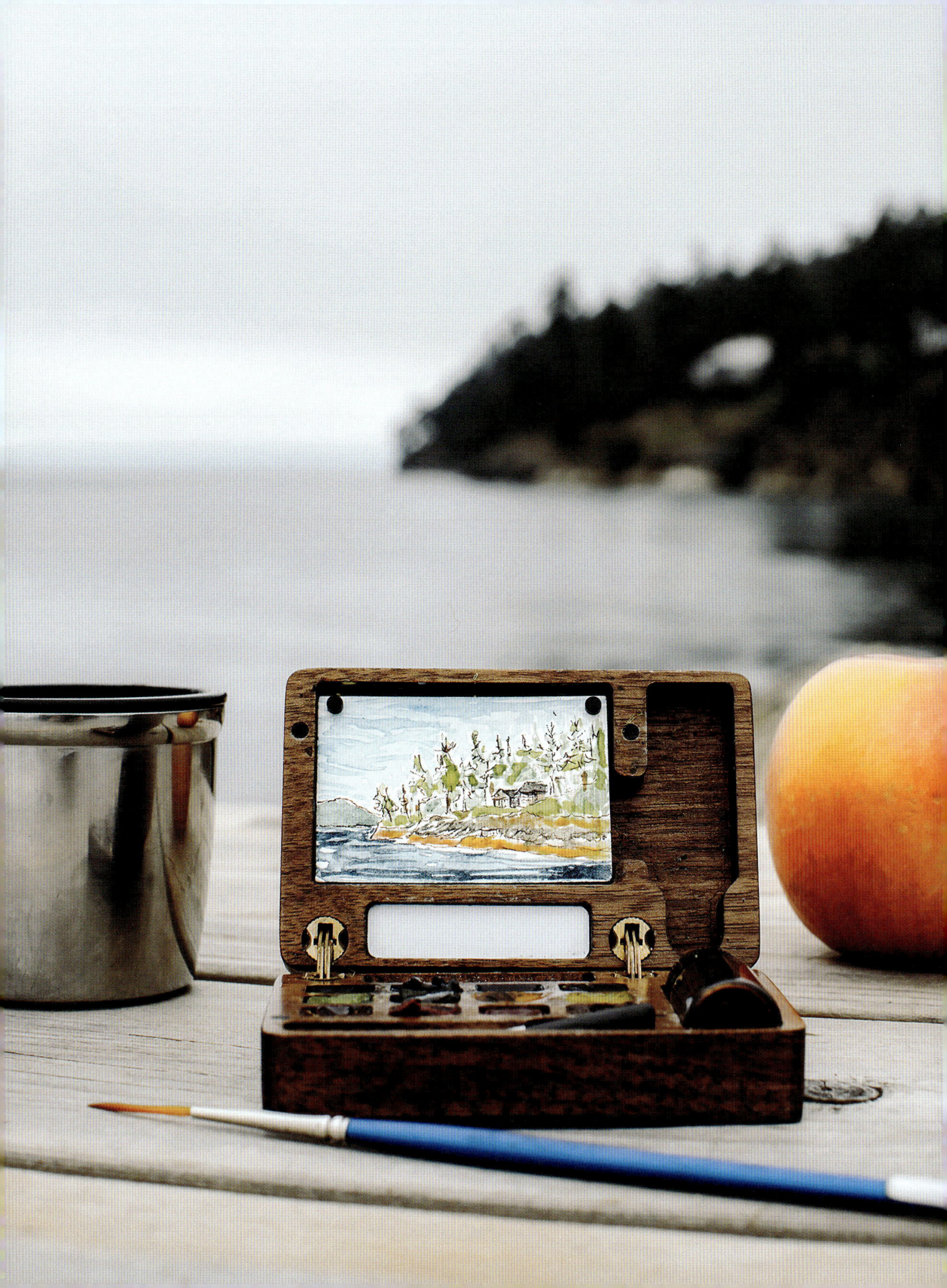

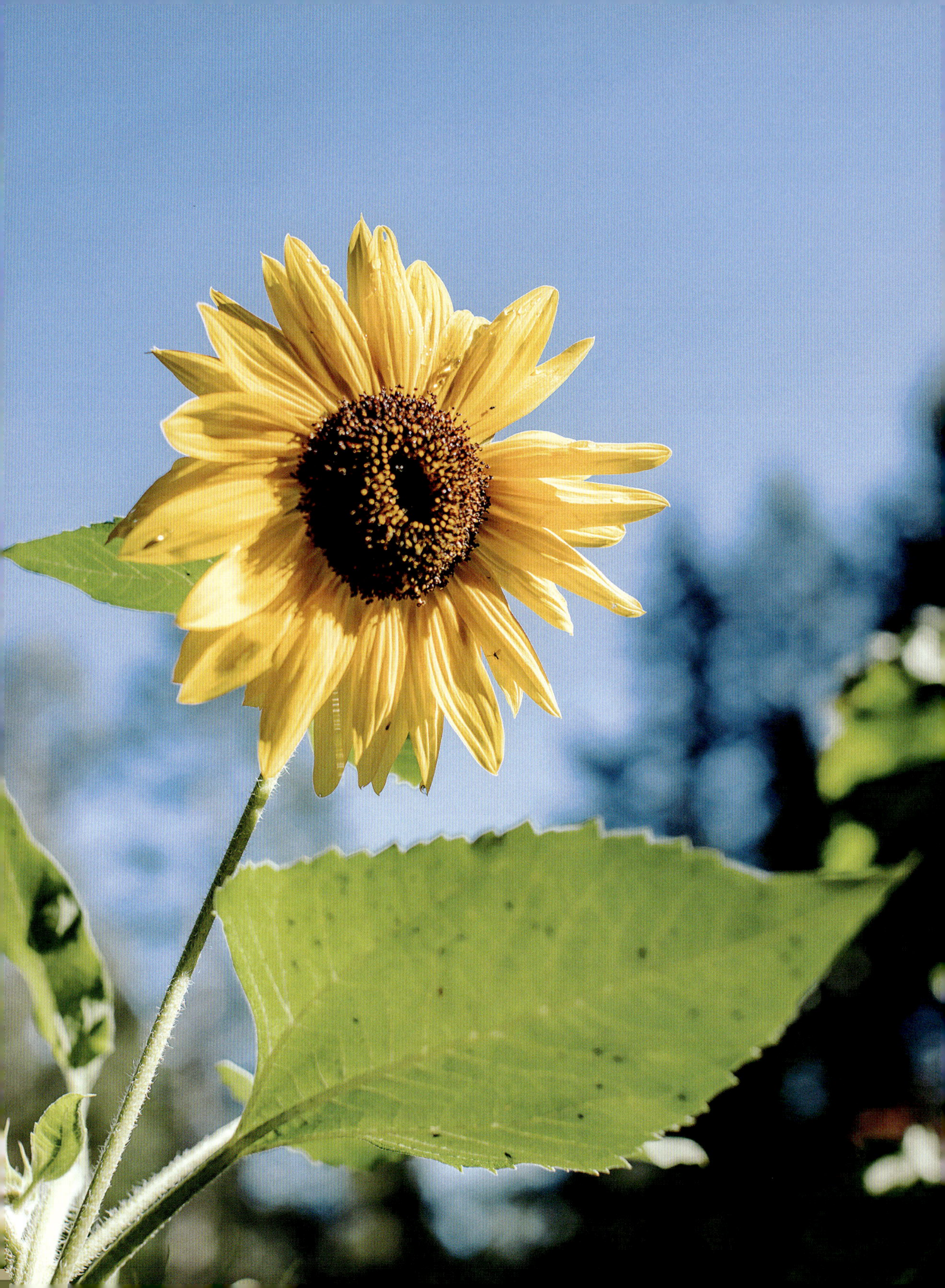

GROWING YOUR OWN COLOR

Growing a dye garden is a wonderful way to level up your botanical paint making! Adding dye plants to a vegetable garden adds diversity and beauty to your garden. Many dye plants attract pollinators, and flowers like marigolds are the perfect companion plants to protect vegetables from pests. Many dye plants can be eaten, used medicinally in salves or made into wonderful teas, such as calendula. Of course, many gardens are already growing sources of vegetable dye, as seen in some of the recipes in this book (onions and red cabbage).

If space is limited, dye plants can be grown in small pots, like on sunny balconies. My dye garden started in a very small portion of my vegetable garden, with the calendula and marigolds. Now I'm growing Japanese indigo, weld, madder root, Hopi sunflowers, dyer's chamomile, goldenrod, cosmos, coreopsis and so on! Research is essential to identify which plants can be grown in your region, as well as to recognize any dye plants that may be considered noxious or invasive in certain areas.

Some plants like madder root take a few years of growing before their roots are harvestable for dye. Growing your own dye plants is a labor of love, but I receive so much goodness in return. As I write this book, we are in the darkening days of winter and I'm already looking forward to perusing the spring seed catalogs. Planning a garden allows me to daydream of the return of warmer days and all the joy that comes with planting and tending the seeds of new color.

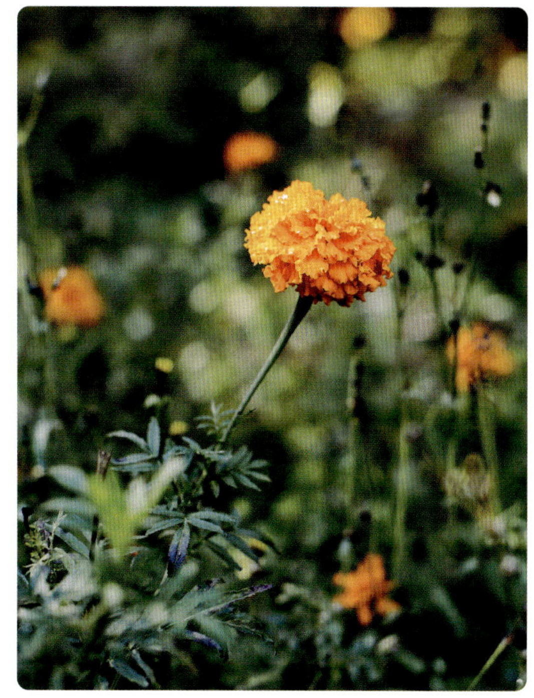

SUGGESTED DYE GARDEN PLANTS

- *Coreopsis*
- *Cosmos*
- *Marigold*
- *Weld*
- *Japanese indigo*
- *Madder*
- *Calendula*
- *Dyer's chamomile*
- *Hopi sunflowers*

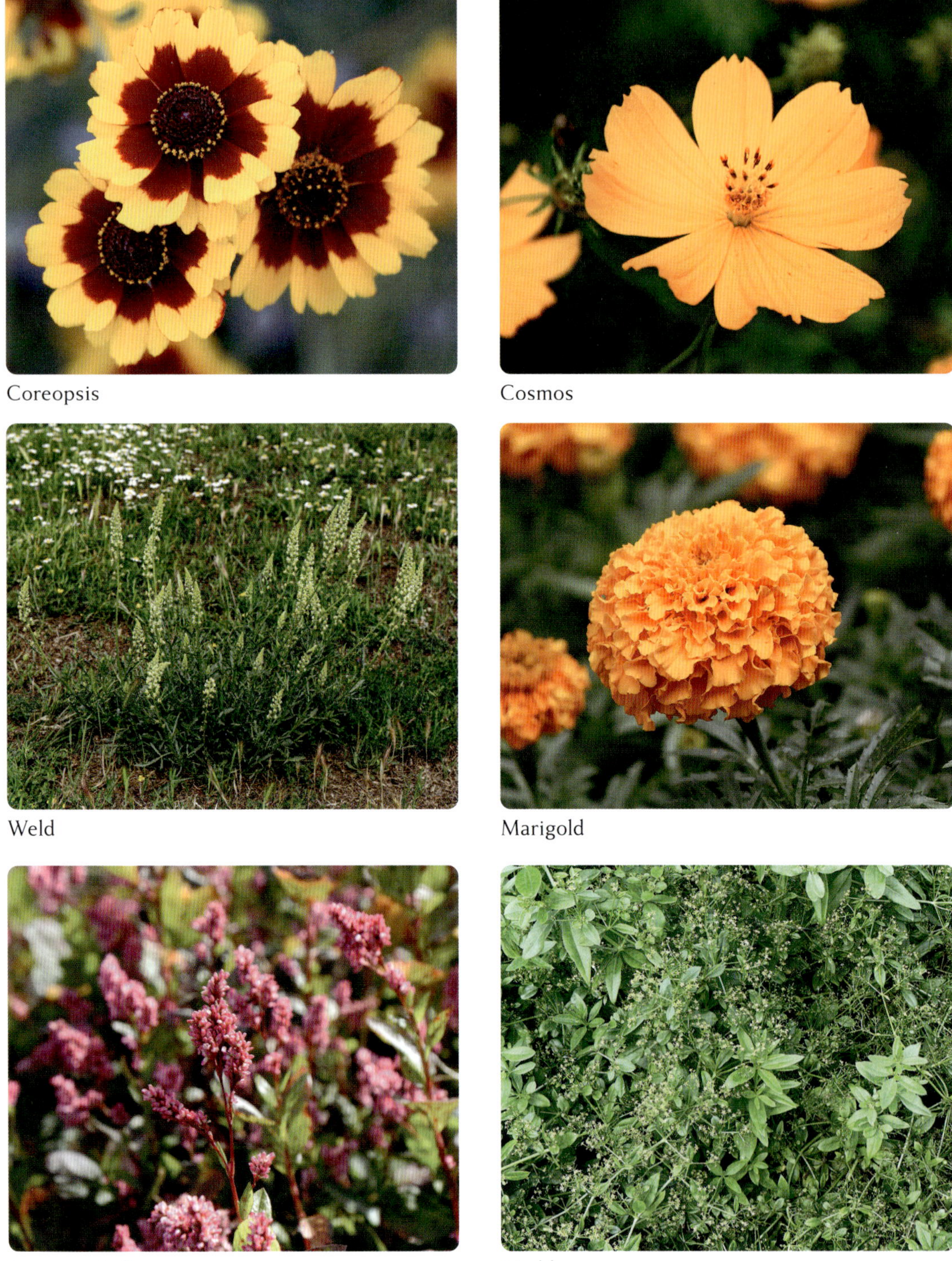

Coreopsis

Cosmos

Weld

Marigold

Japanese indigo

Madder

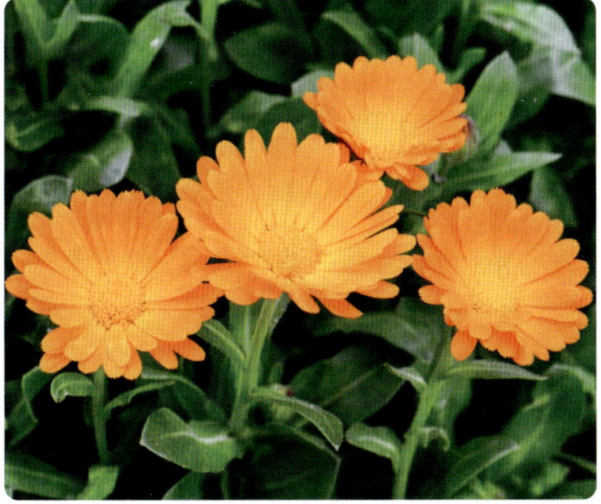

Calendula

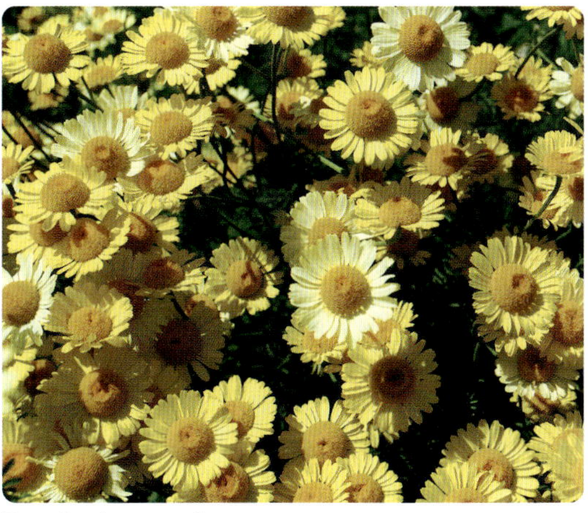

Dyer's chamomile

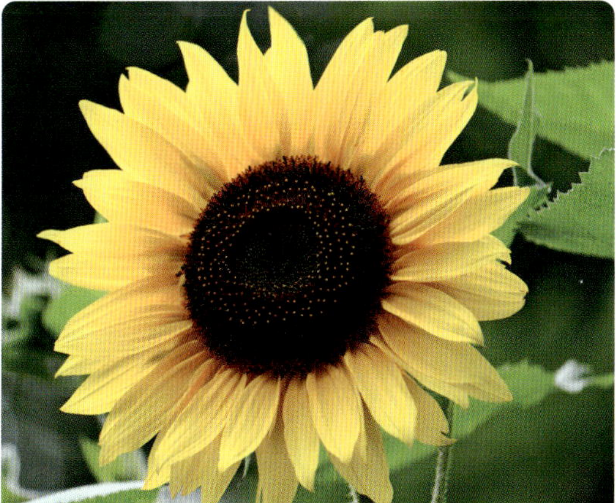

Hopi sunflowers

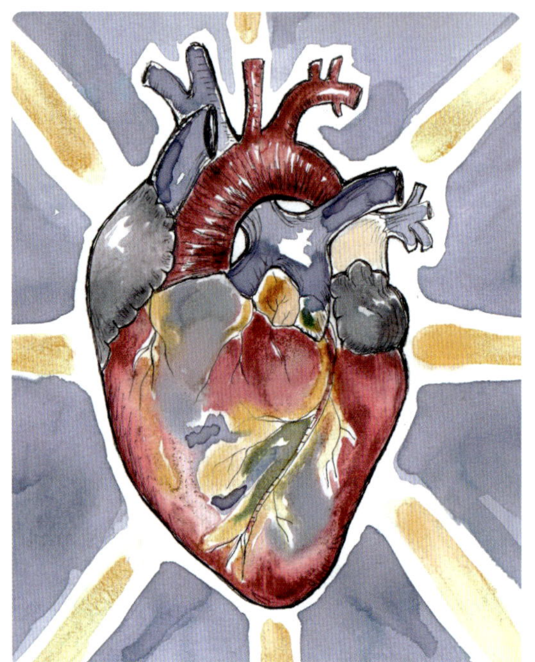

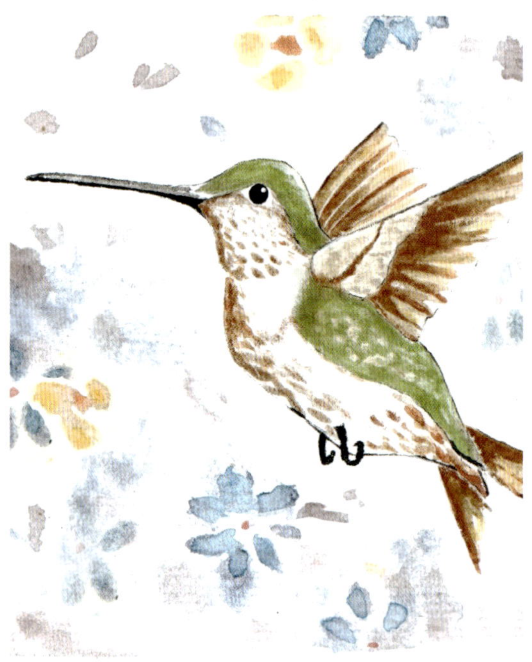

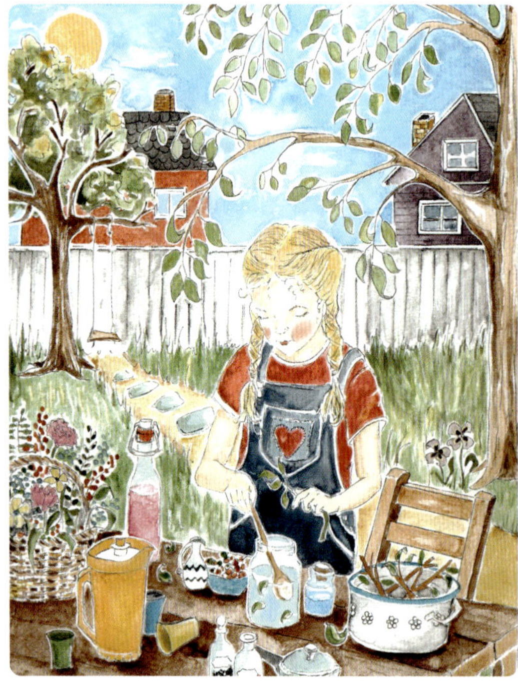

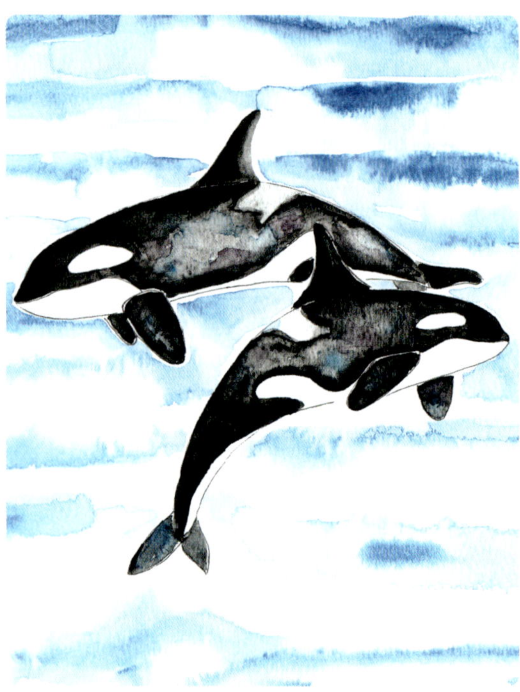

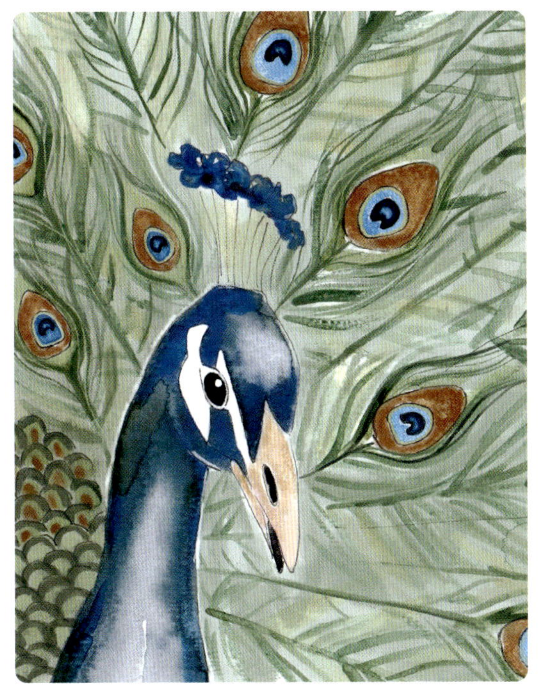

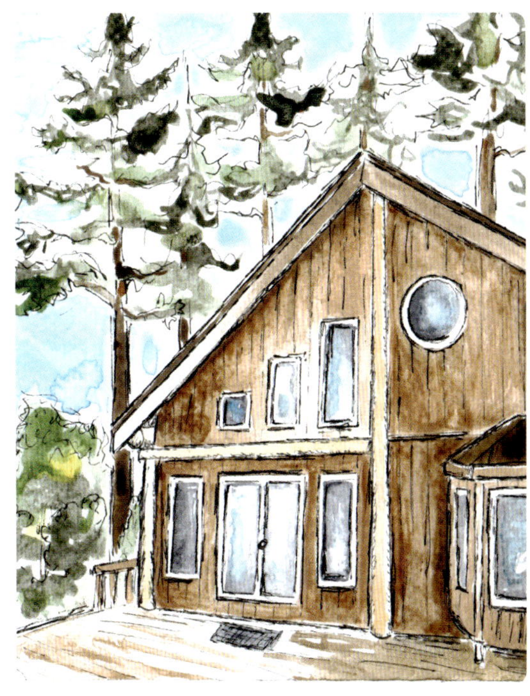

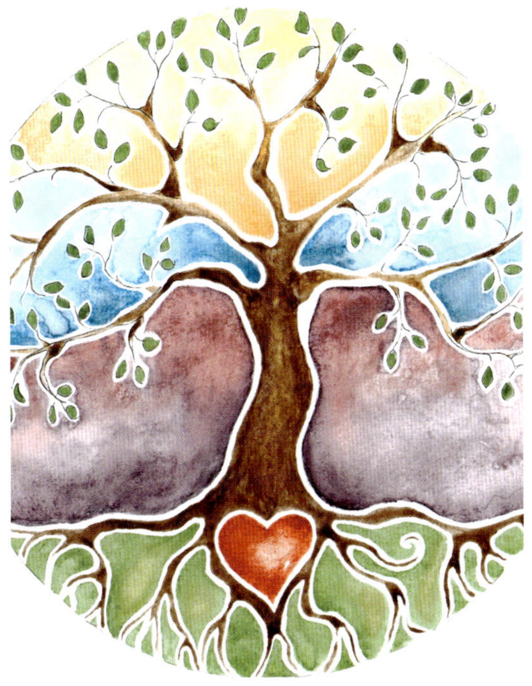

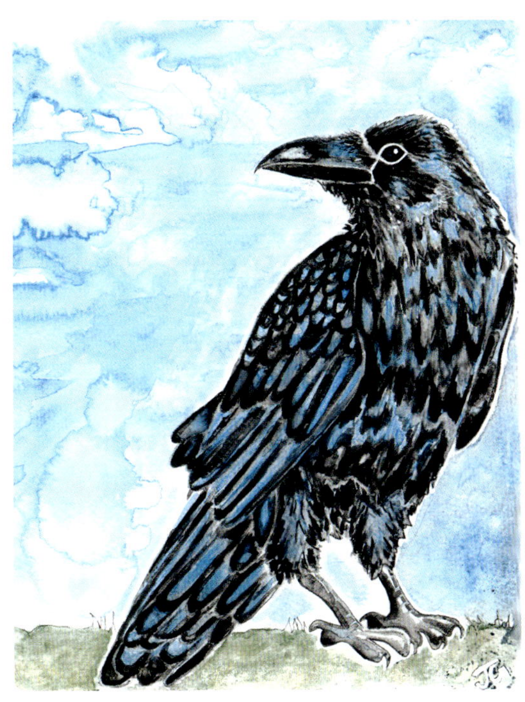

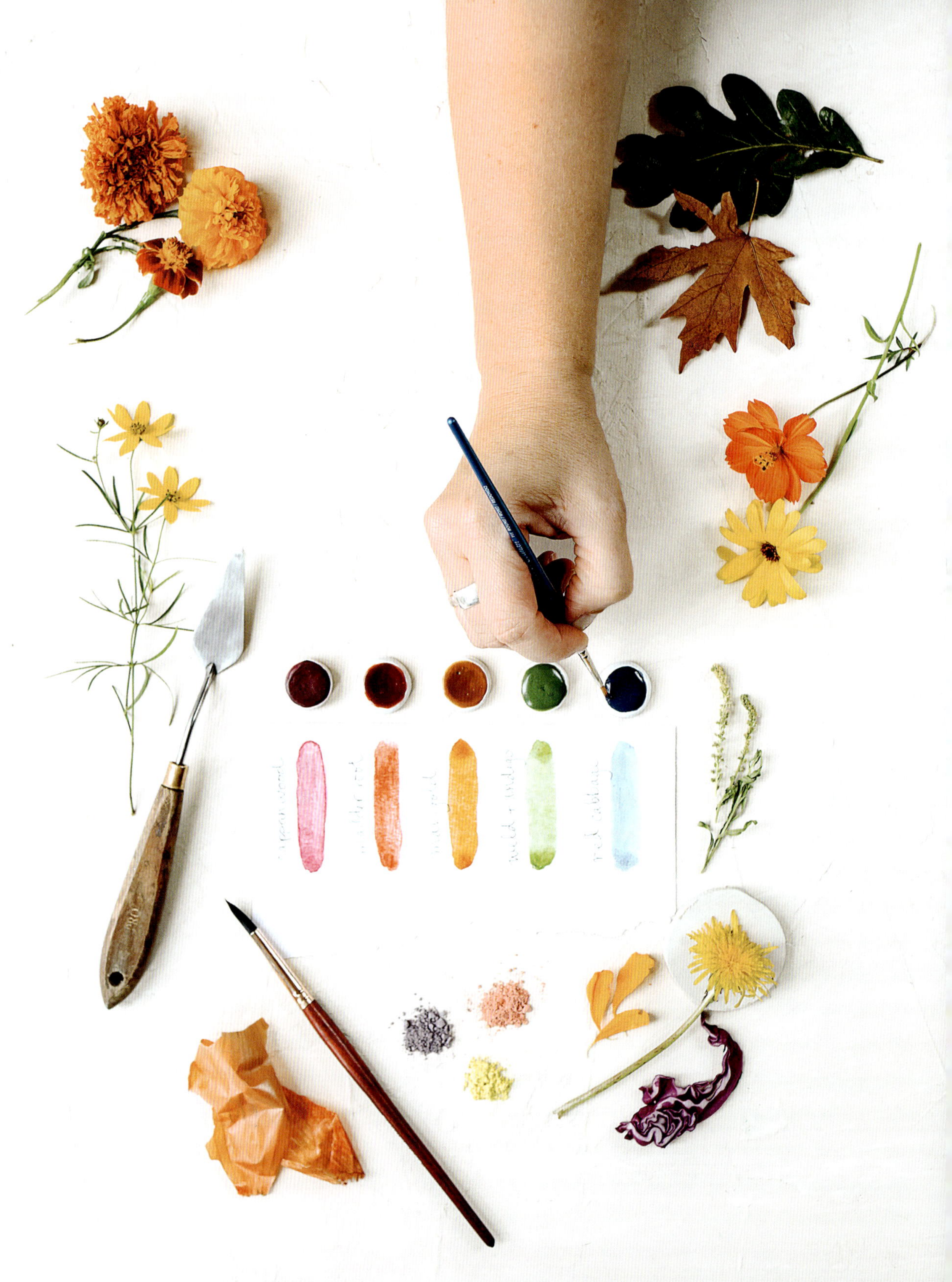

ACKNOWLEDGMENTS AND SPECIAL THANK-YOUS

It has been a true honor to write this book and share my passion for natural paint making with you. It is my sincerest hope that this book has helped you, in some capacity, with your own botanical paint-making journey. At the very least, I hope that you have found some beauty or inspiration here. I recognize that I'm just one of many artists, both throughout history and around the world, exploring the world of natural pigments. The beauty of this craft lies in our unique contributions, while we are all *united* by our love and respect for nature, plants and color.

In many ways, it feels like I've only just scratched the surface of the world of botanical colors, as there's always more to learn and new plants to explore. What I am certain of, however, is that every time I work with a plant's color, it feels like a sacred creative collaboration between myself and nature. I've come to also realize that sharing nature's beauty with others is my way of honoring and thanking Mother Nature for taking such good care of us.

Ultimately, creating homemade watercolors is more than just creating paint; it can be a deeply personal experience that nurtures our souls. It is also a beautiful reminder of the pure and simple joy of creation, and one that fosters a deeper connection and appreciation to the natural world all around us.

I'd like to thank Maiwa School of Textiles and, in particular, their inspiring online natural dyeing workshops. What I learned there inspired me to further develop my skills and eventually learn how to make my own botanical watercolors. Maiwa's online supply store has been an invaluable resource for paint-making supplies, as well as a source of high-quality dye plants.

Thank you to my online community for the ongoing encouragement and support I have received throughout my creative adventures. Your presence has been an integral part of my evolution as a natural paint maker.

I want to thank my family for their love and support, and their patience, especially at times when the kitchen was taken over by my paint-making experiments! And to my children, in particular, for teaching me the importance of play and wonder. May I never outgrow these lessons.

Lastly, and lovingly, to my mom and dad, for allowing their girl to run *wild*, to play in the dirt, and for all the nurturing they have provided. This goodness has led me to where I am today—a *grateful* apprentice of nature.

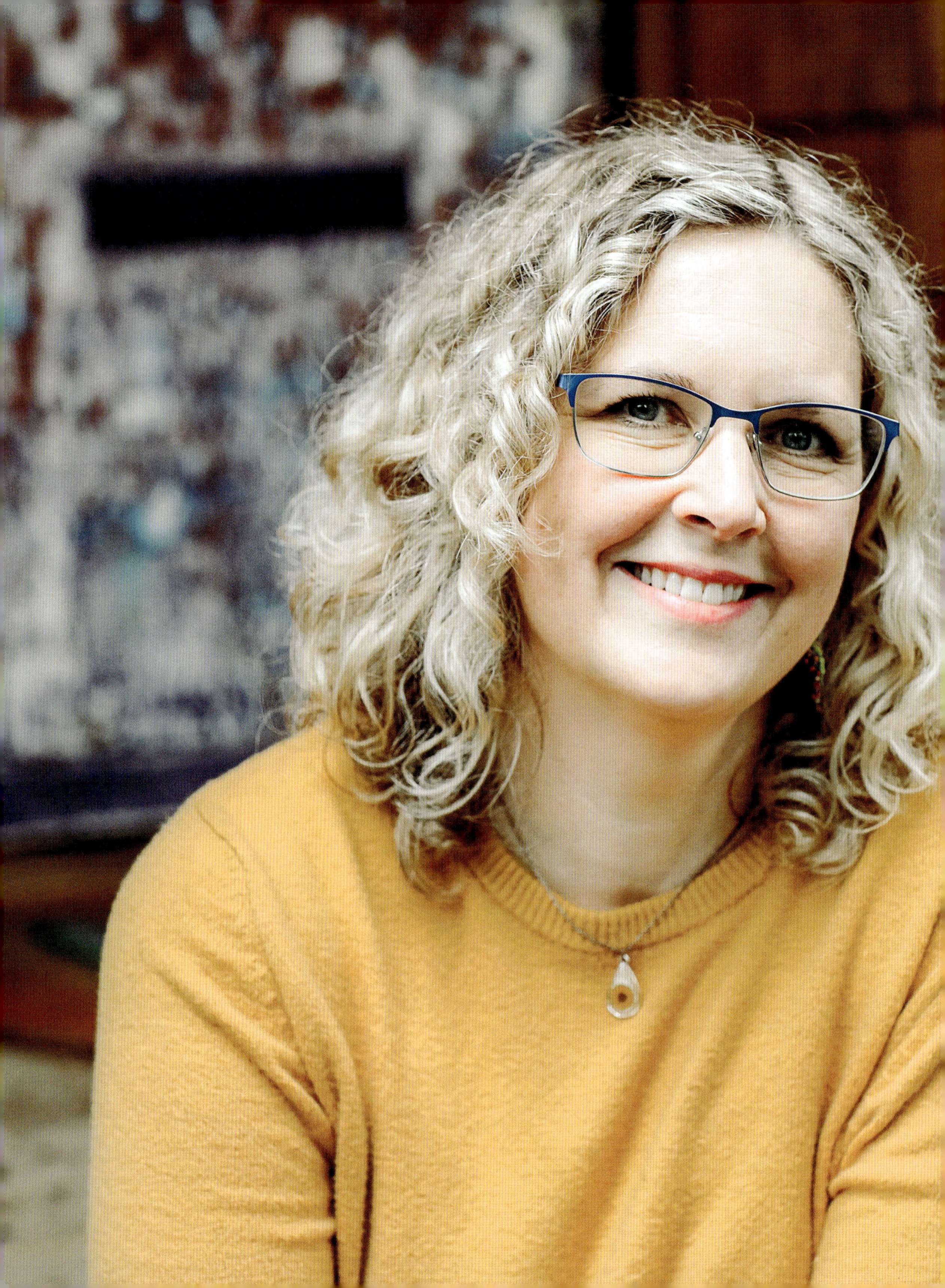

ABOUT THE AUTHOR

Joanne grew up on Canada's west coast, where she forged a strong connection to the ocean and surrounding rainforests. Joanne didn't take a direct path to becoming an artist; instead, she began her career as an archaeologist in the wilderness of British Columbia, specializing in shell midden analysis. Although her early career was in academia, Joanne's creative spirit and passion for art have always been integral to her life. Over the past decade, her focus shifted to raising a family and creating art full-time. Driven by a desire to work with more eco-friendly art materials, she delved into the world of natural dyes and botanical paint making. Joanne gratefully resides on a small island in the Salish Sea, where she continues to explore sustainable methods to use nature's colors in her art. Although she lives on a small island, Joanne thoroughly enjoys connecting and sharing her love of nature and color with a larger global community through her various social media accounts at Joanne Green Art.

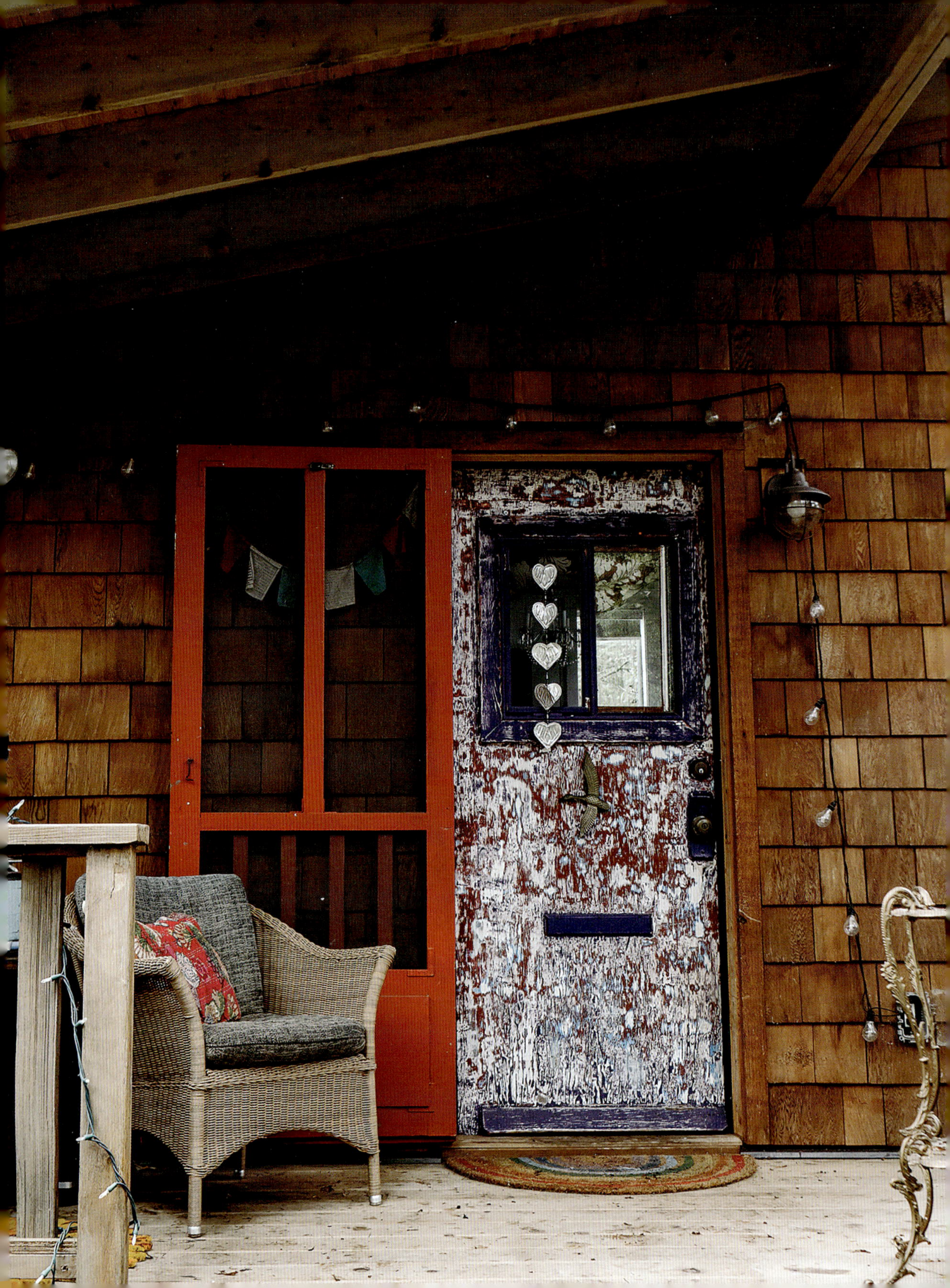

INDEX

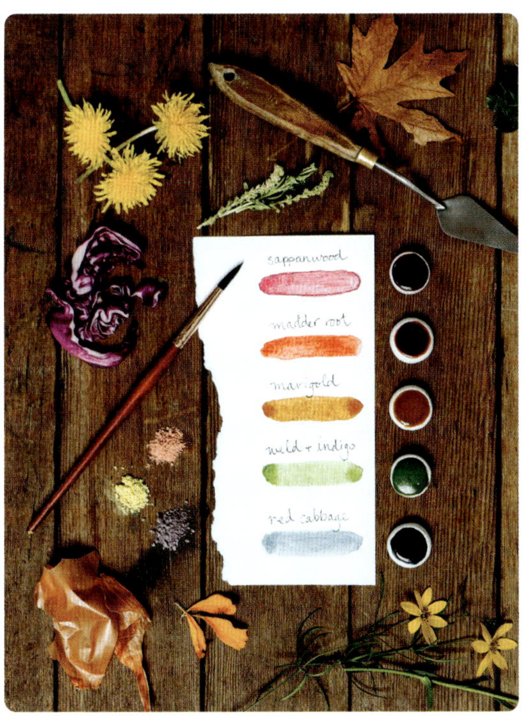
sappanwood
madder root
marigold
weld + indigo
red cabbage

PH indicator test strips, 27, 45, 129

PH modifiers, 28, 129–130

PH neutral water

   Black Walnut (Dark Brown), 105–107

   Logwood (Purple), 113–114

   Sappanwood (Magenta), 115–117

   Sunflower Seeds (Deep Rose, Grey, Umber Brown), 93–95

Phycocyanin, 19

Pigment extraction, methods for. *See* Heat reduction method; Lake pigment method

Pigments. *See also* Paint pigment(s)

   in basic color palette, 139

   from chemical compounds within plants, 17

   inorganic, 21

   sensitivity to light, heat or changes in pH, 21

   sourcing, 17

   storing and caring for powdered, 61, 135

   storing powdered, 61

Pink(s)

   butterfly pea flower food grade powder for, 79

   hibiscus flower food grade powder for, 79

   red cabbage food grade powder for, 79

   sappanwood and, 115

Plants. *See also* specific names of plants

   chemical compounds associated with, 18–19

   dye garden, 143–145

   exploring toxicity of, 83

   extracting dye from, 37

   responsible and safe harvesting of, 22

   toxicity of, 22, 83

Plant "tea"

   dye extraction for creating, 37

   filtering, 38

   in heat reduction method for extraction, 41

   transforming into paint pigment, 41–61

Plein air painting, 140

Pomegranate juice, 78

Pomegranate peel and Pomegranate Peel (Yellowy-Green)

   chemical compound in, 19

   More Ways to Make Green, 125–126

   recipe, 77–78

Pomegranate seeds, 78

Powdered pigment, storing and caring for, 61, 135

Prehistoric cave paintings, 17

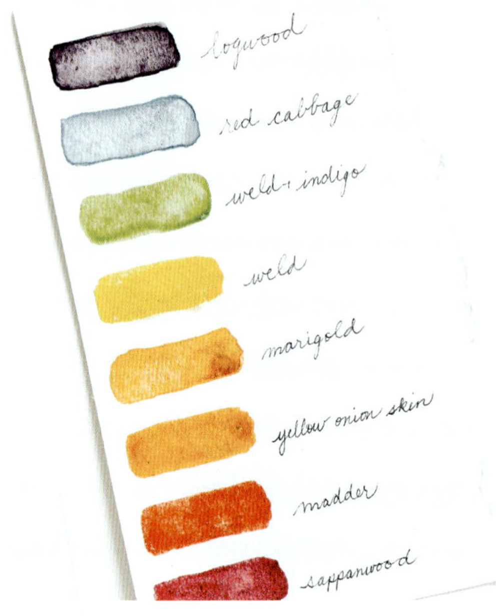

Purple(s)

   hibiscus flower food grade powder for, 79

   Logwood (Purple), 113–114

Q

Quercetin, 18

R

Rags, 27

Red(s)

   beet food grade powder for, 79

   Madder Root (Red), 91–92

   for your color palette, 139

Red cabbage and Red Cabbage (Blue)

   chemical compound in, 18

   color chemistry of, 129

   food grade powder, 79

   making a rainbow of colors from, 129–130

   recipe, 67–69

   recipe review on using, 69

Red onion skins

   chemical compound in, 18

   Red Onion Skin (Green), 41, 71–72

Respirator, 27

Natural Watercolor Paint Making